Prophets of the Great Spirit

PROPHETS
OF THE
GREAT SPIRIT

NATIVE AMERICAN
REVITALIZATION MOVEMENTS
IN EASTERN NORTH AMERICA

ALFRED A. CAVE

UNIVERSITY OF NEBRASKA PRESS
LINCOLN AND LONDON

Library of Congress
Cataloging-
in-Publication
Data
Cave, Alfred A.
Prophets of the great
spirit: Native American
revitalization movements
in eastern North
America / Alfred A. Cave.
p.   cm.
Includes bibliographical
references and index.
ISBN-13: 978-0-8032-1555-9
(cloth: alk. paper)
ISBN-10: 0-8032-1555-X
(cloth: alk. paper)
1. Indians of North
America—East
(U.S.)—Religion.
2. Prophets—United
States. 3. Indians of North
America—East (U.S.)—Rites
and ceremonies. I. Title.
E98.R3C38   2006
299.7′161′0974-dc22
2005024227

Designed by R. W. Boeche.
Set in
Quadraat Sans
by Bob Reitz.
Printed by
Thomson-Shore, Inc.

To the memory of my grandparents,
John A. Watts
Ruth D. Watts

Contents

Preface

The British victory in the so-called French and Indian War led directly to a series of conflicts—some full-scale wars, others guerrilla actions—fought for control of the interior regions of North America. In the years between Pontiac's rebellion in 1763 and Tecumseh's defeat in 1813, the trans-Appalachian West was transformed from a vast, forested region inhabited by Indian nations and a handful of European traders and missionaries into a land dominated by Euro-American farmers and planters. In 1828, when the celebrated and controversial Indian fighter Andrew Jackson was elected to the presidency of the United States, the Old Northwest and most of the new "Cotton Kingdom" of the Southeast had long ceased to be Indian country. The white population west of the mountains had increased many thousand fold after 1763, reaching four million by 1830. New states—Ohio, Kentucky, Tennessee, Alabama, Mississippi, Indiana, Illinois, Michigan—replaced formerly independent and sovereign Indian nations. Through the Indian removal program, Jackson and his successor would eliminate most of the remaining Native American ethnic enclaves east of the Mississippi. The Native American population in eastern North America in 1830 probably numbered around one hundred thousand. It is estimated that by 1840, less than ten thousand remained.[1]

Reflecting on western expansion, nineteenth-century Euro-American commentators—politicians, preachers, scholars—generally celebrated this massive dispossession of indigenous peoples as the triumph of the will of God and of scientific progress over savagery and superstition. Indians as a people, they claimed, were a backward and unprogressive lot who had failed to properly exploit the land's great bounty. They congratulated themselves that those Indians who were capable of improving themselves would profit from their contact with white Christians. They placed great stock in programs to civilize "savages" but were comforted by the thought that the less tractable of the Indians could remove themselves from harm's way by selling their land and moving westward. Thomas Jefferson pronounced his generation's final judgment on the Indian question. Native Americans, he declared, must ultimately either give up their tribal lands and habits and live as other American citizens, subject to the laws of the states and the customs of their neighbors, or be driven into "the stoney mountains." Jackson's contribution was to carry out that mandate with greater thoroughness and ruthlessness than his predecessors. While his Whig and evangelical critics deplored the brutality of Indian removal, they shared with Jackson a common objective: the elimination of Native American cultures through the "civilizing" of "savages."[2]

Euro-Americans during the eighteenth and early nineteenth centuries were generally insensitive to Native American reactions to the "civilization" program, dismissing those who failed to respond positively to the demand that they relinquish most of their land and all of their culture as hopelessly backward and simple people. Few gave any thought to the possibility that Indians might summon up the spiritual and intellectual resources needed to frame ideological arguments to counter Euro-American insistence that mankind's betterment and their own best interests required their physical dispossession and cultural extinction. But while some Indians—for a variety of reasons ranging from conviction to necessity to an eye for the main chance—embraced white material culture and even converted to Christianity, many others remained committed, with varying degrees of passion, to the preservation of their old identities and old values. Some, paradoxically, sought to counter Euro-American cultural imperialism by borrowing Euro-American religious ideas and employing them as weapons in ideological struggles against the invaders.

This book tells the story of nativist prophets in eastern North America who sought to explain the catastrophic events that had befallen Native American peoples. They strove to arm the beleaguered with renewed spirit power, power that would come from the Creator. The European presence on the continent had had a devastating effect on Indian societies. Affliction had began with first contact, for Europeans brought to the continent deadly pathogens from which the Native peoples had no natural immunity. Within the first century of colonization, epidemics reduced Indian populations by about 90 percent. The malign effects of alcohol, of intensified warfare, and of the disappearance of game associated with the fur trade, as well as the progressive loss of land to the European invader, soon exacerbated the impact of epidemic disease. Growing economic and military dependency upon European trade goods threatened the integrity of indigenous societies. The expansion of white settlements imperiled their continued existence as independent communities. The ongoing crises had profound spiritual dimensions, for the failure of shamans to cure the sick, restore lost natural bounty, or arm warriors with invincible power offered alarming evidence that the forces and entities that once had sustained their way of life were no longer with them. Those who cherished a Native American identity were thus in great need of new answers and new visions. Many found those answers and those visions in the teachings of prophets.

Most accounts of Indian resistance and accommodation focus on the deeds of war chiefs and peace chiefs and chronicle battles and treaties. With some notable exceptions—the writings of Anthony Wallace, David Edmunds, Gregory Dowd, Richard White, and Joel Martin come to mind—Native American religious leaders have generally received only passing mention in the histories of the early frontier. But the importance of spiritual beliefs and practices in shaping the lives and guiding the behavior of Native

American peoples must not be underestimated. Many authorities have told us that word *religion* cannot easily be translated into any of the languages of the indigenous inhabitants of North America, as Indian worldviews were holistic and did not postulate a separate structure of reality for the spiritual. This point can and has been misconstrued. Native Americans were not devotees of a simple, pure, and childlike nature worship devoid of dogmas and innocent of concepts of evil. Their beliefs and practices were both complex and diverse. Their quests for power from "other-than-human beings" that would sustain, heal, and empower both individuals and communities took many forms, but they were never simple. Rather, they were always of grave importance, for the people believed that their survival depended upon relationships with beings of supernatural power. In Native American ritual and lore can be found rich veins of material to support both the view which holds that religion serves to resolve inner psychic conflicts and relieve personal anxieties and the arguments of those who find the true significance of religious practices in their functionality in a broader social context—that is, in their role in not only explaining the world but in symbolizing and thereby affirming the values that hold society together and give it meaning.

Among Native Americans, as among many other peoples, both personal and communal identity rested upon an ideological foundation that related mundane events to spiritual forces. Individual and collective crises thus always possessed a spiritual dimension and required a resolution that opened anew access to sacred power. Those accustomed to associating "religion" with the otherworldly need to set aside certain preconceptions if they are to understand Native American revitalization prophets. It cannot be emphasized too strongly that, for Native American peoples, economic security and material prosperity depended not on human efforts alone but on the favor and support of the spirit beings who sustained communal life. While specific beliefs and practices varied, both collective rituals and individual spiritual quests were commonly thought to be essential to the survival of the people. Great ceremonies, such as the Green Corn Dance, brought world renewal and assured the fertility of the soil. Hunters commonly attained power through vision quests and were aided by spirit guardians. They often placated the souls of the animals they killed, and thereby appeased the Master of Animals, through rites of thanksgiving. Access to sacred power attained through proper ritual was also vital to chiefs and warriors. Those who possessed it prevailed; those who did not perished.

The prophets whose work we will investigate in these pages lived in communities in which the sacred power that had once sustained the lives of the people seemed to many to have turned against them. Through the reshaping of a once-distant creator into a powerful, activist deity they often called the Great Spirit, and through the exposure of some old, accepted practices as malign and forbidden, these religious innovators sought to re-store and transform their world. They were both restorationists and revolutionaries. They brought to their communities visions of a future wherein Native peoples would once again live in the manner the Great Spirit intended.

Acknowledgments

I have incurred many debts, both personal and professional, in the course of writing this book. Since this volume is partly (although not exclusively) a work of synthesis, I must acknowledge that I have been deeply influenced by a number of scholars who have studied revitalization movements throughout the world. I trust that in both text and endnotes I have given account of my dependence upon their good work. Portions of the study have been presented at the Annual Conference of the American Society for Ethnohistory, at the MacNeil Center for Early American Studies of the University of Pennsylvania, and at the Humanities Institute of the University of Toledo. I am grateful for those venues and for the trenchant comments and helpful suggestions of the participants of those sessions. Augmented versions of those papers have been published in Ethnohistory and in the Journal of the Early Republic. I am grateful to these journals for permission to draw upon those materials in the present volume. The University of Toledo provided two generous sabbatical leaves that made possible the completion of this study. I thank the editors of the University of Nebraska Press for their invaluable support of this project, and I acknowledge with special gratitude the press's reviewers, Bruce E. Johansen and Anthony F. C. Wallace.

Finally, a special debt of gratitude is due to the secretary of the University of Toledo's Department of History, Deborah MacDonald, for many things, but most immediately for her great assistance in preparing the manuscript for the press.

Introduction

In 1824, eleven years after the defeat and death of his brother Tecumseh, the Shawnee prophet Tenskwatawa issued his final recorded revelation. He warned Michigan governor Lewis Cass that if whites continued to dispossess Indians, the Great Spirit's "poor and miserable" children the Shawnees would carry the sacred flame that burned at the center of their tribal bundle back to their ancestral homeland and release it. Within four years, the ensuing conflagration "will be visible to the entire world. Then Indians grown desperate by a consciousness that their end is approaching will suffer the fire to burn and to destroy the whites, upon whom they will call, tauntingly, to quench it." Everyone, whites and Indians alike, will perish. "After the destruction of the world by this fire," Tenskwatawa declared, "the Great Spirit will cause it to be reformed and re-peopled." The Shawnee prophet's apocalyptic vision was embedded in his recollections of traditional Shawnee lore, but it was clearly not part of that tradition. Instead, it emanated from the prophet's own vision of divine judgment, his ultimate conviction that whites and Indians alike had grievously offended the Creator. It also probably reflected his exposure to stories told by Christian missionaries about the end of the world.[1]

Three years later, in a similar but somewhat less ominous proclamation, the Kickapoo prophet Kenekuk also invoked the Great Spirit. Hoping to postpone the removal of his people to lands west of the Mississippi, Kenekuk warned Gen. William Clark that he must proceed cautiously, as the Great Spirit had given the land they then occupied in Illinois to the Kickapoos. Their relocation, Kenekuk declared, must not occur until the Great

Spirit gave a new sign to his prophet. The general must bear in mind that the Creator "holds the world in his hands" and has the power "to make the earth shake, or turn it over."[2]

Tenskwatawa and Kenekuk were part of a long line of Native American religious visionaries who, from the mid-eighteenth century onward, warned Indians and whites that they must not offend the Great Spirit. The prophets of the Great Spirit were the products of diverse cultures and differing historical circumstances, and the content of their messages varied greatly. Some called for holy war against whites, while others were prophets of peace. Some were advocates of limited acculturation and called for acceptance of some aspects of Euro-American culture, while others declared that the Great Spirit demanded total cultural separation from whites. But these visionaries had two things in common: they called for the restoration and preservation of a way of life that was passing, and in so doing they claimed to speak for the creator of the universe, a supreme being described as an awesome and majestic figure, omnipotent, omnipresent, righteous, jealous, and judgmental. He had punished his Indian children for their transgressions. He would soon afflict whites as well. He could work miracles on a vast scale. Indians were his chosen people. Their obedience to the teachings of his prophet would be rewarded by the restoration of the world that had been lost. But further disobedience would lead to unimaginable new catastrophes. The Great Spirit was the God of creation, the God of history, and the God of eternity, rewarding the righteous and punishing the wicked in this life and in the world to come.

Although the prophets whom we will investigate in this study were nativists who sought the restoration and preservation of Native American values and customs, their concepts of the Creator and his role in human life were revolutionary. The "Great Spirit" they invoked and portrayed as the omnipotent, omnipresent creator and ruler of the universe cannot to be found in the traditional Native American tribal folklore that has been compiled over the centuries. Indian stories of the creation and of human relationships to the spirit world are rich and varied, full of lore about gods, spirits, ghosts, animals, and culture heroes. If they speak of a sky-god creator at all (and sometimes they do not), that deity plays only a minor role in the daily lives of the people. Nor can descriptions of an all-powerful and ever-present "Great Spirit" be found in sixteenth- and seventeenth-century European accounts of Native American religious beliefs and practices. The indigenous people of North America did not conceive of the supreme being as an anthropomorphic celestial deity who personally ruled the world and intervened regularly in human affairs. The Great Spirit spoken of by the prophets was born in the eighteenth century.[3]

Although the prophets endowed the Great Spirit with attributes derived from stories they heard about the Judeo-Christian Creator, the idea of a supreme god was nonetheless familiar to many Native American peoples. Their sacred narratives describe a great variety of gods "in an upper world" ranging from the zoomorphic (in one case, a Great Condor) to the highly abstract (e.g., a Holy Flame of Life). Some of those deities were said to be the ultimate sources of life and power. Among the peoples we will visit in this investigation, the Lenapes (Delawares) honored the sky god Kishelemukong, "he who created us by his thoughts." The seventeenth-century Shawnees spoke of a Supreme Being or Creator whom they sometimes called "the Finisher." The Muskogees (Creeks) worshipped a creator whom they named "the Maker of Breath." Elsewhere, as one authority notes, Native American high gods included the Winnebagos' Ma'ura, who made man in his image "but appears only as a voice and a ray of light," as well as the Zuni deity Poshayaank'i, who lives in mist, has an almost human shape, but "looks like fire." We have also the Pawnees' Tirawa, "a mighty power in human form" who could be "seen or heard or felt by human beings only through sixteen lesser powers, especially Wind, Cloud, Lightening and Thunder," as well as the Sioux's Wakan Tanka, knowable also only through sixteen manifestations. "In his person as *Wakinyan Tanka*, the Thunder Being and giver of revelation," the Sioux supreme being "is shapeless but winged, headless but beaked; all of his young come from a single egg, and when he devours them they become his many selves." Yagasati, supreme god of the Beavers of the Pacific Northwest, "is both male and female, motionless but the creator of all motion."[4]

In traditional Native American sacred lore, however, the high god or ultimate deity was not always the creator of this present world. The spirit beings who did the actual work of creation were sometimes not only humble but bumbling. In the Northeast we frequently encounter the Earth Diver myth, which explains our present world as the work of an animal-being (often portrayed as a muskrat or beaver, sometimes a waterbird) who with much difficulty carried up from the watery primal deep the mud from which the earth would grow and placed it on the back of a great turtle. In the West, the spider motif, which regards the universe as the work of a great spider that wove it out of her body, is also commonplace. Even more commonplace throughout North America was the belief that the present order of things was not the work of a supreme being but of a less lofty and often irresponsible spirit "known in the ethnological literature as the Transformer, Culture-hero, Trickster," whose "role is to transform the world into its present shape and to bestow upon mankind all the various aspects of culture." In this formulation, as Paul Radin has noted, the supreme being and primal creator was "beneficent and ethical" but "unapproachable directly, taking little interest in the world after he has created it," whereas the Transformer, Culture-hero, or Trickster was "utterly non-ethical," sometimes malicious, and "only incidentally and inconsistently beneficial." He was, however, "approachable" and often intervened "in a very human way in the affairs of the world."[5]

Whatever the image of the supreme being, and whatever that deity's relationship to a Trickster or Culture-hero, Native

American high gods seldom received directly individual human supplications, and they were never accorded exclusive worship. Nor were they represented as jealous gods who punished humans who had recourse to other supernatural beings. Although differing greatly in nature and behavior, these Native American deities, in traditional lore, were distant and aloof beings, not to be relied upon to meet immediate human needs. In some cases they were believed to possess great power, the ultimate source of all life and motion, but not easily accessible to humans. In others the Creator god was neither omnipotent nor omniscient but, like humans, depended upon access to a mysterious, impersonal force. In traditional Native American communities, the essential object of religious practice was obtaining sacred power for the good of the individual and the well-being of the community, and that power was seldom, if ever, obtained directly from the high god. Instead, sacred power was generally sought through the intercession of lesser spirit beings, for that power was believed to be immanent in many objects in the physical world, both animate and inanimate. However conceived, the supreme being might well be addressed in prayers of thanksgiving at the great annual communal rituals, and there be acknowledged as the source of all being, but otherwise it played little role in the daily spiritual life of the people.[6]

The prophets whose work we will describe and analyze in this book were all the products of encounters, confrontations, or accommodations with the agents and the culture of a powerful and disruptive alien people. They were products of histories marked by dispossession, demoralization, disease, and despair. All were influenced by alien ideas conveyed to them by missionaries and other spokesmen of the Christian religion. They all borrowed from its teachings and rejected its claims. They founded syncretic religious movements that blended traditional and borrowed spiritual concepts. Some scholars have emphasized the non-indigenous aspects of their teachings. One study of the Delaware prophets, to cite an example, concludes that "by the mid-eighteenth century, the Delaware had internalized white culture to the extent that they could not distinguish it from their own." In this interpretation, the Delaware nativist revival led by Neolin and others was not "an out-growth of indigenous tradition" but must rather be understood "as a basically European innovation expressed in native idiom."[7] In support of that view, one can point to the fact that the prophets made use of certain ideas about God, the Devil, heaven, hell, and divine providence that were not only borrowed from Christian teachings but—on the surface at least—appear to have few if any counterparts in traditional Native American belief.

But we need to be skeptical of claims that the prophets were alienated from, or unaware of, their roots. Preoccupation with their indebtedness to Christian teachings can too easily divert us from the important task of placing their prophetic messages within their proper contexts. If we are to understand Native American revitalization movements, we must also, as Elizabeth Vibert points out, seek to explain "why the prophetic response seemed a natural and rational one to the prophets and their followers." A vital key to the prophets' appeal is found in their invocation of the familiar and in their skillful incorporation of borrowed concepts within a nativist framework. We must therefore focus our attention on their "ability to tap all of the ambiguous power of enduring symbol and myth and ritual" by blending elements that drew on "age-old patterns" as well as those that were clearly "innovative."[8]

Revitalization movements and syncretic religions are world-wide phenomena that are usually—although not exclusively—associated with European colonialism. The literature, both descriptive and theoretical, dealing with those movements is ex-tensive.[9] Despite this wealth of scholarship, the basic definitions in Anthony F. C. Wallace's 1956 analysis remain the most useful. Revitalization leaders, Wallace wrote, "seek to construct a more satisfying culture" through a reordering of "the mazeway," which he defined as perceptions of "nature, society, culture, personality and body image." Of the several categories or "subclasses" Wallace identified, two are particularly relevant to eastern North America. Nativistic movements "are characterized by strong emphasis on the elimination of alien persons, customs, values, and/or materials from the mazeway." Millenarian movements "emphasize mazeway transformation in an apocalyptic world transformation engineered by the supernatural." As to the roots of these movements, in an ultimate sense they are the result of severe social dislocations that produce unrelieved stress in individuals. However, they generally originate "in one or several hallucinatory visions of a single individual. A supernatural being appears to the prophet-to-be, explains his own and his society's troubles as being entirely or partly a result of the violation of certain rules, and promises individual and social revitalization if the injunctions are followed and the rituals practiced, but personal and social catastrophe if they are not." In North America, charismatic nativist leaders from the mid-eighteenth century onward called for the restoration of "the old culture by ritual and purification." But, as Wallace notes, "revival movements are never entirely what they claim to be, for the image of ancient culture to be revived is distorted by historical ignorance and by the presence of imported and innovative elements."[10]

There is another, perhaps more fundamental reason why revitalization prophets seldom if ever prescribed a total return to all of the old customs and beliefs of their people. Bryan Wilson has noted that the mass movements inspired by nativist prophets throughout the world provide "a pattern of sustained social action stimulated by new supernatural interpretations of contemporary processes of social change."[11] Crucial to those patterns of "sustained social action" are new understandings not only of the alien and the intrusive but also of the traditional and the familiar. The prophets whose work we shall investigate sought to explain the catastrophes that had befallen their people.

Accordingly, they endeavored to identify and excise those past practices and transgressions that had presumably offended those supernatural beings whose goodwill and benevolent interventions were essential to individual and collective well-being. In their identification of the sources of corruption in their traditional culture, the prophets employed some traditional explanations (taboo violations, lapses in rituals, witchcraft), but they often also utilized religious concepts and values borrowed from the same alien culture whose influence they sought to eliminate. In particular, revitalization leaders throughout the colonial world and across the centuries have been inclined to judge their own traditional religious practices by standards derived from European dualistic monotheism, with its emphasis on obedience to the will of God and avoidance of the wiles of Satan. The cry of the early-twentieth-century Altaic prophet Chet Chepan that shamans "pray to the devil instead of the one-all-powerful God who lives high in the sky" and thereby bring suffering and disgrace to their people would have been perfectly comprehensible to the mid-eighteenth-century Delaware prophet Neolin and to the early-nineteenth-century Shawnee prophet Tenskwatawa. [12]

We will not, however, find uniformity in the North American prophets' use of the idea of "one-all-powerful God who lives high in the sky." Max Weber's caveat about the limited value of general laws in the understanding of human history is also applicable to the overuse of generalizations and definitions, such as monotheism, in the study of revitalization movements. "For the knowledge of historical phenomena in their concreteness," Weber warns, "the most general laws, because they are most devoid of content, are also the least valuable. The more comprehensive the validity—or scope—of a term, the more it leads us away from the richness of reality since in order to include the common elements of the largest number of phenomena, it must be necessary to be as abstract as possible and hence *devoid* of content." [13] The common elements in prophetic teachings are not unimportant, but in and of themselves they do not provide the key to understanding the prophets and their appeal. That understanding requires close attention to the distinctive and the idiosyncratic. Some prophets to a greater degree than others affirmed various old beliefs and practices and incorporated much that was traditional in both their preaching and ritual. Their Great Spirit, although in fact a new deity, could be seen as an old god of creation come back to earth in time of crisis. Other prophets—without acknowledgment, and in some cases contrary to their professed intentions—abandoned much that was fundamental in the culture and established a new religion that departed radically from the past. Their "Great Spirit" had no clear, identifiable antecedent. Neolin may be thought of as an example of the former; the Seneca prophet Handsome Lake is an example of the latter.

The prophets combined both elements in unique ways. The interplay of the indigenous and the alien in their teachings reflected concrete and immediate social needs arising from very specific historical circumstances. Prophetic teachings and innovations were no less varied. Tenskwatawa and Handsome Lake, to cite two well-known examples, differed radically in their interpretations of the will of the Great Spirit. To explain their differences, one must weigh not only personal histories but also far broader historical factors and underlying cultural patterns. Theorists have long recognized that armed revolts against oppression, in the words of Michel Foucault, "have easily been able to find their expression and mode of performance in religious themes: the promise of beyond, the return of time, the waiting for a saviour or the empire of the last days, the indisputable reign of the good." Such themes, Foucault suggests, often "have furnished throughout the centuries not an ideological cloak but the very way to live revolts." [14] We must recognize, however, that those themes of liberation through sacred power were also employed by prophets who, on the surface, did not appear to be leading revolts. These prophetic advocates of peace and accommodation were in fact resisters. They sought to fashion nonviolent modes of revitalization that would set clear limits, culturally as well as geographically, on white incursions and thereby save the people.

The prophets spoke to immediate hopes, needs, and fears. They explained past defeats and present deprivations. They prescribed means whereby the favor of the Great Spirit could be regained and the land claimed anew for his true children. Some prophets inspired, even led, wars of resistance, while others rejected violence but offered access to sacred power in times of defeat and dispossession. Some prophetic innovations died with their prophet, while others endure to this day. The reconstruction of the prophets' voices is sometimes problematic, as we hear some only in the incomplete and sometimes garbled accounts of white observers. Others are remarkably well documented. All command our attention, for they shed invaluable light not only on Native American responses to crises but also on the various uses of ideology and spirituality in sustaining the lives and cultures of beleaguered peoples.

The Delaware Prophets

David Brainerd, Presbyterian missionary to the Delawares, had little respect for his prospective converts. Indians, he declared, were "unspeakably indolent and slothful" and "have little or no resolution or ambition. Not one in a thousand of them has the spirit of a man." High strung, frail, and humorless, Brainerd might well have been a model for the typical British missionary described some years later by Sir William Johnson: "well meaning but Gloomy," determined "to abolish at once their most innocent Customs, Dances, Rejoycings." Sir William, the Crown's superintendent of Indian affairs for the Northern District, complained that, in comparison to their French Jesuit rivals, British missionaries were both ignorant and tactless in their dealings with Indians. Since he spoke none of the local languages, young Brainerd relied on an interpreter. He avoided close contact with Indians and boarded with nearby white settlers when in Indian country. When he called at their villages he sometimes employed a dramatic and confrontational strategy, interrupting religious rituals and challenging the local spiritual leaders to use their witchcraft against him. [1]

In one instance, however, the village shaman did not follow the usual practice of ignoring the missionary's presence. In his diary, Brainerd recorded that in the summer of 1744, while visiting a Delaware village on the Juniata River, he was accosted by a bearskin-clad figure wearing "a great wooden face, painted one half black, the other tawny." Its mouth was "extravagant, cut very much awry." The apparition shook his tortoise rattle and danced toward Brainerd "with all his might." The missionary cowered, for "although it was then noonday, and I knew who it was, his appearance and gestures were so prodigiously frightful" that they invoked fear of "infernal powers." Never before, he confessed in his diary, had any sight "inspired such images of terror in my mind."

Brainerd's confrontation with the shaman then took an unexpected turn. To his surprise, his antagonist, who spoke English, treated him with "uncommon courtesy" and suggested that they talk of matters of the spirit. Sitting together in "a house consecrated to religious uses . . . the ground beat almost hard as a rock with their constant dancing," Brainerd learned that his companion believed that God had called on him to revive "the ancient religion of the Indians." The shaman tried to explain his experience, to tell the missionary how, after leading a pointless and dissolute life, he withdrew into the woods and, after months of solitude, received his calling. Brainerd interjected that his companion's vision came from the Devil, not God, as all Indian religious beliefs and modes of worship were diabolical in origin. He warned that their adherents would suffer the eternal fires of hell. The shaman protested. There was no devil, not in Indian belief, nor was there a hell. Christianity, he told the missionary, might be fine for whites, but God wanted Indians to follow their old ways.

The shaman puzzled Brainerd. Impressed by his sincerity and honesty, the missionary reflected that "there was something in his temper and disposition that looked more like true religion than anything I ever observed among the heathen." But the shaman stubbornly refused to consider accepting the Christian faith. Brainerd was disappointed but not worried. He did not regard his companion as a serious competitor. The shaman's own people, Brainerd concluded, scorned their holy man as "a precise zealot that made a needless noise about religious matters." The Delawares, he insisted, were essentially a profane, degenerate, and irreligious people.[2]

David Brainerd did not understand the Delaware Indians, and he was not inclined to inquire too deeply into their beliefs. His account of his conversation with the shaman is striking for its lack of insight into the nature of the shaman's experience. There is reason to suspect that the shaman may have been telling the missionary about his vision quest. Had he undertaken a "sky journey" to the Creator similar to that later experienced by the prophet Neolin? We cannot be sure, as Brainerd dismisses the matter, declaring that the Delaware holy man was mistaken in believing that God had inspired him. One wonders exactly what the shaman was trying to tell Brainerd. One thing is clear: had the missionary been more willing to take the shaman's experience seriously, he would have gained some valuable information. His assumption that the shaman's message would fall on deaf ears within his own community was wide of the mark.

After Brainerd's untimely death in 1747, at the age of twenty-nine, his younger brother John, a Yale graduate ordained to the Presbyterian ministry in 1748, took up his work among the Delawares. John shared his brother's disdain for Indian habits as well as his hope that their faults could be remedied by conversion to Christianity. John was more vigorous than David, however, and established closer associations with the Delawares. Listening carefully to the talk in the villages he visited, he soon sensed that he had Native American competitors who were not, as his brother had imagined, scorned as "zealots" by their people. They were instead winning support for a new story of human origins that redefined the relationship of Native Americans to the spirit world and to the white man. In place of the old origin myths, with their diverse agents of creation and their implicit assumption that all humans have a common ancestor, Brainerd's Indian informants now claimed that an omnipotent Creator-God had made Indians, Negroes, and whites separately and that, far from being a distant or absent deity, he actively favored people of color. Not only were whites not superior to Indians, but they were morally suspect, as they had enslaved the Negroes and now plotted to take the Indians' land "and make slaves of them and their children." Some of his informants confronted Brainerd with the charge that he himself intended to subjugate the Delawares and become their "king." In response to his protest that his concern was only with their spiritual salvation, Brainerd's nativist critics replied that his efforts were misplaced. While it might be true that the Great Spirit had "given the white man a book and told him that he must worship by that," Indians had not been so instructed. Christianity was therefore a religion for whites only, containing nothing of value for God's more favored peoples.

Given this atmosphere of distrust, Brainerd could not obtain much specific information about the activities of the nativist prophets who were so effectively undermining his efforts. He did hear rumors about "a revelation lately made by a young squaw in a trance." The prophetess had claimed that "the Great Power" had instructed her to denounce the use of "poison" by tribal leaders. Brainerd conjectured that the practice she challenged was a form of witchcraft. We have reason to suspect that the prophetess's message was far broader than he realized. She may have been a leader in a movement to oust local leaders who collaborated with the British, a movement that foreshadowed Delaware belligerency in the French and Indian War.[3]

Frontier Prophecies

Other reports from missionaries and traders provide tantalizing but sketchy evidence of religious ferment in frontier Indian communities. In 1737, Pennsylvania's Indian agent Conrad Weiser wrote of a "seer" at Otseningo on the Susquehanna River who had declared that the Great Spirit was angry with the Indians because of their trade with Europeans and their growing addiction to European rum. He had already driven away the game upon which Indians depended. If Indians did not now forsake their collusion with aliens, the Great Spirit would "wipe them from the earth." Moravian missionaries, fluent in various Algonquian languages, learned of prophetic stirrings elsewhere on the Susquehanna. They reported that a Munsee holy man named Papoonan, while mourning the death of his father, had a vision in which he learned that a great deity which he identified as the Creator had been deeply offended by Indian abandonment of their "ancient customs and manners." Like later prophets, Papoonan, in the name of the Creator, denounced the use of alcohol. Unlike some contemporary and later prophets, he also preached peaceful coexistence with whites. Late in life, Papoonan joined the Moravian community on the Muskingum River in Ohio and apparently accepted some, if not all, Christian teachings, but the heart of his message remained a call for the restoration of a traditional economy grounded in communal sharing and modest utilization of native resources. The prophet warned of the Creator's anger that many Indians were now as greedy and selfish as the invaders. Desire for white trade goods had made them "proud & covetous, which causes God to be Angry & to send dry & hot summers & hard winters, & also Sickness among the people, which he would not do if they loved one another and would do as he would have them." This warning that emulation of Europeans and acceptance of their economic values had brought down upon Indians the wrath of the Great Spirit would soon be the dominant motif in the teachings of the prophets, echoing over and over again in the future pronouncements of Native American holy men. Later prophets would be less accepting of even the most altruistic of Christian missionaries.[4]

　　An example of growing anti-Christian fervor is found in the work of another Susquehanna visionary described in the Moravian reports. Wangomend, often referred to as the Assinisink prophet, regularly called his followers together in emotionally charged mass meetings. Combining traditional religious practices and new innovations, the faithful sought catharsis through all-night dancing, "at the conclusion of which Indians wept," and then offered "prayers to the sun at dawn." They observed "a special thanksgiving festival" celebrated "by spectacularly painted and flower-bedecked men and women." The faithful, adhering to a long-standing Delaware custom, gave public testimony concerning the "Dreams and Revelations" that had given them renewed spirit power. Wangomend's message, which would be echoed by other prophets in the years to come, was that Indians corrupted by the whites were doomed to burn in hell. In his preaching, Wangomend made use of a chart illustrating the specific torments that would be inflicted upon rum drinkers in the world to come. He told the Moravian missionary David Zeisberger that, during a hunting trip, he had been visited by a great buck which had warned him that continued emulation of whites would bring disaster to Indians. Survival would be possible only if "they cherished their own customs" in accordance with the will of "the great and good spirit" who called on them to renounce everything that was of European origin. Wangomend told another Moravian missionary, John Heckewelder, that the Great Spirit had allowed him "to take a peep into the heavens, of which there were three, one for Indians, one for the Negroes, and another for the white people." Whites were not well treated in the afterlife, however, "for they were under chastisement for their ill treatment of the Indians, and for possessing themselves of the land which God had given to them. They were also punished for making beasts of the Negroes, by selling them as the Indians do their horses and dogs." The Assinisink prophet denounced those who listened to Christian missionaries.[5]

News of the prophets' teachings soon spread throughout Native American frontier villages in Pennsylvania and the Ohio country. The reports of the Brainerds, Weiser, Heckewelder, and

Zeisberger not only bear witness to growing nativist anger against whites but also reveal that by the mid-eighteenth century, Native American religious innovators were using, for their own purposes, new concepts of heaven and hell and of a supreme, omnipotent, and judgmental creator deity that were derived in part from missionary accounts of the Christian God, concepts they blended with traditionalist beliefs about the efficacy of both ritual ("frantic dances and singing") and individual vision quests ("Dreams and Revelations").

The prophetic movement culminated in the teachings of the Delaware prophet Neolin in the early 1760s. Neolin, as we have seen, was not the first of the nativist revitalization preachers, but the reports we have of the teachings of his predecessors are terse and vague. Prior to Neolin, white observers paid little attention to Indian "prophets," but Neolin's claim that he had spoken to the Creator and had received instruction on the means to be employed "to drive the white people out of their country" came to the attention of the British at a time of extreme tension on the western frontier.[6] Neolin's teachings were quoted extensively by the war leader Pontiac and provided spiritual support to the nativist uprisings of 1763–64. The account of Pontiac's description of Neolin's trip to heaven, recorded by a French trader during the siege of Detroit in 1763, is one of the most remarkable and underappreciated documents of the period. Neolin and his disciples had extensive contact with whites and were far less secretive about their beliefs than were their predecessors. Hence, reports of his teachings provide us with the only reasonably comprehensive view we have of an eighteenth-century Native American prophetic movement.

The Delawares

Before considering Neolin's message, we must digress to place his teachings in historical context. The Delaware prophets were the product of a century of upheaval and dislocation. Although recognized as a distinct group by both the Dutch and the British, the Delawares, more properly called the Lenapes, spoke several dialects of two distinctive eastern Algonquian languages, Munsee and Unami. Prior to the mid-eighteenth century, the Delawares had no identity as a tribe or nation. The center of Lenape life was the village, generally inhabited by a few hundred members. Some villages were loosely linked together in transitory alliances generally formed to counter an external threat, but for the most part local autonomy prevailed.[7]

In the early seventeenth century, the Lenape homelands were located in the Delaware valley of New Jersey, in eastern Pennsylvania, and in southeastern New York. The Lenapes fared poorly in their early interactions with European colonizers. Dependent upon the fur trade for access to those European goods that were now necessities, the they had exterminated most of the fur-bearing animals in their locale by the 1640s. When Dutch traders at New Amsterdam turned to the interior tribes, particularly the Iroquois nations, for peltry, the Delawares were marginalized. As Duane Champagne notes, "because the Delaware were not unified or strong enough to force open trade territories from the interior nations, they became increasingly impoverished near the European settlements. They began to sell handicrafts, corn, meat and land in order to obtain the European goods on which they had grown dependent."[8]

Poverty and pressure from both Europeans and Indian rivals forced the Delawares westward. They suffered severe attrition from both infectious European diseases, to which they had no immunity, and from the intensified intergroup warfare that soon followed after involvement in trade with Europeans. Alcohol also took its toll. Within a century, the Lenape population declined from an estimated ten to twelve thousand at the time of contact to no more than three thousand. Contemporary accounts spoke of both depopulation and demoralization as basic realities of Lenape life in the European colonial era. The western migrations of the Delawares were marked by severe disruptions in established social patterns. As William Newcomb notes, "geographical displacement" of the various Lenape communities occurred unevenly "as small groups sold their land or were forced from it at various times. The scattered, decimated, and unorganized bands . . . soon gathered, or were gathered, as they had never been in pre-European times. The 'towns' that grew up in the river valleys of Pennsylvania in the early decades of the eighteenth century were not formed from homogeneous cultural units."[9]

The prophetic movement began in those refugee villages whose inhabitants, of diverse background but sharing a common sense of loss, were receptive to a call to renewal. The process of dispossession and removal continued throughout the eighteenth century. Although Delaware land rights had been recognized and honored by William Penn and the early Quaker settlers, their successors were less principled and more materialistic. Lenape bands in eastern Pennsylvania were forced to relinquish the Tulpehocken and Brandywine valleys and were resettled in territories on the Susquehanna and its tributaries claimed by the Iroquois and occupied by several other refugee groups. In the Lehigh valley, the Delawares were defrauded and dispossessed by the notorious "Walking Treaty" of 1737, in which speculators associated with Penn's heirs invoked the authority of a fraudulent deed, allegedly given many years earlier to William Penn, to lay claim to some twelve hundred square miles of Lenape land. "By 1740," Anthony Wallace writes, "the Delaware had lost most of their own territory, and were forced to live on the lands of their haughty uncles, the Six Nations, or on the lands of equally haughty Europeans. Their condition was pitiful: drunken, disillusioned, dependent, and hostile." Continued pressure from white settlers, sometimes aided and abetted by corrupt Iroquois sachems, combined with the shortage of game and general privation on their remaining eastern lands, impelled many Lenapes to abandon the

Susquehanna and Wyoming valley. Many found refuge in new communities on the upper Ohio.[10]

Out of the turmoil of Delaware dispossession and migration emerged new political leaders who, often inspired by the prophets, forged a new sense of ethnic identity and independence in the refugee villages of the West. Driven from their lands in the East, a majority of the Lenapes resettled in the Ohio country in the 1750s. While the Delawares were still resident in the East, the Iroquois, with British encouragement, had attempted, with mixed results, to deny Delaware self-determination, designating a "Half King" to supervise their affairs and hold them in a subordinate status. Iroquois intervention as enforcers for white land claimants had contributed to Delaware dispossession, but their control over their presumed Lenape subjects was never as complete as colonial pretense and later historical myth maintained.[11]

In the Ohio country, as William Newcomb notes, the Delawares rose "Phoenix-like, from the ashes of their subjugation and removal and . . . forged themselves into a tribe that was able to defy the Six Nations and the Europeans." Scarooyaday, an Oneida appointed to act as the Six Nations' "viceroy over the Ohio Delawares," had little real authority and served more as a negotiator than as a proconsul. The British soon recognized that the Iroquois had no effective control in the West, and in their efforts to shore up their own influence in the Ohio country they asked the Iroquois to designate a "King of the Delawares" with whom they might deal. Bowing to necessity, the Iroquois recognized the authority of Shingas, a Delaware sachem who had won the respect of his compatriots as a strong and independent leader. Colonial authorities and the Iroquois both came to regret the choice, for Shingas, no puppet, would soon send war parties in support of French efforts to exclude the British from the trans-Appalachian West. The Delaware bands remaining in the East also sought independence. Some followed the leadership of Teedyscung, who in 1755 emerged as the self-styled "King of the

Delawares." While the Iroquois and the British both conceded Teedyscung's right to negotiate on behalf of the eastern Lenapes, neither recognized his claim to title to the Wyoming valley. Teedyscung and his followers would also, for a time, give support to the French during the French and Indian War. [12]

The bungling of British major general Edward Braddock was partly responsible for Delaware belligerency during that conflict. When Shingas sought guarantees of Indian rights in the Ohio country, Braddock replied that "no savage should inherit land." [13] The general also haughtily declined Delaware and Shawnee offers to accompany his troops on his campaign against the French in western Pennsylvania, a blunder that contributed to, if it did not cause, his disastrous defeat and death near the forks of the Ohio in 1755. The British humiliation inspired not only Delawares and Shawnees but also some Senecas and Cayugas from the Iroquois Confederation to join the French. However, French failure to provide adequate support for their Native American allies impelled both the western and eastern Delaware, as well as other Indian belligerents, to make peace with the British before the war's end. That peace was grounded in a British promise, later dishonored, to withdraw from their Ohio valley bases and respect Indian land rights in the West. [14]

Soon after the French capitulation, the overbearing behavior of the British victors triggered renewed Indian insurgency. Despite the warnings of seasoned Indian agents and traders such as Sir William Johnson and George Croghan, British commander Lord Amherst terminated the policy of reaffirming kinship ties with Indian allies through gift giving. Johnson warned Amherst that failure to continue to bestow presents on Indian allies would be seen, not as a necessary postwar economy measure, but as evidence of "contempt, dislike and an inclination to reduce them so low as to facilitate [British] designs of extirpating them." [15] Amherst, convinced that Indians could easily be whipped into submission by a few British soldiers, not only ignored that warning but seized lands rightfully belonging to the Iroquois to reward some of his officers. He also authorized sharp increases in the prices charged for goods sold to Indians. The underlying cause of Native American unrest was, of course, the perception, reinforced by Amherst's arrogance and insensitivity, that the victors threatened not only their lands but their lives. It was rumored that "the British planned to annihilate them as punishment for siding with the French in the late war." [16]

Although often blamed for the outbreak of Pontiac's rebellion, Amherst was only one of a number of British official who made clear their intention to "dominate and master a conquered continent" and in the process deny to Indians "recognition, honor and respect." [17] While early efforts by an anti-British Seneca faction to organize a pan-Indian uprising had failed, the Ottawa war leader Pontiac in 1763 led a coalition of tribes in an assault on the British in the Old Northwest. The Ottawas, French allies in the recent war, had heard many stories of British malice and in particular thought that infectious disease, which struck their camps near Detroit in the winter of 1762–63, was the result of the "Conjurations of the English," who planned to use such means "to kill all the Indians." [18] Soon other uprisings, led by other regional leaders, struck British outposts from the Susquehanna valley of Pennsylvania to the upper Great Lakes and the Illinois country. The teachings of the Delaware prophet Neolin played an important role in that insurgency.

Neolin's Vision and Traditional Delaware Religion
We know neither the date or place of Neolin's birth nor much of his personal history. The prophet resided in Tuscarawas Town in the Ohio country during the years when Delaware refugees in the West forged a new national identity. His message, first reported in 1762, drew upon but greatly amplified the teachings of the earlier Delaware visionaries. It reflected both an intensified anger against whites, particularly against the British, and a commit-

ment, perhaps not present in earlier prophetic messages, to a new concept of Indian solidarity that unified old antagonists and created a new racial identity.

The fullest account we have of Neolin's teachings is contained in a report, written by a French resident of Detroit, of a story told by Pontiac to his followers during the siege of 1763. Pontiac spoke in detail of Neolin's journey to heaven, of his meeting with the Creator of the universe, whom he called the Master of Life, and of the message that the Creator instructed him to carry back to his Indian children. Neolin had learned in a dream that he must visit this supreme being, so he accordingly set off equipped for "a hunting journey, carrying" provisions, and ammunition, and a big kettle. "After walking eight days towards [the] celestial realm," he halted at sunset, as usual, at the opening of a little prairie upon the bank of a stream that seemed to him a suitable camping place. As he was preparing his shelter he beheld three roads—wide and plainly marked—at the other end of the prairie where he camped." Although somewhat surprised by that, Neolin "went on working on his shelter, so as to be protected from the weather, and made a fire." But as he cooked his meal by campfire in the gathering twilight, he was astounded to see that "the three roads became all the brighter the darker it grew, a thing that surprised him to the point of fear." As he reflected on that strange phenomenon he came to realize that one of those roads must lead to the Master of Life, the object of his quest, so the next morning he set out upon the broadest of the roads. Pausing to catch his breath after half a day of walking, Neolin "suddenly saw a great fire coming out of the earth." As he approached, the flames soared higher. Terrified, he retraced his route and, back at the prairie, "took another road which was narrower than the first one." But after a few hours' travel he once again encountered an inferno and, trembling, made his way back to the beginning. Setting out upon the third and narrowest trail, he journeyed for a day without encountering anything of note, then "suddenly he saw before him what appeared to be a mountain of marvelous whiteness, and he stopped, overcome with astonishment." Approaching the mountain, Neolin "could no longer see any road and was sad." Looking around, he finally beheld a woman "of radiant beauty, whose garments dimmed the whiteness of the snow. She was seated." As he gazed upon that apparition, she spoke to him in his own dialect and explained that to approach the Master of Life he must first disrobe, leave all his possessions behind, and bathe in a nearby river.

Neolin followed her instructions and, naked, then tried to climb the mountain. But it was perpendicular, pathless, and smooth as ice." Unable to make any headway, he appealed to the woman in white. She told him that he must use only "his left hand and his left foot" in the ascent. The climb was difficult, but Neolin somehow made it to the top "by dint of effort." At the summit, the woman disappeared. He was now without a guide. He saw to his right "three villages. He did not know them for they seemed of different construction from his own, prettier and more orderly in appearance."

After some reflection, Neolin walked toward the most attractive village, but halfway there he remembered that he was naked and stopped, confused and uncertain as to what to do next. Then "he heard a voice telling him to continue and that he ought not to fear, because, having bathed as he had, he could go on in assurance." At the gate to the village he was greeted by "a handsome man, all dressed in white," who promised to take him to "the Master of Life." His guide showed him "a place of surpassing beauty." There Neolin encountered a figure "who took him by the hand and gave him a hat all bordered with gold to sit down upon." He was reluctant, "for fear of spoiling the hat, but he was ordered to do so, and obeyed without reply." Since only whites usually wore such headgear, the order suggested that deference to such people was not part of the divine scheme.

Neolin was now in the presence of the Master of Life, who

declared: "I am He who hath created the heavens and the earth, the trees, lakes, rivers, all men, and all thou seest and hath seen upon the earth. Because I love you, ye must do what I say and love, and not do what I hate." Neolin learned that the Creator was displeased with his Indian children and that the sufferings that had plagued them were the result of their transgressions. The Master of Life denounced their addiction to the white man's alcohol and deplored their practice of polygamy and witchcraft. He was also offended by sexual promiscuity and constant strife. But the gravest Indian transgression was toleration of European intruders. "This land where ye dwell I have made for you and not for others," Neolin was told. "Whence comes it that ye permit the Whites upon your lands? Can ye not live without them?" Because Indians had abandoned their old way of life and embraced the evil that whites embodied, the Master of Life "had led the wild animals to the depths of the forests," leaving his own true people dependent on the invaders. But, the Creator declared to Neolin, "ye have only to become good again and do what I wish, and I will bring back the animals for your food."

The Master of Life then revealed that to regain his favor and restore the game animals that once sustained his people, the Indians must resist further European incursions. "As to those who come to trouble your lands, drive them out, make war upon them. I do not love them at all; they know me not, and are my enemies. . . . [S]end them back to the lands which I have created and let them stay there." Indians must now pray only to the Master of Life, using the prayer he now gave Neolin, and abandon their practice of calling upon other deities and spirit-protectors, "because in 'making medicine' one talks with the evil spirit." Finally, the Creator called for Indian unity and assured his children that "when ye shall have need of anything, address yourselves to me; and as to your brothers, I shall give it to you as to them; do not sell to your brothers what I have put on earth for food. In short, be good and ye shall receive your needs. When ye meet one another exchange greetings and proffer the left hand which is nearest the heart." On his return from his journey to heaven, Neolin announced that the Master of Life had promised that, if his commandments were kept, he would restore the good life his people had enjoyed before the European invasion of the continent.[19]

Other sources confirm the accuracy of Pontiac's account of Neolin's message. Missionary John Heckewelder learned from Indian informants that the prophet revealed that the Master of Life required that they "put off entirely . . . the customs which you have adopted since the white people came among us; you are to return to that former happy state, in which we lived in peace and plenty, before these strangers came to disturb us." They were not to tolerate white incursions on the lands the Creator had given them. A key to victory over whites was sobriety, for whites "for the sake of increasing their gains and diminishing our numbers" had used alcohol to destroy them. Even more important was the restoration of communalism; Indians must share the Creator's bounty. "Do not sell to your brothers what I have put on earth for food." Finally, the Great Spirit warned that he could do nothing for his children without a reformation in their religious practices. Indians must now engage in the pure worship of the Creator, praying only to the Master of Life, using a formal prayer he had given to the prophet. But prayer alone would not be enough. They must also repudiate their shamans and the forces those shamans invoked, "because in making medicine, you talk with the evil spirit." If all those commandments were obeyed, Neolin promised, "the great Spirit [will] give success to our arms. . . . [H]e will give us strength to conquer our enemies."[20] Similar accounts of the prophet's teachings are to be found in the journal of the Quaker trader James Kenney, in the captivity narrative of John M'Culloch, and in the correspondence of a French officer, Neyon de Villiers.[21]

The warriors at Detroit who listened to Pontiac's account of

Neolin's visit to heaven heard much that was familiar, for the story drew upon powerful and ubiquitous themes in traditional Native American spiritual lore. The prophet's quest was undertaken in response to a dream. As Herbert Kraft notes, "the most vital and intimate phase of Delaware religion was a belief in dreams and visions, and in the existence of personal guardian spirits. The vision was the point of contact, a line of communication between the supernatural world and the sphere of everyday life."[22] Equally familiar was the idea of a sky journey culminating in a religious revelation. Historian Gregory Dowd tells us that "throughout the Eastern Woodlands, Native Americans commonly believed that their rituals and ceremonies had once been gifts, donated by benevolent forces. According to some myths, culture heroes had received these ceremonies after crossing into other dimensions of the universe. Such crossings were always dangerous and themselves required ritual. . . . Successful passage to and from the upper world . . . required supernatural aid and ceremony. Such travel entailed risks but could bring great rewards."[23] The description of an encounter, on the road to heaven, with a flaming inferno drew upon that traditional belief in the exceptional difficulty and danger of such travel. The figure of the woman in white who taught Neolin the means of ascending the crystal mountain of heaven and the man in white who led him into the presence of the Master of Life were immediately recognizable, for it was understood that sky journeys were not possible without a spirit guide. The strange method employed to climb the mountain suggests use of a ritual to gain access to the higher realm. Finally, Neolin's revelation of commandments that, if observed, would bring about the restoration of game and the defeat of the invader was comprehensible within a tradition which held that the acquisition of power was the primary purpose of a spiritual quest.

Even so, it does not follow that we can explain Neolin's prophecy simply as an expression of indigenous beliefs. Although his trip to heaven in the particulars outlined above resembles a shamanic sky journey, other aspects of his message are clearly alien to Delaware tradition. Despite their opposition to cultural accommodation with Europeans, Neolin and other nativist preachers of revitalization were not calling for a strict return to traditional spiritual practices. Their invocation of the power of an omnipotent, omnipresent, supreme, and Jehovah-like deity who had presumably punished his Indian children for their adherence to certain well-established traditional practices, such as polygamy and the medicine dance, posed a serious threat to traditional ways of dealing with the spirit world. To understand the import of Neolin's message, we must digress in order to review what is known about Delaware religious beliefs and practices in the mid-eighteenth century.

Like other Eastern Woodland Indians, Neolin's people were a deeply religious folk who regularly sought guidance and assistance from the spirit world. But the spiritual power that was so important, both to the individual's well-being and to the Lenape communities, did not usually come directly from a supreme being. Delaware conceptions of the Creator's nature and role were varied. Delaware creation stories recorded in the seventeenth century conformed to the commonplace Eastern Woodland Indian belief in "a pre-existent sky world" and offered no particular explanation of an "absolute beginning." [24] The myths that spoke of that sky world usually dealt with the origins of the earth and of humans and were inconsistent in their explanations of those origins. Some, drawing upon the ubiquitous Earth Diver myth, spoke of the present world as the handiwork of a tortoise who carried the island that humans would later occupy on its back, having lifted land out of the primal waters that covered the universe. In one version told among the Delawares, the first men and women sprouted from the root of a tree that grew in the middle of the earth. [25] Other early Delaware informants, echoing the Iroquois cosmological myth, related that a pregnant woman who fell from the sky at the dawn of time created the world. [26]

In eighteenth-century sources we encounter Kishelemukong, a male sky god "who creates us by his thoughts."[27] It is likely that earlier European commentators misconstrued stories about the creation event as statements about the nature of an ultimate creator. It is not to be assumed that Kishelemukong was a post-contact innovation, as this creator-deity was not modeled after Jehovah. Kishelemukong was not the omnipresent, omnipotent, and judgmental god whom Neolin would later call "the Master of Life." The Delaware Creator contemplated his creation but did not rule it directly.[28] A Delaware informant told C. C. Trowbridge in 1823 that while the Creator remained on earth for a short time after the creation and exercised "moral superintendency of all affairs therein," he soon departed and never returned.[29] Moravian missionary Heckewelder related that the Delawares believed they must look to "the subordinate spirits . . . between God and man" for help and protection, for the Creator had turned the world over to those spirits.[30] The Delawares addressed the Creator during their great public rituals,[31] but in their everyday lives they spoke to the "agents to whom he [the Creator] has given charge of the elements, and with whom the people feel they have a close personal relation, as their actions are seen in every sunrise and thunderstorm, and felt in every wind that blows across woodland and prairie."[32]

Individual access to sacred power was fundamental to traditional Delaware religious practice. Through vision quests in adolescence, Delaware males commonly obtained protection and empowerment from various spirit beings. An early European observer of the Lenapes, writing in 1656, reported that their young men generally made contact with an "idol" at age fifteen.[33] In the following century, Moravian missionary David Zeisberger reported that young Delaware males undertook their vision quests between the ages of twelve and fourteen.[34] Contact with the supernatural through the vision quest was essential to the Delawares, as it brought success to the hunter and prowess to the warrior.[35]

For that reason, parents sometimes drove their teenage sons from their homes and forced them to take refuge in wilderness areas believed to be frequented by spirits. Those few Delaware males whose vision quests failed to obtain the guidance of a spirit were regarded as marginal people, devoid of power and deficient in manhood. [36] Zeisberger reported that the Delawares explained that they received spirit power from a great variety of entities, ranging from celestial objects to insects. He was surprised to learn that some Lenapes claimed that their visions were gifts from such "ridiculously insignificant creatures as ants." Although the form these entities assumed might on occasion strike Europeans as bizarre, the role they played in Delaware life cannot be over-stated. [37] Those whose vision quests were successful fabricated small representations of their guardians, which they wore on a chain around the neck. [38] They believed, as Zeisberger related, that they were now endowed with "a particular power" so great that they could not only "perform extraordinary exploits" but were invulnerable to harm. [39]

While all Delaware males sought personal access to the spirit world through the vision quest, those called to serve as shamans experienced visions of "extraordinary potency." Through those visions they were able to personally manifest "the holiness of the other world," expressed through remarkable physical transforma-tions in which they sometimes turned into animals and at other times left their bodies altogether to embark on sky journeys to the spirit realm. [40] Shamanic rituals played a vital role in the life of the community, for through them the people collectively received "vital energy" from the spirit world. "The dramatic actions, the emotional chants, the terrifying masks, and the elaborate dances all bring about contact with a spiritual energy that sustains society." [41] Shamanic power was utilized in other, more personal ways as well. Among the Delawares, some shamans specialized in divination and in rainmaking. Others made love potions or pre-pared "medicine" to assist hunters in locating and killing game.

Many were devoted to the curing of illness, perhaps the shamans' most important function. Among the Delawares, women as well as men served as shamans. They tended to be elderly and were well paid for their services in wampum, peltry, tobacco, and other valued substances.[42]

Despite the crucial role of the shamans, they possessed no monopoly on supernatural power, which in the Lenape world was open to all through dreams and visions. As C. A. Weslager notes, "An individual who received his guardian spirit in a vision could appeal to this spirit as his own special protector for aid and comfort in times of trouble, and sometimes to foretell coming events. The guardian spirit, usually an animal or bird, took a personal interest in his affairs, whereas the creator and the subordinate *Manetuwak* were so busy controlling other natural forces that they might not be able to concern themselves with the affairs of one individual."[43]

The Manetuwak were four spirits, located at each of the cardinal directions, to whom the Creator had assigned responsibility for the world's natural forces. The Delawares addressed these Manetuwak as grandparents. Three grandfathers presided over the North, the West, and the East, and Koo-hum-mun-nah, Our Grandmother, was the guardian of the South. These powerful deities, aided by the sun and the moon, which were venerated by the Delawares as Elder Brothers, controlled the weather and were objects of human supplication. In the great semiannual communal rituals of the Delawares, the Green Corn Dance and the Big House Ceremony, the Creator and the four great Manetuwak played a prominent part. They were invoked in the chants that accompanied the intense drumming and dancing and were also mentioned in individual prayers during communal ceremonies. But in their descriptions of the spirits that influenced their lives, the Delawares spoke more often of lesser spirits. Among these were Thunderbeings, described as "huge birds with human heads whose duty it was to water the earth." They were manifested in thunder and lightning and were said to protect the world from the Great Horned Serpent, an evil reptile who had once lived in the sea. Spirit protectors had killed the Great Horned Serpent, but pieces of its flesh were preserved in medicine bundles and possessed great power. Also of great importance were the Masked Being, sometimes described as the Keeper of Animals, a spirit being who controlled the activities of game; the Earth Mother, "whose duty it is to carry and nourish the people and the animals"; and " 'mother Corn,' who has dominion over all vegetation and is envisioned as an elderly woman who resides in the far heavens." Communal well-being depended upon gaining the favor of those spirits and on neutralizing the power of various malevolent beings. Delaware songs, dances, and sacrifices of "burnt meat, tobacco, cedar and other substances" were all intended to gain the assistance of nature spirits. In these observances, those spirits, not the distant Creator, offered protection to those who successfully invoked their power.[44] The public recitation of visions obtained from such guardian spirits was an important aspect of all the major Delaware religious ceremonials. The guardians were the mainstay of traditional Delaware spirituality.[45]

Neolin's teaching that the supreme deity was a jealous male sky god who both created and ruled the world thus departed from Delaware tradition. Neolin related that the Creator had warned that when "ye conjure and resort to the medicine dance, believing that ye speak to me; ye are mistaken,—it is to the Manitou that ye speak, an evil spirit who prompts you to nothing but wrong, and who listens to you out of ignorance of me." To some extent that warning could be understood in the context of traditional beliefs about witches. Neolin's condemnation of certain shamanic practices made eminent good sense to traditionalists who believed that shamanic power, being morally neutral, and subject to manipulation could be used malevolently. Fear of witchcraft, which Native Americans understood as the misuse of supernatural power, was widespread in the troubled and demoralized Native

American communities of the mid-eighteenth century. Neolin drew on those anxieties but also radically modified understandings about the nature of shamanic power. The Great Spirit, he believed, had revealed that the quest for such power apart from the worship of the Creator was a great evil. [46]

This is notable, for Christian missionaries from the earliest years of contact had endeavored to persuade Native Americans that all shamanic practices were of diabolical origin. Their efforts to link village medicine men with the Devil were generally unsuccessful at first. While recognizing the possibility that shamanic power could be used to maim and kill as well as heal, Indians commonly insisted that their own spiritual leaders were benefactors who used their access to spirit power for the good of the community. While European documents from the early contact period contain some accounts of Indian efforts to use shamanic power against external enemies, none of the many accounts penned in England's North American colonies in the seventeenth century offer any indications of witchcraft hysteria or of extensive witch killings within Indian tribes. Indian testimony about witchcraft invariably pointed outward, implicating either Europeans suspected of spreading disease through sorcery or Indian enemies suspected of using witchcraft against their foes and rivals. [47] By the mid-eighteenth century, however, we find evidence of extensive witchcraft anxiety within Native American communities. In his journal entries for 1761, trader James Kenny recorded a rather obscure, possibly garbled, story told to Frederick Post by Indian informants who claimed that an "infernal Spirit" posing as a child had been found by a Nanticoke Indian woman who "kept and fed" it "until in time it grew of a short & thick size" and began killing other children. Although the demon was put to death many times, it kept coming back to life, so the Nanticokes finally agreed to "obey it & serve it" and thereby gained access to its malevolent power. [48]

Zeisberger reported extensive fear of sorcery among the

Delawares. He learned that they were persuaded that "the sorcerer makes use of a 'deadening substance' which he discharges and conveys to the person that he means to 'strike,' through the air, by means of the wind or of his own breath, or throws at him in a manner which they can neither understand nor describe." A Delaware who believed he had been struck by that invisible "deadening substance" seldom survived. The victim "is immediately seized with an unaccountable terror, his spirits sink, his appetite fails, he is disturbed in his sleep, he pines and wastes away, or a fit of sickness seizes him, and he dies at last a miserable victim to the workings of his own imagination." Witches could also make use of "a little piece of an old blanket or something else. This they rub in their hands until formed into a ball. Naming the one who is marked for death, they throw this ball at him, saying that he shall die. They call this shooting the witch ball. Any person wishing to get another whom he hates out of the way will hire a sorcerer or several of them to do it, paying them in wampum."[49]

In his denunciations of shamans and their "medicine," Neolin reflected and drew upon this heightened anxiety about witchcraft. He was neither the first nor the last revitalization leader to do so. John Brainerd had reported in 1751 that a Delaware prophetess in the Wyoming valley claimed a revelation from the "the Great Power" that warned against the "poison" (probably medicine bundles) used by their "old and principal men."[50] In 1775, Wangomend, the Assinisink prophet, called upon the Delawares in the Ohio valley to ferret out and execute the witches in their midst. His campaign failed because of disagreements about the identity of the presumed malefactors.[51] As we will see later in this study, in the early nineteenth century the Shawnee prophet Tenskwatawa, whose teachings closely resembled Neolin's on many key points, briefly led witch hunts among the Delawares in Indiana and the Wyandots in Ohio.[52] While witchcraft hysteria seldom led to witch killings, the belief that disease, famine, and other misfortunes might well be the product of shamanic abuse of supernatural power—a conviction that most if not all Native Americans shared—led in times of trouble to the suspicion that medicine men and tribal leaders who possessed medicine bundles were guilty of witchcraft.[53]

Neolin, however, did not subscribe to the traditional understanding of the nature of witchcraft. It is important to note that he did not denounce medicine men for their abuse of the sort of power possessed by all shamans; instead, he reported that the Great Spirit had revealed that those who taught the medicine dance were in collusion with the "Evil One." We have here a vision of a dualistic spirit world with the Master of Life in opposition to a hated "evil spirit." Who was Neolin's "Evil One"? The prophet may have been influenced to some degree by traditional Lenape stories about the Mahtantu, a trickster figure who spoiled the Creator's perfect work by such malicious acts as adding thorns to berry bushes and creating stinging insects and poisonous reptiles. But the Mahtantu did not play the commanding role that Neolin assigned to the "Evil One," who on closer analysis resembles the Devil of Christianity. Moravian missionary George Loskiel noted that the Lenapes had "no idea of the Devil, as the Prince of Darkness, before Europeans came into the county." In his warnings against the medicine dance, Neolin in effect portrayed a form of devil worship. That idea is one that he probably picked up from contact with Christian missionaries, as his "Evil One" has no real counterpart in the traditional Lenape pantheon.[54]

While Neolin's teaching about witchcraft resonated to some degree with traditional beliefs, his doctrine of hell did not. While an earlier Delaware religious teacher had assured David Brainerd that belief in a place of eternal torment in the afterlife was a Christian superstition that had no counterpart in Native American lore, Neolin threatened those who failed to heed his message with hellfire.[55] The prophet and his followers, M'Culloch reported, relied upon a diagram of the afterlife that portrayed a heaven and hell corresponding not to Native American conceptions but to Christian teachings. In his drawing, Neolin included one area where the fortunate "went immediately after death to heaven" and another populated by the "abandonedly wicked" who were dispatched immediately on the road that leads to hell. There were other areas, reminiscent of the Catholic purgatory, "where the wicked have to undergo a certain degree of punishment, before they are admitted into heaven." Between heaven and that place of temporary affliction lies "a pure spring of water, where those who have been punished . . . stop to quench their thirsts, after they have undergone purgation by fire."[56]

Moravian missionary Heckewelder, who also had seen a copy of Neolin's map of heaven and hell, learned that when explaining the meaning of the design, the prophet claimed that Indians could no longer enter paradise through the usual, broad avenue, as it was "now in the possession of the white people." Instead, they were forced to traverse a narrow and treacherous pathway that was "both difficult and dangerous for them to enter, there being many impediments in their way, besides a large ditch leading to a gulf below, over which they had to leap." The evil spirit lay in wait at the ditch, seized Indians who faltered, and carried them away to a parched and hungry wasteland where he sometimes "transformed men into horses to be ridden at his pleasure." Indian appeasement of whites, the prophet declared, led not only to misery in this life but to torment in the life to come. Pointing on his map to the lost route to paradise, Neolin would exclaim that by disobeying the Great Spirit's wish that America be occupied by Indians alone, they had lost not only their lands but their access to heaven. No longer could they travel on "our own avenue, leading into those beautiful regions which were destined for us. Such is the sad condition to which we are reduced."[57] M'Culloch related that as Neolin preached in that vein the prophet wept copiously and incessantly.[58]

Some scholars have advanced the argument that Neolin replaced taboo with a new sense of sin borrowed from Euro-

American Christians. While not invalid, this to some extent over-simplifies and overstates the case. [59] While many of the commandments of Neolin's Master of Life are reminiscent of those of the Judeo-Christian God—no doubt a reflection of missionary influence—the new ritual observances Neolin sought to establish do not quite fit the pattern of a religion grounded in concepts of guilt, repentance, and atonement. Although he denounced certain traditional shamanic rituals, the prophet instituted numerous new ritual practices that reflected a Native American—not a Euro-American—understanding of the relationship of human beings and spiritual forces. He required his followers to buy, and use twice a day, a prayer stick on which had been carved the prayer given him by the Master of Life. He also asked that they purchase from him a parchment he called "the Great Book of Writing." This was not a scripture, however, but rather his map that charted the route to heaven. Neolin introduced a ritual handshake as well as rites of purification involving both sexual abstinence and use of an emetic probably derived from the Black Drink of the Southeast. Finally, he placed a prohibition on the use of flint and steel in making fires and of firearms in hunting game, and he called for the elimination of foodstuffs of European origin from the Native American diet. Observance of these rituals and prohibitions, Neolin declared, would give his followers that infusion of sacred power essential to ridding the land of the corrupting presence of the white man. [60] The concept of ritual observance as the gateway to the attainment of supernatural power was not borrowed from Christians; it was fundamental to Native American spirituality. Here again we find in Neolin's teachings an interweaving of traditional and syncretic elements.

It is not sufficient, however, to note that the Delaware prophet invoked both traditional and borrowed ideas about God, the Devil, and witches in his call for a reformation in Native American religious practices. Neolin's message must be understood within its historical context. It came at a time when the Lenapes and other dispossessed and threatened peoples were not only angry about past losses but also desperately worried about the future. Neolin provided hope, and an ideological basis for resistance, by proclaiming that unity against the intruders would be rewarded by the favor and protection of the Creator. His revelation that the Delawares were enduring privations because of their transgressions drew in part on the commonplace Native American assumption that grave misfortunes would befall those who offended the spirits. They believed, for example, that offenses against the Master of Animals (among the Lenapes represented by the Masked Being) would be punished by the disappearance of game. But Neolin added new elements into the customary explanations of worldly misfortune by emphasizing moral as well as ritual offenses, by identifying the Creator as the source of wrath for such transgressions, and by extending punishment into the world to come. Much of his message about the Great Spirit appears on the surface to be Christian in origin and therefore alien, but that message was well suited to the changed circumstances of Delaware life.

Emphasis on divine providence and on salvation both communal and individual served immediate and pressing needs. By replacing, or at least supplementing, the traditional vision quests, healing ceremonies, and communal rituals of renewal with a religion of moral commandments reinforced by the promise of heaven for the righteous and of hellfire for the disobedient, the prophet armed his followers with a powerful means of shoring up the discipline their beleaguered and divided communities desperately needed if they were to resist further white incursions. The idea of a historic divine providence, inexorable and just, reinforced that discipline and added a badly needed measure of hope for this world. Even the new emphasis on moral guilt, seemingly alien to a people accustomed to relating to spirit beings in terms of ritual and taboo, was empowering, for as Richard White notes, "the great advantage of accepting guilt is that it restores power to the guilty party. To take the blame is, in a sense, to take control."[61] The nativist doctrines that condemned Indians for their compromises with whites and threatened utter catastrophe if emulation of European ways did not cease complemented borrowed concepts about God and divine providence nicely, as together they affirmed that through reformation the future would indeed belong to the Great Spirit's chosen people. Neolin's denunciations both of those who engaged in the medicine dance and of those who compromised with Europeans reflected and served political needs, for traditionalist village leaders were an impediment to tribal and pan-Indian unification, and accommodationist leaders had accepted dispossession and exile. Receptivity to Neolin's teachings was an outgrowth of disaffection with leaders who had either failed to protect or had sold out.

Neolin and Pontiac

The prophet's teachings spread throughout the Delaware bands. On March 1, 1763, James Kenny noted in his journal that he had learned from a Delaware informant that their "Whole Nation" had agreed to follow Neolin. They were training boys "to the use of the bow and arrow" and hoped, after a seven-year transitional period, to "Clothe themselves with Skins" and eat only traditional foods obtained in the old way. They would then "quit all commerce with the White People." The movement, Kenny reported, was restricted to the Delawares, as "none of the other Nations" had accepted "the Scheme."[62] But Neolin's message was not intended only for the Delawares, for it was grounded in the concept of Native American racial unity in resistance to the evils brought by whites. The obstacles to acceptance of Neolin's pan-Indian appeal were substantial. As Dowd has noted, the Delaware prophets' call for unity against whites, grounded as it was in a vision of a divinely sanctioned Indian racial identity, represented a radical departure from "the heritage of Indian diversity and of highly localized, familial, and ethnically oriented government."[63] Pan-

Indian prophetic movements threatened village-based political and spiritual leaders. The prophets' rejection of the autonomy and primacy of local cultures, their vision of a single, unified Indian race, and their deep antipathy for traditional religious practices disrupted not only customary kin-based political and social relationships but also challenged accepted understandings of relationships with the spirit beings who sustained human life.

The call to forsake the use of trade goods of European origin was also quite radical in its implications and practical applications, for dependence upon those goods had been an integral part of Indian life for more than a century. Neolin and his contemporaries lived in a cultural world whose material aspects reflected the Euro-American presence. Indians wore European-style clothing mixed with traditional leggings and breechcloths, were warmed by trade blankets, hunted and waged war with firearms, and often lived in Euro-American-style log cabins furnished with iron pots, glass mirrors, and other non-indigenous ornamentation. White traders lived and worked in most Indian villages. Trade with whites had long been an integral part of the Indian economy. Time and time again from the early seventeenth century onward, efforts to oppose European expansion had failed because potential allies of Indian resistance leaders made common cause with whites in order to protect their access to the trade goods that were believed to confer both power and prestige on their possessors.

Even so, Kenny was mistaken in his assumption that the prophetic movement would not spread beyond the Delawares. Within a year, Neolin's message had reached demoralized and disaffected tribes as far west as the Illinois country. Neolin's preaching helped provide the spiritual foundation not only of Delaware unity but also of a nascent pan-Indian resistance movement. In 1763–64 Neolin's gospel played a major role in the insurgency mounted by Pontiac and other war leaders who sought to unite diverse tribes in an uprising against British occupation of the trans-Allegheny regions. The appeal of Neolin's message of hope and resistance in Native American communities inhabited by dispossessed refugees and indigenous peoples fearful of loss of power and autonomy is understandable. The old religions of medicine men and shamans had failed to protect against disease, hunger, and defeat. They harkened back to a time that had passed. To many Native Americans who pondered the meaning of recent events, the old ways now seemed to be devoid of power. The new religion of Christ, which had seemingly empowered the white man, was for most a strange and alien faith, identified with the invader and not suited to Indians. But the message of the prophets brought word from a powerful deity, the Creator himself, who promised salvation to the Indian in both this world and the next. The revitalization gospel offered not only an explanation of suffering and defeat but also a promise of victory and restoration. It brought hope to those who had despaired.

The precise nature of the relationship between Pontiac and the prophet remains somewhat problematic. While the Ottawa war chief appealed to Neolin's teachings in his exhortations to the warriors besieging Detroit in 1763, he may have distorted the prophetic message to exempt the French, whose military assistance he hoped to receive, from condemnation as enemies of the Master of Life. [64] His version of the prophet's teachings also placed more emphasis on armed resistance, and less on nativist cultural renewal, than we find in other accounts. Pontiac and his supporters' warriors realized that they could not immediately repudiate all trade with Europeans, give up use of guns, and restore the ancient lifestyle. Some scholars have concluded therefore that Pontiac's objective was the restoration of "the middle ground," that is, of relationships with whites based on extensive trade, fictive kinship cemented by gift giving, and mutual political accommodation. [65] But that probably understates the depth of Pontiac's commitment to Neolin's teachings. We must bear in mind that, in addition to being a war chief, Pontiac was the spiritual leader of a medicine society called the Metai. He had been deeply moved by Neolin's proclamation that the Creator favored Indians and regarded whites as intruders on the lands of his chosen people. In his pan-Indian call to arms, Pontiac constantly invoked the authority of Neolin's vision.

Pontiac and the other insurgents of 1763 failed in their efforts to expel the British from the major forts at Detroit, Pittsburgh, and Niagara. However, they destroyed all of the other trans-Allegheny posts as well as numerous isolated white settlements. Although finally constrained to seek peace, they were never decisively defeated on the field of battle. The British commanders who fought to pacify the Old Northwest soon recognized that they could not carry out Lord Amherst's demand that all conspirators be executed and all Indians subjugated. Amherst was recalled, and his successor, Gen. Thomas Gage, finally agreed to a series of treaties in 1764–65 that essentially restored the prewar status quo. As Ian Steele notes, "an unprecedented balance of power had been achieved, the war had become a stalemate; and the peace was a traditional accommodation."[66] Never again would an Indian uprising do as well.

The success the insurgents enjoyed early in the uprising was made possible by intertribal cooperation. While Pontiac and other regional leaders failed to unite all of the tribes, the coalitions they forged for a time were fairly formidable. But they also proved ephemeral. Dwindling support from his Indian allies forced Pontiac to abandon the siege of Detroit. As he sought to rally support for a new offensive, a rival Ottawa leader, Manitou, arrived at the gates of Detroit in July 1764 to seek the reestablishment of friendly relations with the British. Manitou, whose name means "spirit," also claimed divine sanction for his demands. Denouncing Neolin's prophecy as a lie, Manitou declared that the Great Spirit had told him that the earth had been made for all peoples, whom he expected to live together in peace and harmony. In Manitou's prophecy, the Creator promised to consign to hellfire those Indians who refused to "follow the Advice and obey the will of their Brother." [67] Manitou's peace overture failed, but in the following year Pontiac himself was persuaded to seek peace. He urged Native Americans in the Illinois country, where previously he had gone to seek support for a continued a pan-Indian uprising, to end the war. Elsewhere, severe privation, a smallpox epidemic, and tribal dissension undermined local resistance leaders such as the Shawnee Charlot Kaske, who had earlier rejected Pontiac's call for a truce.

In Neolin's last recorded vision, around Christmas 1764, the Great Spirit called upon him to use the Quakers as intermediaries to negotiate peace with the British. Rebuffed in his efforts to carry out that mandate by Pennsylvania officials suspicious of the "Quaker Party," Neolin attended Indian agent George Croghan's April 1765 conference and, according to Croghan's journal entry, called upon his Indian brethren "to be as one people" with the whites.[68] After that speech, in which he apparently either modified or repudiated his earlier nativist doctrines, Neolin faded from view, and we know little of his later years. Presbyterian missionary Charles Beatty conversed with him about religious matters in 1766 and reported that the former prophet seemed to be intensely interested in Christian teachings. For a time Neolin lived with the Shawnees, a people profoundly influenced by his nativist doctrines. A 1772 report places him among the Delawares once again, now securely ensconced in an English-style house with a stone fireplace and a cellar. After that the record is silent. Neolin's prophetic mission apparently ended with the termination of the uprising. We know neither the date nor the place of his death.[69]

The Prophetic Heritage
Neolin's vision of a renewed and united Indian people sustained by the favor of the Great Spirit was not realized in his lifetime or thereafter, but the armed uprisings that Neolin and other prophets helped to inspire and rationalize remind us anew not

only of the crucial role of ideology in shaping human responses to historic change but also of the ingenuity of indigenous peoples in appropriating alien ideas to serve their own ends. The most significant contribution of the Delaware prophets to Native American spirituality is found in their appropriation of Judeo-Christian ideas about a Creator-God and their recasting of that deity as the Great Spirit. But the high god they proclaimed was not necessarily the heavenly father of all mankind. Some denied that he had created white people. A French observer, writing a year after Pontiac's death, reported that the Ottawas now spoke of two "Masters of Life." One, a handsome brown man, had created Indians; the other, an ugly, bearded white, was the maker of Europeans.[70]

Whatever conception of human origins the Delaware prophets held, revelations about the Creator's plan for mankind constituted the most significant and radical aspect of their message. The Great Spirit, like the Judeo-Christian God, had a grand design, but it was one in which his Indian children would occupy this continent. The new doctrine of the Great Spirit as ruler and judge of those whom he created provided powerful ideological support to advocates of armed resistance such as Neolin and Tenskwatawa. But, as we shall see, belief in obedience to the Great Spirit's will was also indispensable to later revitalization prophets such as the Seneca Handsome Lake and the Kickapoo Kenekuk, who rejected violence and preached coexistence. That sense of historical providence and of the ultimate triumph of divine justice, so fundamental to later Native American religious movements such as the Ghost Dance, has its roots in the teachings of Neolin and his contemporaries.

2

The Shawnee Prophet

Despite the collapse of Pontiac's rebellion and Neolin's subsequent silence, not all prophetic voices were stilled. Wangomend and others, some of whose names we do not know, continued to call for the regeneration of the Native American way of life and to warn of the wrath of the Great Spirit. Moravian missionary David Zeisberger reported from the Pennsylvania frontier in 1767 that local nativist prophets had persuaded his prospective converts that all of their sufferings were the result of their failure to honor the "ancient way of living." They also commonly charged that the Moravians and other missionaries plotted the enslavement of all Indians. One of those unnamed prophets at Newcomerstown, Ohio, also warned that if his people listened to the Christians there would be an immediate drought followed by a cataclysmic flood. Since some contamination had already occurred, he prescribed an austere diet of corn and water to avert disaster. When the community was struck by an epidemic, Newcomerstown leaders proposed to raise two young boys on such a diet, believing that through fasting they would receive exceptional spirit power. Another road to deliverance was prescribed by the Delaware holy man Scattameck, who taught his followers to use a powerful emetic to "cleanse" themselves of the corruption that came from association with Euro-Americans.[1]

Scattameck's message was received with particular enthusiasm among the Shawnees, one of whose principal villages in the Ohio country, Wakatomica, came to be known among whites as "vomit town." Rebuffing the efforts of missionaries to lead them to Christ, Shawnees generally concurred with Red Hawk, a Shawnee chief who refused to listen to Christian teachings on the grounds that the Creator did not intend Indians to live as whites but had given them "another way." In the wars of resistance of the late eighteenth century, the Shawnees were in the vanguard of efforts to build a pan-Indian confederacy.[2]

Shawnee militancy reflected the ongoing influence of prophetic teachings. James Moore, taken captive by the Shawnees in 1784, recounted that the leader of the village medicine society claimed that the Great Spirit had revealed that he was angry that Indians had "forsaken the ways of their fathers." Contact with whites had made them "more proud and less kind."[3] At a religious festival in a Shawnee village in the early 1790s, Oliver Spencer, also a white captive, listened as a tribal elder declared that the Creator abominated whites as "murderers and oppressors." The hunger and disease afflicting Indians, the elder advised, were the result of the anger of the Great Spirit for granting those murderers asylum in lands made for Indians. The speaker rejoiced, however, in the recent defeat of the American army led by Gen. Arthur St. Clair. Through such acts of resistance, the Shawnees and their allies could win anew the "favour of the Great Spirit." Soon, he prophesied, the lands that the Creator originally gave to the Indians, lands that had once provided "abundantly" such blessings as corn, buffalo, elk, deer, and other game as well as "the most valuable medicinal plants," would be restored to them. Those warriors who fell in battle against the whites were destined to a happy immortality, for in death they would be given a "passport to the boundless hunting grounds in the far, far west, beyond the great waters where the Great Spirit would never suffer the 'pale faces' to enter."[4] The speaker's indebtedness to Neolin and other prophets is obvious in the emphasis on the omnipotence and omniscience of the Great Spirit, the unity of all his "red children," the accursed nature of whites, the punishment of Indians for their collaboration with the Great Spirit's enemies, and finally in the closing references to a hunting land in a realm "beyond the great waters" which promise that resistance would be rewarded by salvation not only in this world but in the world to come.

The Struggle for a Shawnee Homeland

The Shawnees, who spoke an Algonquian language described as "expressive, stately, eloquent, and beautiful," were closely related to the Kickapoos, a people with whom, according to their traditions, they had once been united. [5] In historic times the Shawnees were often allied with the Delawares, but they were far less inclined than their Delaware cousins to welcome white missionaries or cooperate with Euro-American authorities. At the time of their first contact with Europeans, in the mid-seventeenth century, the primary Shawnee homelands were in the upper Ohio valley and on the Cumberland, although there were probably Shawnees living elsewhere. A series of events, including conflicts with the Iroquois during the seventeenth century, had led to their relocation and fragmentation, as some bands of Shawnees migrated to the Illinois country, some moved eastward into parts of Pennsylvania and Maryland, and others resettled in the South on the Savannah or joined the Creeks. [6]

In the mid-eighteenth century, Shawnees sought to rebuild a homeland in the Ohio country in the vicinity of the Scioto River. The Shawnee nation that emerged there was a loose-knit confederation of villages, organized into five discrete divisions, each of which played a distinctive role in the life of the tribe. The Chillicothes and the Hathawekelas were politically dominant, vying with one another in supplying tribal chiefs. The Kispokos and the Pikowis supplied war leaders, with the latter also responsible for certain duties related to religious rituals. However, overall spiritual leadership as well as conduct of diplomacy was generally entrusted to the Mekoches. That division was responsible for providing shamanic healing as well as religious guidance.

In addition to divisional affiliation, every Shawnee held membership in a clanlike society. There were about a dozen such organizations. Decision making in Shawnee society was shared, with women's councils advising male leaders both in peacetime and wartime. In time of war, the regular civil, or peace, chiefs were replaced by war chiefs as the principal leaders. Despite the Shawnees' reputation as fierce warriors, they considered war an unnatural state and celebrated the return of peace with stunning ceremonies that included both song and an elaborate dance whites called the "feather dance." The female civil chief was entrusted with special responsibilities to plead for negotiation and forbearance in dealing with adversaries so that wars might be averted if possible.[7]

Historian John Sugden writes that the Shawnee pioneers in the Ohio valley believed that by reuniting the people in the place of their ancestors they would regain the favor of the Creator. "Once they were unified, the Great Spirit would smile on them again, and as long as they remained unified in the Ohio country he would protect them. For the Shawnees, regrouping on the great river was also a search for grace."[8] In defense of that homeland, Shawnee warriors fought in the 1763 uprisings, attacking white settlers in the trans-Allegheny regions of Pennsylvania and Virginia. They were among the last to make peace.

That peace was short lived. In 1768, in the Treaty of Fort Stanwix, the Iroquois sold to the British the Shawnee hunting grounds in what is now Kentucky, along with western Pennsylvania and portions of western Virginia and eastern Ohio. Although the Iroquois had no rightful claim to those lands, Shawnee efforts to prevent white occupation of Kentucky through peaceful means proved unsuccessful. In 1769 Daniel Boone led a probe into that newly acquired territory, "killing game in a profligate manner, saving only the furs and hides and leaving the meat to rot." A

Shawnee war party expelled Boone and his men, confiscating their horses, guns, and peltry but giving each of the white interlopers "two pairs of moccasins, a doeskin for patch leather, a little trading gun, and a few loads of powder so that they would not starve on their way back to the settlement." [9] The Shawnees told Boone: "Don't come here anymore, for this is the Indians' hunting ground, and all the animals, skins, and furs are ours; and if you are so foolish as to come here again, you may be sure the wasps and yellow-jackets will sting you severely." [10] Undeterred, Boone returned, only to be expelled again in 1771. In 1772–73 he spearheaded the first efforts to establish permanent British settlements in Kentucky. [11]

Boone was soon followed by droves of hunters, speculators, and settlers. Many of those newcomers regarded all Indians as subhumans to be killed on sight. Sir William Johnson, reviewing early reports from the white settlement in Kentucky, concluded that "those who daily go over the Mountains of Virginia . . . have a hatred for, ill treat, rob, and frequently murder the Indians." [12] When several border ruffians imprisoned by Gov. Francis Fauquier of Virginia for killing Indians without provocation were freed by their fellow frontiersmen in 1767, British general Thomas Gage complained that "all the people of the Frontiers from Pennsylvania to Virginia inclusive, openly avow, that they will never find a Man guilty of Murther, for killing an Indian." [13] Gage described the frontiersmen as a "People . . . near as wild as the country they go in" and "by far more vicious and wicked" than the Indians they sought to dispossess. [14] In the same vein, Gov. John Penn of Pennsylvania had complained a year earlier that "no jury in any of our frontier counties will ever condemn a man for killing an Indian. They do not consider it in the light of murder, but as a meritorious act." [15] That attitude was not limited to the frontier. On January 10 and 11, 1768, near Middleburg in eastern Pennsylvania, a German immigrant rum dealer, Frederick Stump, aided by his servant John Ironcutter, murdered six itinerant Iroquois and then assaulted their camp, killing four others, whom they scalped. Historian Randolph Downes notes: "Although Stump was apprehended and jailed in Carlisle, he was rescued by a mob on March 11, 1768. He was never tried." [16] Some years later, the great Shawnee resistance leader Tecumseh, expressing the fundamental reason for his distrust of whites, declared: "They do not think the red man sufficiently good to live." [17]

Conflicts over land exacerbated racial hatreds. The Shawnees fought back as whites invaded their territories, sometimes killing Indians at random. Throughout the Ohio country and on "the dark and bloody ground" called Kentucky, whites moving onto lands claimed by virtue of the Iroquois "sale" at Fort Stanwix were first harassed and then sometimes killed by Shawnees and other tribesmen. Attacks on frontier settlers prompted retaliatory attacks on Indians. One set of racial killings in the Ohio valley in 1774 triggered "that brief orgy of irresponsibility, cruelty and despair" historians call Lord Dunmore's War. [18] In late April, several whites led by Michael Cresap, a local land speculator, shot and scalped a Shawnee and a Delaware in a canoe on the river. Both of the victims were the employees of a white trader. A day later, Cresap and his men butchered several Shawnees who had stopped to trade at Cresap's homestead on the Ohio River below Wheeling. Cresap later claimed that a letter from Dr. John Connolly warning of an impending Indian attack had persuaded him that they were in fact at war with the Indians. Connolly, a Virginia justice of the peace who had been sent to Pittsburgh to assert Virginia's claim to authority there, was a hard liner opposed to concessions to Indians. The evidence suggests that Connolly, a land speculator with interests in Kentucky, sought deliberately, through rumormongering, to provoke hostilities.

On May 31, another massacre, this time of Indians trading, as they were accustomed, at a farm on the Virginia side of the river, claimed eight to ten more lives. The victims were residents of a small and peaceful Mingo village on Yellow Creek near the present site of Steubenville, Ohio. [19] The village's headman, Tachnedorous, known to whites as John Logan or Logan the Great Mingo, hitherto a staunch advocate of peace and accommodation with whites, lost most of his family in those acts of unprovoked brutality. Thomas Jefferson recorded his cry at war's end: "There runs not a drop of my blood in any living creature." [20] Obligated by custom and by his own deep grief to retaliate, Logan led a war party against white settlers on the Muskingum River and appealed to the Ohio Shawnees to join in a general war of retribution against the "Long Knives." Lacking support from the Delawares or the Iroquois, who made clear their intention to remain at peace with the whites, the Ohio Shawnee leaders prudently declined.

Examination of the circumstances leading to Lord Dunmore's War and its aftermath sheds much light on the subsequent political failure of Shawnee moderates and on the roots of Shawnee nativist militancy. About a dozen Shawnee warriors, relatives of the massacre victims, did accept Logan's call. After Logan's small band had killed thirteen white settlers, Lord Dunmore, governor of Virginia, invaded Shawnee country. He did so in the face of Shawnee efforts to avert further bloodshed. The governor understood the circumstances that had prompted Logan's actions and deplored the excesses of the local Indian haters. The killings at Yellow Creek, Lord Dunmore declared, were "marked with an extraordinary degree of cruelty and inhumanity." [21] But Dunmore previously had yielded to pressure from speculators and had advised his superiors that the Proclamation of 1763 protecting Indian territory was unenforceable, as he lacked the means to keep Virginians from occupying western lands. He was not willing to antagonize speculators and squatters. Accordingly, he rejected the efforts of Ohio Shawnee chiefs who sought a negotiated settlement and supported Connolly's call for military reprisals. Connolly claimed that Logan's frontier raids proved that a powerful Shawnee confederacy had already declared war. In actual fact, "the Ohio Shawnee in 1774 were a weakened, isolated and fragmented group" whose leaders were committed to coexistence with whites. [22] The more militant, nativist Shawnees had moved westward to avoid further contact with the colonists.

In an attempt to set the stage for peace talks, the Ohio Shawnee leaders shielded the traders in their midst from Logan's fury and escorted them back to Pittsburgh. It was of no avail. As Pennsylvanians deplored Dunmore's intransigence and as British military officials fretted about the potential cost, the Virginia militia in August 1774 crossed the Ohio and put half a dozen Shawnee villages to the torch. Some authorities assert that the "massacre of Logan's family was planned by Lord Dunmore or other Virginians with the expectation that the inevitable retaliation by Indian kinsmen would so terrorize the frontiers that Virginia would be forced to conquer the Shawnee and the Delaware and terminate the presence of these tribes in Kentucky and western Pennsylvania." That cannot be proven. Even so, it is clear, as Anthony Wallace writes, that this war "was not about Cresap, or Logan's murdered family. It was about the taking of Indian land." [23]

In October, a Shawnee counterattack on Virginia forces at Point Pleasant ended indecisively. To forestall further militia attacks on their towns and fields, Cornstalk and other Ohio Shawnee leaders once again sought peace. Although the terms for ending the war were never committed to paper, it appears that the governor forced Cornstalk and his compatriots to acknowledge the loss of Kentucky. Some accounts claim that the Shawnees also agreed to send hostages to Williamsburg as a guarantee of their future acquiescence to white occupation of that contested land. Whatever terms Cornstalk accepted, most Shawnees remained unreconciled to the loss of Kentucky and to the continued intrusion of whites in their homeland. [24] Moreover, in the years to come, Cornstalk and other Shawnee advocates of coexistence would find their efforts to keep the peace repeatedly undercut by murderous whites who regarded all Indians as enemies. The persistence of the nativist, anti-white prophetic tradition and the emergence of militant pan-Indian movements led by Shawnee warriors and later by the prophet Tenskwatawa and his brother Tecumseh must be understood in part as a consequence of the failure of the moderates.

The Shawnees and the New Republic

The outbreak of war between rebellious colonists and Great Britain posed a dilemma for Native American leaders responsible for maintaining their own independence. Some heeded the colonists' early warning to remain neutral. A few later were persuaded to support the American rebels. Many more, however, responded to British blandishments and fought to eject Anglo-Americans from contested frontier lands. To promote the cause, General Gage sent word to the Shawnees that King George had ordered Lord Dunmore and the Virginians to respect their land claims. [25] Indian belligerency, orchestrated but never controlled by imperial agents, was marked by a high degree of intergroup cooperation, as warriors from tribes as diverse as the Shawnees of the Ohio valley, the Cherokees and Creeks of the Southeast, and the Ojibwes of the northern Great Lakes took up arms to protect their homelands. In a futile effort to preserve Indian neutrality, American revolutionary authorities, during a conference at Pittsburgh in the fall of 1775, had promised to respect the independence of the Indian nations and forgo any claim to lands north and west of the Ohio River. As we will soon see, that promise lacked credibility.

The Shawnee chief Cornstalk, leader of the Mekoche division, embraced the neutrality policy urged by the Americans but encountered substantial opposition from other Shawnee groups angered by the loss of Kentucky. In 1777 a number of Chillicothes, Pikowis, and Kispokos joined with other belligerents in a series of bloody attacks on white frontier settlements. The Shawnees' close neighbors, the Mingos, heaped scorn on those who advocated peace. Seeking to explain his problems to the Americans, Cornstalk that fall journeyed to Fort Randolph at the juncture of the Kanawha and Ohio rivers. The commander there, Capt. Matthew Arbuckle, declaring that "I am well satisfied that the Shawnee are all our enemies," had imprisoned two Shawnees who had come to the fort professing friendship for the Americans. When Cornstalk's son Elinipisco arrived to ask for their release, he was also seized. When Cornstalk arrived, Captain Arbuckle refused to confer but placed him in confinement as well. The captain reported to Gen. Edward Hand at Fort Pitt that he would jail "as many as may fall into my hands" as a guarantee of Shawnee good behavior. Soon thereafter a group of Virginia militiamen arrived at the fort and falsely accused the Shawnees there of complicity in the death of one of their number. Overcoming the halfhearted opposition of the fort's garrison, they shot Cornstalk, his son, and his associate Red Hawk and mutilated their bodies. American authorities apologized to the Shawnees for that atrocity, but efforts to punish their murderers failed, as no one from the garrison could be found willing to testify against them. General Hand, writing from Fort Pitt, reported to his superior in Philadelphia, "From this event we have little reason to expect a reconciliation with the Shawnees."[26]

Despite the murder of Cornstalk, his sister Nonhelema, a physically imposing woman said to be six and a half feet tall and known to the Americans as the "Grenadier Squaw," continued to urge that the Shawnees remain neutral. Predictably, however, a large number renounced neutrality and attacked American frontier settlements. Nonhelema moved to Fort Randolph, where she served as an interpreter for the garrison. Ultimately "her people disowned her and in old age and poverty she was forced to petition the United States for support." Most of Cornstalk's people relocated at Coshocton, the neutralist Delaware village led by Chief White Eyes. Others moved westward and resettled on the Mad River. In the spring of 1779 a majority of the members of the Kispoko and Pikowi divisions resettled in Spanish Missouri, hoping thereby to escape further conflict.[27]

The commander at Fort Pitt, Daniel Broadbent, urged the neutralist Delawares and Shawnees who had gathered at Coshocton to wage war against the British, insisting that "peace with the Americans could be bought only at the cost of going to war against the English and the Mingoes."[28] He won little support. Shawnees and Delawares of all persuasions were angered not only by Cornstalk's murder but by the massacre, by militia men commanded by General Hand, of six Delawares—an old man, four women, and a child—at Beaver Creek in February 1778. Nonetheless, the Delaware accommodationist chief White Eyes was reluctant to go to war against the Americans. In the face of growing opposition from the militants, he urged continued collaboration on the grounds that the British and their Indian allies would inevitably lose. In November 1778, while carrying messages for Fort Pitt, White Eyes was killed by a group of militiamen. American efforts to blame his death on smallpox met with skeptical responses in the few remaining neutralist Indian communities, as warriors of diverse tribes joined the militants. In February 1779, Shawnees who rejected the neutralist policy joined with resistance leaders from other tribes at the British fort at Detroit to plan action against the Americans. Leaders of the new republic regarded the Shawnees as a particularly virulent enemy. Virginia's war governor, Thomas Jefferson, declared that their extermination might prove to be necessary to secure the frontier.[29]

At the end of the Revolutionary War, an American officer told some Shawnee warriors: "Your Fathers the English have made Peace with us for themselves, but forgot you their Children, who Fought with them, and neglected you like Bastards."[30] The Indian militants—Shawnees, Miamis, Mingos, Delawares, and others— were never decisively defeated by American forces but were rather abandoned by their British allies, who ceded control of the West to the United States in the Treaty of Paris of 1783. Claiming the land by right of conquest, representatives of the new republic initially insisted that Indian nations sign a series of treaties (the so-called Conquest Treaties) legitimizing white occupation. Disregarding a British-brokered agreement entered into with other tribes at Sandusky in 1783 that called for a united front in negotiating with the Americans, a number of Iroquois leaders capitulated to American demands at Fort Stanwix the following year. Although repudiated by the Six Nations council meeting at Buffalo Creek in 1786, the Treaty of Fort Stanwix and the land leases subsequently negotiated by New York authorities soon led to the confinement of the New York Iroquois to a few reservation tracts. At Fort McIntosh in 1785, Delaware and Wyandot leaders had also yielded to demands that they relinquish land.[31]

The western tribes were more resistant. The Miamis refused to negotiate, as did many Shawnees. Shawnee militants sent out war belts in 1784 urging other Indian nations to oppose white intrusions on Indian lands. They joined with the Chickamauga Cherokees in seeking support for a broadly based resistance movement. Those Shawnee leaders who attended a treaty conference called by the Americans at Fort Finney in January 1786 represented only a minority of the Shawnee people. At that gathering, Kekewepelthy (Captain Johnny), who would later emerge as a leader in the northern Indian confederation, protested that the Shawnees were undefeated and still had every right to their land. American commissioners brushed him aside. "According to some accounts they advertised their contempt for the Shawnees by sweeping the Indian wampum from the table and trampling it underfoot."[32] Under pressure, Moluntha, the elderly chief of the Mekoche division, and several others signed a treaty of dispossession that granted almost all of eastern and southern Ohio to the invaders. That treaty was not, however, acceptable to many of the Shawnees. Captain Johnny predicted that if whites tried to claim the lands granted to them under its provisions, "we shall take up a rod and whip them back."[33]

Shawnee dissension over their response to American demands ended abruptly after Moluntha, their most prominent advocate of accommodation, was murdered by a Kentucky militia colonel whose forces looted and burned a neutralist Shawnee village in October 1786. Kentucky authorities responded to Shawnee protests over that atrocity by temporarily suspending the colonel from military service.[34] At Detroit two months after the killing of Moluntha, Shawnee representatives attended a general conference of Indian nations called for the purpose of cementing plans for an Indian confederation committed to united action in resistance to American territorial expansion. Thereafter "the Shawnee were among the most active and ardent supporters of the grand alliance idea." The Shawnee chief Blue Jacket joined with other leaders, including most notably Joseph Brant of the Mohawks and Little Turtle of the Miamis, in denouncing treaty concessions to the United States. Insisting that only their confederation had the right to cede land, the militants repudiated accommodationist tribal leaders and called for the ejection of whites from the Ohio country.[35]

Realization of their inability to finance an all-out Indian war to enforce their demands led the leaders of the new republic to seek to gain through purchase the lands they could not easily seize by force. Advising the Continental Congress that paying Indians for land was both the "cheapest" and "the least distressing way" of expediting national expansion, George Washington warned that negotiators should take care not "to yield nor to grasp at too much." Since the Indians possessed more land than they needed, Washington expressed confidence that, if handled with tact, they could be induced to move westward to make room for white settlers.[36]

Washington was mistaken. The leaders of the newly formed northern Indian confederation insisted on an absolute prohibition of white occupation north and west of the Ohio River. Encouraged by British agents who supplied arms and some provisions from forts they still occupied in the American Northwest, Shawnee, Delaware, Miami, Chippewa, Potawatomi, Kickapoo, Ottawa, and some Iroquois warriors sporadically struck frontier settlements that encroached upon their lands, killing around fifteen hundred Euro-American intruders between 1783 and 1790. We have no estimate of Indian casualties, but they were clearly substantial. The war for the Ohio country saw few pitched battles but it was nonetheless brutal, marked by horrendous atrocities on both sides. Inspired by land hunger, scalp bounties, and racism, frontiersmen, in defiance of national policy, often killed indiscriminately, slaughtering the friendly as well as the hostile. Native Americans were more inclined to take prisoners, some-times adopting captives into the tribe. But they also often put male prisoners to death through slow torture, most commonly by burning them alive over a slow fire, a practice that became more frequent as the struggle intensified, as did the killing of women and children and the practice of ritual cannibalism. "Increasing ferocity," writes historian Wiley Sword, "evidenced by dismemberment and gross mutilation of fallen whites, began to characterize frontier Indian attacks in the later 1780's and early 1790's." For their part, frontiersmen distributed poisoned food to Indians, fashioned razor straps from the skin of Indian dead, and celebrated the exploits of such Indian haters as Col. Hugh McGary, the killer of Chief Moluntha, who on another occasion, after "pretending to befriend a lone Indian encountered on the trail," brained him "with a large club once his fellow traveler's back was turned." [37] The continued killing of peaceful Indians undercut efforts to resolve the Ohio question through diplomacy.

Lacking an effective national force to deal with the crisis, President Washington called on the states to supply militiamen to march with a small federal unit commanded by Gen. Josiah Harmer. Harmer's poorly trained, undisciplined army of 1,450 men blundered through Ohio in the late summer of 1790, burning Indian villages along the way. Falling into an ambush near the

Maumee River, Harmer's force fell apart, with nearly two hundred killed in the rout. Casualties would have been far higher had a lunar eclipse not been interpreted by many of the Miami warriors as an ill omen requiring that they disengage rather than attacking the stragglers. A year later the governor of the Northwest Territory, Arthur St. Clair, raised a new army of some three thousand recruits, of whom a thousand deserted before they encountered the enemy. When Indians attacked the remainder of St. Clair's army in a dawn raid on November 4, 1791, on his encampment by the banks of the upper Wabash River south of the Maumee, the United States suffered the worst military catastrophe in its history. More than half of St. Clair's men were killed or wounded, and the rest fled the field. "In mock tribute to the greed of these white men, who already had usurped so much land, yet sought more, the Indians crammed dirt into the mouths of those slain."[38] Of the Indians who assaulted the American army, only twenty-one were killed and forty wounded.

The northern Indian confederation now clearly controlled most of the Ohio country. In negotiations at Detroit in 1793, the Shawnees and their allies insisted that no peace was possible until all American settlers were removed from the contested territories.[39] With the aid and support of their erstwhile British allies, an Indian "buffer state" (from time to time a British policy objective) might well have emerged out of interracial warfare in the Old Northwest. But the Indian confederation was vulnerable, as the nations that comprised it could not wage a sustained war and also provide for the most basic economic needs of their people. Away from their villages, Little Turtle and Blue Jacket were dependent on the British even for food. Having committed their people to an ongoing war, they were no longer self-sufficient.[40] In a meeting with the British at Detroit in late November 1790, Blue Jacket had declared that without British help the Indians could not remain on their lands in Ohio and Indiana, but "must divide like a cloud separated by a whirl wind, and scatter away to the long running and never tried waters of the Mississippi, and be seen no more among you."[41]

The help they needed was not forthcoming. Although British Indian agents in the West and the fur-trading interests they represented were eager to assist in defeating the territorial ambitions of the new republic, peace with the United States was a higher priority for policy makers in London. The vague assurances earlier given by British spokesmen to Joseph Brant in London and Blue Jacket at Detroit meant nothing when a more formidable American army under the command of "Mad Anthony" Wayne struck the Indian allies at Fallen Timbers near modern Toledo, Ohio, in September 1794. Chickasaw warriors from the South supported Wayne's troops. A year earlier, the Shawnee chief Red Pole had visited the Chickasaws to enlist their support, but they chose to cast their lot with the United States, as did other acculturated Indian groups in the South and elsewhere.

Bloodied but not totally defeated at the Battle of Fallen Timbers, the insurgents sought refuge at the nearby British Fort Miami on the Maumee. The gates were slammed in their faces. As the British stood aside, Wayne, understanding his enemies' vulnerabilities, devastated villages and fields, ultimately forcing the insurgents to sign the Treaty of Greenville the following year. Although somewhat less severe than the earlier "Conquest Treaties," that document opened most of Ohio to white occupation. In the same year, in London, the signers of Jay's Treaty agreed that the British would finally evacuate their outposts in the Old Northwest. Although some Native American militants for many years to come would continue to hope for British aid in their struggles for independence, those hopes had long been without substance.

After Wayne's victory, some Shawnee leaders, believing that further resistance would lead only to disaster, sought other means of preserving their people. Some were willing to modify their traditional way of life to accommodate new realities. They were

therefore receptive to the "civilization" program of the Washington administration. Secretary of War Henry Knox believed that
the solution to the "Indian problem" was the transformation of
warriors into farmers. If Indian communities could be induced to
abandon their reliance on hunting and horticulture and develop
a full-blown agricultural economy, Knox believed, they would
need less land and therefore have no reason to oppose the
expansion of white settlement. Responding to Knox's appeal,
Congress provided some funding to assist in that transformation.
The former Shawnee war chief Black Hoof, leader of the Mekoche,
invoking a provision of the Treaty of Greenville, asked that the U.S.
government provide the assistance needed to convert his village
at Wapakoneta in the Auglaize valley into a Euro-American-style
agricultural community, complete with log houses with chimneys,
modern agricultural implements, and a herd of cattle. Visiting
Washington DC in 1802, Black Hoof secured a promise from
Secretary of War Henry Dearborn that "Your father the President
will take care to have ploughs and other useful tools provided for
such of his red children, as may be disposed to make good use of
them, and he will furnish you with some Cattle and other articles
equally beneficial."[42]

Despite Dearborn's promise, Black Hoof and his followers
received no assistance until July 1807, when Quaker missionary
William Kirk settled at Wapakoneta and undertook an ambitious
program that included not only instruction in white agricultural
techniques but also the construction of a sawmill and planning for
a gristmill. To the dismay of the Wapakoneta Shawnees, Dearborn
fired Kirk in 1808 for presumed irregularities in his accounts. As
David Edmunds notes, "although the Shawnee and many white
Ohioans petitioned the government in Kirk's favor, the Quaker
was forced to leave the Auglaize. At first, Black Hoof's people
attempted to continue on the white man's road, but they soon
became discouraged. With Kirk's departure the Shawnees lost

their primary source of technical advice and their experiment in agriculture waned." [43]

Elsewhere in Ohio and in Indiana, Shawnees who tried to maintain their traditional lifestyle faced sporadic harassment from white intruders unwilling to respect the boundaries set at Greenville in 1795. Those "border ruffians" slaughtered the game upon which the Shawnees and other Native American peoples depended, raided and despoiled their camps and villages, stole their horses, and sometimes murdered the defenseless. In 1800, Michigan governor Arthur St. Clair complained to his territorial legislature that too many whites seemed to believe that, because their Native American neighbors "had not received the light of the gospel, they might be abused, cheated, robbed, plundered and murdered at pleasure." [44] Seven years later, in an address to the Indiana legislature, Gov. William Henry Harrison advised that the failure to punish even one "of the many persons who have committed murder on their people" was a major obstacle to maintaining peace with the Indians of the territory. Despite the governors' concern, Indians remained at risk. [45]

In their anger and despair, some Shawnees looked to the spirit world for deliverance. In conversations with American officials at Fort Wayne in 1803, a Shawnee representative whose name we do not know proclaimed that "the Master of Life, who was himself an Indian, made the Shawnee before any other of the human race." The Creator "gave them all the knowledge he himself possessed, and placed them on the great island, and all other red people are descended from the Shawnee." White people were inferior by nature; the Creator made them from his lesser body parts. "The Shawnee, for many ages, continued to be masters of the continent, using the knowledge the received from the Great Spirit in such a manner as to be pleasing to him, and to secure their own happiness." In time, however, "they became corrupt, and the Master of Life told them he would take away from them the knowledge which they possessed, and give it to the white people, to be restored when by a return to good principles they would deserve it." Soon thereafter, whites, newly empowered with knowledge, appeared in North America. But "after these white people landed, they were not content to have the knowledge which belonged to the Shawnee, but they usurped their lands also." Because of their transgressions, the whites would soon be punished by the Master of Life, who "will trample the long knives under his feet" and "restore to the Shawnee their knowledge and their rights."[46]

The Shawnee Prophet's Vision

In the spring of 1805, some two years after the Fort Wayne revelation, a thirty-year-old Shawnee named Lalawethika (The Rattle), a man hitherto scorned as a braggart, drunkard, womanizer, and coward, fell into a stupor so profound that his family, believing him to be dead, began preparing his body for burial. But Lalawethika suddenly awoke, crying that the Master of Life had given him a vision of the afterlife. Those who drank alcohol or offended the Great Spirit by other transgressions, he revealed, were destined to burn in hell.[47] Barred from the road to heaven, such sinners were condemned to travel to the land of the "Bad Spirit." Upon their arrival there, they were confined in a house of fire. The worst among them were cast into the conflagration and "burned to ashes," while lesser offenders were "only maimed." After a period of torment, all of the sufferers were revived and, having resumed their "former appearance and sense of feeling," were compelled to travel on "to another house," to burn again. That process was "repeated a number of times." The sufferings of the damned were not, however, eternal. In time their sins burned away, and even the wicked would "go to the residence of the Great Spirit," where they would be "permitted to enjoy in a small degree the happiness allotted" to the righteous. By contrast, however, the souls of the worthy dead journeyed immediately to heaven, which Lalawethika described as "a rich, fertile country, abounding in game, fish, pleasant hunting grounds, and fine cornfields." In that land of plenty "they plant, they hunt, they play at their usual games & in all things are unchanged." [48] After recounting his vision, he declared that the Master of Life had called upon him to show Indians the way to renewal and salvation.

Lalawethika was an unlikely choice for such a mission. A triplet born in 1775 in the Shawnee village of Old Piqua in western Ohio, he was the son of a noted war chief, Pukeshinwau, who had been killed at the battle of Point Pleasant in 1774. The fallen warrior left a large family: a wife, Methoataaskee; six sons (including the triplets, one of whom had died shortly after birth); and three daughters. When Lalawethika was about four years old, his mother left her children to join kinfolk elsewhere. Raised by an older sister, Tecumapease, the future prophet remained in the shadow of two older brothers, the valiant Chiksika, who had fought at Point Pleasant and would die in 1788 in an assault on a white settlement, and Tecumseh, a strong, handsome young man of great promise. Of the prophet's childhood, Edmunds writes: "Either abandoned or ignored by parent figures, he overcompensated for his insecurity through boastful harangues on his own importance. To add to his woes, while playing with a bow and iron tipped arrows, he suffered an accident and lost the sight of his right eye. Moreover, during his adolescence, Lalawethika acquired a taste for the white man's firewater, a habit that both increased his bragging and decreased his popularity among the Shawnees." With his brother Tecumseh he fought against "Mad Anthony" Wayne at the Battle of Fallen Timbers, but unlike his brother he acquired no reputation as a warrior. After the Treaty of Greenville, the brothers left Ohio for the White River country of Indiana. There the future prophet married, but he had much difficulty supporting his wife and three children. Inept as a hunter, Lalawethika, under the tutelage of an aging shaman named Penagashea (Changing Feathers), sought to become a healer. His efforts to succeed Penagashea after the latter's death in 1804 met with indifferent success. As Edmunds notes, "many tribesmen questioned if a man who so often had broken the sacred Shawnee laws could ever wear the mantle of healer or prophet."[49]

A tradition preserved by the Winnebagos holds that Lalawethika told his followers that, under the influence of the Devil, who "misled him," he had initially disregarded the Creator's call and had continued to drink, womanize, and brawl even after his vision of heaven and hell. The Creator accordingly sent a messenger to escort him back to heaven so that he would be reminded of his mission. When he arrived there, in order to "make him see all his bad characteristics and his evil mind," God "took out his heart and showed it to him. It was all furrowed up and bad to look upon. 'Did I create you thus?' said the Creator." Chastised, Lalawethika returned to earth, vowing to obey the Great Spirit. But when he tried to carry out the work entrusted to him by explaining "the mysteries" to his people, no one would listen to him. "He is just getting crazier all of the time," they said of him. Even his brother Tecumseh believed that he was a fraud and told him to shut up. He finally won their attention and respect by placing a small war club on the ground and promising that if anyone could lift it up he would say no more about his mission. No one could. Tecumseh immediately thereafter became his strongest supporter.[50]

In the late spring of 1805, Lalawethika revealed the contents of a series of visions which, he claimed, contained divine instructions on the means of restoring the well-being of the Shawnees and their brethren. As Indian agent Thomas Forsyth recorded the Shawnee prophet's teachings, Lalawethika called for a radical cultural and economic separation from Euro-Americans. The first step to renewal was the elimination of the material trappings of white culture. Indians must immediately shed all non-Indian clothing and get rid of alien domesticated animals. All cats were to be given to whites, as were all dogs "not of their own breed" (horses were not included in the prohibition). The prophet directed that "no Indian was to eat any victuals that were cooked by

a White person, or to eat any provisions raised by White people."
He forbade consumption of the flesh of domestic animals as well
as bread made in the European manner. Banning most commerce
with whites, Lalawethika called for the abandonment of reliance
on the Euro-American cash economy through the restoration
of traditional Indian modes of exchange. "No Indian," Forsyth
reports, was to "offer skins or furs or anything else for sale"
but should instead obtain "such articles as they want" through
bartering. The prophet declared that if the "Indians were to
endeavor to do without buying such merchandise as much as
possible," the Great Spirit would reward them by restoring the
game. "Then," he promised, "by means of bows and arrows, they
could hunt and kill game as in former days, and live independent
of all white people." In maintaining that independence, Indians
were permitted friendly relations and trade connections with
"the French, English, and Spaniards," but "they were not to
know the Americans under any account but to keep them at a
distance." They must never patronize American traders or sell any
provisions to settlers. Only if he were starving could they give
food to an American. They must never shake hands with him. [51]
Anthony Shane, a trader and interpreter of mixed Indian and white
ancestry who was acquainted with the prophet, confirmed much
of Forsyth's account, noting the prophet's insistence that Indians
not live as whites but rather "have all things in common." [52]

    In his reflections on the nature of evil, the Shawnee prophet,
echoing earlier nativist visionaries, declared that the Great Spirit,
whom he also called the Master of Life, was not the creator of the
white man. Whites were the work of a malevolent Great Serpent.
In recounting his visit to heaven and the revelation of the creation
of mankind given to him there, the prophet declared that after
making the first Indians, "the Great Spirit then opened a door and
looking down, they saw a white man seated upon the ground. He
was naked and destitute of hair upon his head or his body and had
been circumcised. The great Spirit told them that the white man

was not made by himself but by another spirit . . . over whom . . . he had no control." He added that the serpent responsible for making white men was trying to undo all of creation and sought to kill "the real people." [53] The prophet and his adherents thus held that Euro-Americans were enemies of the Great Spirit, who intended that his own Indian children occupy all of the land in America. The Creator, they declared, had promised his prophet that he would reward Indian obedience to his commandments by turning over the land "so that the white people would be covered." [54]

To pave the way for that transformation, the prophet sought to reform Indian life, which in his view had been corrupted and debauched by contact with whites. He called for the strict and total prohibition of alcohol. He forbade intermarriage with whites, directing that Indian women living with white men were "to be brought home by their friends and relations, and their children to be left with their fathers, so that the nation might become genuine Indian." He insisted, in Shane's words, that the young must "always support and cherish the aged and the infirm." [55] But the prophet did not simply endeavor to restore traditional values, for, as Forsyth noted, he ordered that "no Indian was to take more than one wife in the future." While those who were polygamous were permitted to keep their wives, the prophet asked them to remember that "it would please the Great Spirit" if they had only one (although, by some accounts, the prophet himself had three). [56] He condemned sexual promiscuity and ordered single men to marry. He declared that husbands should discipline their wives with a rod if they failed "to pay proper attention" to their work. Women who were so punished were not to bear a grudge. [57] The prophet's conception of gender roles departed from Shawnee tradition in some ways. In organizing his community at Prophetstown in 1808, he eliminated the traditional Shawnee "council of women leaders whose resolutions in the areas of diplomacy, peace, and war held equal significance with their male colleagues," in effect depriving women "of any form of ruling power."[58] But he invoked tradition in opposing any change in occupational roles, arguing that Quaker efforts to teach men to work as farmers would destroy Indian manhood.[59]

White commentators, relying on Indian informants, reported Lalawethika's teachings in some detail and, as their accounts generally agree, probably fairly accurately. They were less thorough, however, in noting his creation of new religious rituals, not understanding the crucial role of ritual in Native American spirituality. Informants reported that the prophet insisted on the destruction of medicine bags and also banned all of the traditional "medicine dances and songs." In their place he inaugurated, among other innovations, a new dance that Forsyth mistakenly believed was merely recreational. That dance, later known as the Dance of the Lakes, was actually a highly charged invocation of sacred power. The prophet also directed that the faithful were to gather in an assembly where "everyone was to make open confession to the Great Spirit in a loud voice of all the bad deeds that he or she had committed during their lifetime, and beg for forgiveness." Thereafter they were to offer morning and evening prayers to the Creator. Neglect of that devotion, the prophet warned, would offend the Great Spirit. His followers were also to keep an eternal flame.[60]

The prophet established a number of other rituals, some apparently inspired by contact with Christian missionaries or with peoples such as the Wyandots, who had once been under Catholic missionary influence.[61] One of those quasi-Christian rituals, public confession of sins, has already been mentioned. John Tanner, a white captive living among the Ojibwes, witnessed a ritual vaguely reminiscent of the Catholic rosary. Describing the visit of two messengers from the Shawnee prophet, Tanner related that they carried "an effigy of the prophet" concealed in a blanket, which also contained four strings of beans. After delivering a lengthy sermon on the prophet's teachings, the messengers displayed the strands of beans, claiming that they were made from the prophet's own flesh. Those strings "were carried with much solemnity to each man in the lodge, and he was expected to take hold of each string at the top, and draw them through his hand. This was called shaking hands with the prophet and was considered as solemnly engaging to obey his instructions, and accept his mission, as from the Supreme."[62]

By 1808 Lalawethika was known by a new name, Tenskwatawa, meaning either "the open door" or, as Shane translated it, "he who opened the sky for men to go up to the Great Spirit." [63] In both his teachings and his ritualistic innovations, the prophet offered his adherents a new syncretic religion that borrowed some Christian ideas alien to Shawnee tradition, including belief in an omnipotent and omnipresent Creator, in heaven and hell, in sexual repression, and in patriarchy. [64] But he also affirmed the traditional belief in the importance of ritual as the means of accessing sacred power. His proscription of contact with objects and persons of Euro-American origin resonated with the customary avoidance of acts that gave offense to powerful spirit beings. His appearance and behavior when in communion with the spirit, described by a white observer as "truly hideous," was that of a great shaman. Stephen Ruddell, a white captive raised by the Shawnees, recalled that Tenskwatawa, clad in wildcat skins and carrying the shoulder blades of a deer, would enter "a darkened wigwam" and "would remain in his incantations whole days and whole nights without eating, drinking or sleeping." Ruddell testified that the prophet's "powers of endurance when thus engaged were really remarkable."[65]

In keeping with the pan-Indian tradition established by Neolin and other nativist prophets, Tenskwatawa called for the unification of all Indian peoples. His message inspired the political movement and military alliance usually identified with his brother, the celebrated war chief Tecumseh. As Edmunds has noted, "it was Tenskwatawa, not Tecumseh, who provided the basis for Indian resistance."[66] The prophet's movement had three major thrusts: the revitalization of Native American communal life everywhere through the elimination of practices offensive to the Great Spirit and through the institution of new rituals to win his favor; the establishment of a new, separatist sacred community free of corruption; and the forging of a pan-Indian alliance to preserve Indian lands from further white encroachments.

Fundamental to the prophet's call for the regeneration of the Shawnees and related peoples was his insistence on a thoroughgoing religious reformation. Tenskwatawa's warning that Indians must pray only to the Master of Life and shun all other spirits recalled the teachings of Neolin, and, like Neolin's, went against the grain of traditional practice. The Shawnees had customarily sought, for the well-being of the community, the favor and support of deities similar to those invoked by the Delawares and other related Algonquian peoples: the Sun, the Four Winds, the Earth Mother, Corn Woman, Thunderbirds, and star people. They commonly sought the intercession of "witnesses" in their efforts to communicate with the Creator himself. Among the "witnesses" said to enjoy access to the Creator were tobacco, fire, the sky, stars, certain plants, and the medicine bundles the prophet wished to destroy. Traditional Shawnees believed that the Creator, as one scholar notes, could not "maintain the universe" by himself, as he was not omnipotent, but was instead dependent upon the proper behavior of human beings to avert chaos. In one tradition, he warned the Shawnees that he did not "know how long the place where you live will survive," as its continuation would be possible only if they were faithful to essential spiritual practices.[67] The destruction of the world through human error or malice was a very real possibility to the Shawnees, and ceremonial observances were believed to be essential to survival. In the Green Corn Ceremony and the Spring Bread Dance they won the continued favor of the spirit beings who assured the fertility of the soil. They believed that failure to observe those rituals properly would bring drought and starvation. To traditional Shawnees, communal well-being depended not on prayers to the Creator, who was neither omnipotent nor omniscient, but on proper ritual practice. In those practices the Shawnees closely resembled other Algonquian peoples.

The Shawnee concept of the nature of creation and of the Creator was, however, rather distinctive. Many Native American peoples believed that the material universe was preexistent and eternal, without a beginning or an end but subject to great transformations. Their creation stories explained the origins of mankind but not the creation of the material world. The Shawnees, however, spoke of both primal creation and destruction. The traditional Shawnee Creator, sometimes called "the Good Spirit," sometimes referred to as "the Finisher," had brought the world into being out of total, primal darkness. He first created clouds, then light, which emanated from two great glowing deities, the sun and the moon, and also from numerous lesser spirits seen as stars. Below the now-luminescent heavens the Creator made water and land, which he divided into the four great cardinal directions. Humans and animals, in some versions of the Shawnee creation story, were first created as sky beings and later placed upon the earth after it dried out. The universe from the sky above to the waters beneath the earth teemed with supernatural beings, some benevolent to mankind, others dangerous. The Creator made mistakes. His early human prototypes were nonfunctional because he put the genitalia in the wrong places, first on the forehead, then in the armpits. Only on the third attempt did he finally succeed in making people capable of reproduction.[68]

Tenskwatawa's Shawnee contemporaries believed that the first world made by the Creator was destroyed in a flood. The present creation was the result of collaboration between the Finisher and the single survivor of the deluge, an old woman. That survivor, whom the Shawnees named Our Grandmother, persuaded the Creator to create a new earth and assisted him in the process. The Creator descended from the sky, raised a turtle out of the watery void, placed dirt on the turtle's back, formed islands, and surrounded them with waters. After the second creation was completed, Our Grandmother was given responsibility for supervising the Creator's chosen people, the Shawnees. At some point in the nineteenth century, Our Grandmother eclipsed the Finisher in Shawnee consciousness. Twentieth-century ethnographic reports identified her as the Shawnee Creator and as the prime object of their worship. Voegelin, for example, related that his Shawnee informants, representing three separate bands, all reported that the Creator and supreme being in their pantheon was Our Grandmother. They indicated, however, that Our Grandmother did not live in the highest sky realm. "There appears to be some feeling for a level above the Creator, but its resident is absent in current mythology." One informant made a fleeting reference to "an otiose deity" who created the world before the time of Our Grandmother. [69] But the most popular modern Shawnee creation story portrays Our Grandmother descending from the void above into the primal waters, settling on the back of a turtle, and then forming both the heavens and the earth. For a time she remained upon the earth, accompanied by a dog and by her grandson, a troublesome young man to whom she granted "unwholesome license." She subsequently ascended into the sky, "from which place she dispenses medicine and other benefits to mortal visitors." [70]

Tenskwatawa's prophetic visions did not come from Our Grandmother or from the Finisher. The prophet spoke for the "Master of Life," the Great Spirit of the Delaware prophets. He warned that the Creator was a jealous god who had told him that the work of creation must not be attributed "to any but me." Tenskwatawa also drew on the earlier prophetic tradition in his dualistic view of the spirit world. He spoke of a shape-shifting "Evil Spirit" with "power to transfer his own spirit into animals and men, whenever he has criminal designs against anyone." But that evil spirit, like the Devil of Christianity, was less powerful than the Creator, who could render him harmless "at any time." Those who obeyed the commandments revealed by the prophet thus had no reason to fear the evil spirit. In his 1824 interview with C. C. Trowbridge, Tenskwatawa, in explaining Shawnee beliefs and practices, interwove older Shawnee beliefs about the Creator and the events of creation with the new belief in the prophets' Great Spirit. He drew upon the familiar turtle island theme, relating that after the Master of Life created the true people (Indians), he told them "to go to an island that rested on the back of a great turtle that they were henceforth to call Grandfather." Tenskwatawa also repeated the traditional Shawnee story that the Creator left his people soon thereafter, saying that "he would not be seen by them again, and that they must think for themselves, and pray to their grandmother, the Moon," who was present in the form of an old woman. He explained that the Creator had appointed Our Grandmother and her grandson "subordinate deities" directly responsible for supervising the Indians. But in his 1824 interview Tenskwatawa also declared that those times were past, telling Trowbridge that Indians were now commanded to direct their prayers to the Creator alone and acknowledge him as the sole source of life and power. The Creator was no longer absent from the world of men.[71]

Unfortunately, we have no direct report of the content of Tenskwatawa's sermons on creation and on the Great Spirit from the crucial years 1805 to 1813. We do not know whether the story of the withdrawal and return of the Shawnee Creator embedded in the prophet's 1824 interview reflects his original message. It seems likely that he combined traditional stories with his new teaching then as he did in his conversations a decade later with Trowbridge, but we cannot be sure. We do know this, however: whatever the prophet's explication of the relationship of the primal Creator and the secondary deity known as Our

Grandmother, the most radical aspect of his message was his uncompromising opposition to traditional shamanism. This was the key to his teachings about the will of the Creator.

Numerous sources testify to the high status and exceptional power of Shawnee shamans. Writing in the late twentieth century, anthropologist James Howard reported that "even today the Shawnee tribe as a whole is regarded as a nation of wonder-workers by the Creeks, Seminoles, Alabamas, Koasatis, Cherokees, and other southeastern groups." [72] From sources contemporary with Tecumseh and the prophet we learn that it was believed that Shawnee warriors who possessed shamanic gifts could sometimes defeat the enemy by transforming themselves into large, ferocious animals or could escape harm when outnumbered by becoming small, flying insects. They could kill the foe by transmitting poison at a great distance or by enveloping them in a magical, woven halter. "The Delaware, who lacked such power, on occasion . . . were compelled to call on the Shawnee for aid." [73] Jedidiah Morse, writing in 1822, related that the Shawnees themselves believed not only that their shamans possessed "the art of restoring the dead" but that at the time of their migration into this continent the Shawnees "enjoyed the art of walking on surface of the ocean, by which they crossed from the east to America without Vessels." [74]

The prophet's account of the initiation rites once said to have been observed by the Shawnee "Juggling Society" suggests the ongoing influence of archaic shamanic traditions, for it is reminiscent of Siberian lore about the dismemberment and rebirth of shamans. [75] In the rites of admission to a Shawnee shamanic brotherhood, the initiate, usually a boy around eight years old, was first knocked unconscious with a club and then cut into pieces. His head was set aside, but the other parts of his body were fed to dogs, who were then driven away. The head was then taken into the society's lodge, "where it was laid on a bed of leaves as the elders sang. The dogs were called back. These animals, being overcharged with food which they had eaten, were kept near the head, where they vomited and discharged all that they had eaten. This mass was covered with leaves, the society danced around the bed to the right in quick succession, during which the oldest men sang very violently, and at the end of the dance they seated themselves." The dead boy then miraculously reappeared, having "exactly the same appearance as before he was killed" but now endowed with exceptional power. He "took his place among the members."[76]

That initiation story conveyed in a powerful manner the sense that the Shawnee shaman was no longer an ordinary mortal. While the Shawnees did not share the secrets of the Juggling Society with whites, the evidence available to us suggests that its members, among other things, performed the Shaking Tent Ceremony, a practice rooted in classic shamanism and widespread among northern Algonquian peoples. The tent or lodge constructed for this ceremony was usually about twelve feet high and covered with hides affixed to four poles that supported the structure. On entering the tent, the shaman sang a sacred song that summoned spirit animals. Their presence was made manifest by a violent shaking of the tent, which swayed back and forth "as in heavy gale." The shaman then heard the voices of the spirit animals, which advised him on matters such as the location of lost possessions or the proper cures of whatever diseases might be currently afflicting the people.[77]

Breaking with long-standing belief and tradition, Tenskwatawa portrayed the traditional shaman not as a healer but as a killer in league with the Devil. His message was not entirely new. As we have noted, the Delaware prophets of the preceding century had also on occasion condemned the medicine dance and certain other shamanic practices as diabolical. More recently, Lalawethika's mentor, Penagashea, had warned against the dangers of witchcraft.[78] The prophet's concept of witchcraft, like Neolin's, departed from the customary notion that witches were simply malicious or self-seeking individuals who abused power inherent in sacred objects that in more responsible hands would be used benevolently. He was persuaded that all who used medicine bundles were in league with the Great Serpent, and thus he rejected the traditional distinction between shamans and witches. The Shawnee prophet challenged a fundamental precepts of traditional Shawnee religion: the belief that the well-being of the people required both the preservation and use of "sacred bundles" and the performance of the medicine dance to invoke sacred power.[79]

Medicine bundles played a vital role in the religious practice of many Native American peoples. As Timothy Willig notes, "at no time prior to the advent of the prophet would members of the Algonquian cultures have gone without their sacred bundles. These buckskin pouches contained sacred elements through which the manitous empowered and protected their proper bearers, and to be without the sacred bundles invited disaster."[80] To the Shawnees they were of particular significance. A Shawnee myth related how victory over a dreaded enemy had been won after a medicine bundle had been opened to reveal the wooden figure of a boy who came to life and foretold the Shawnee triumph by shooting magic arrows at a specter of the foe.[81] The Shawnees also believed that some sacred bundles, when opened by a shaman of the Turtle clan, could end drought by summoning the Thunderbirds to produce rain.[82] The prophet himself, in his conversations with Trowbridge in 1824, related a traditional story that told how, immediately after their creation, the Shawnees were guided through an impassable ocean to the island that was to be their homeland by singing to their sacred bundle for twelve days. On the twelfth day, their founder, Old Man, told them that "the Great Spirit had promised to grant them all they desired and that they must pray to him to remove the water which impeded their journey to the island. Soon after the water was dried up & they saw nothing but sand." Old Man then designated a guardian of the bundle, who was also to be leader of the people. Tenskwatawa may have exempted the sacred tribal bundle from his condemnation of individual bundles, since it figured prominently in his vision of the end of the world.[83]

Visitors to the Shawnees often remarked on their exceptional reverence for their sacred bundles, a reverence that generally has included bundles of all sorts. Thomas Morris, writing in 1764, reported, "They carry their God in a bag, which is hung in front of their encampment, and is viewed by none but the priest; if any other presumes to advance between the front of that encampment and that spirit in a bag, he is put to death; and it was told that a drunken French soldier, who had done so, was with some difficulty saved."[84] Anthropologist C. F. Voegelin, after extensive fieldwork among the Shawnees in the 1930s, concluded that "ultimate insight" into Shawnee religion "must rest on a study of the sacred bundles," which, he concluded, "overshadowed" even the Creator in importance. Voegelin's informants were reluctant to speak of the bundles, for they were both mysterious in nature and origin and awesome in power. But Voegelin did learn that the Shawnees believed that they were the direct gift of Our Grandmother, that they were the most potent of all the means of communicating with her, that she revealed her will to the Shawnees through them, and that she would recall them shortly before the end of the world. Proper care and use of the sacred bundles assured the prosperity and security of the people. They were of such central importance in the spiritual life of the Shawnees that Voegelin concluded that during the ceremonial dances, the Shawnees "talk of Our Grandmother, but think about the bundles."[85]

In traditional Shawnee belief, much good was said to come from the power contained in these bundles; however, their possessors could also torture and kill through sorcery. In troubled times, some came to suspect that shamans were abusing the power inherent in medicine bundles. Like other Native American peoples, the Shawnees feared shamans who used their power, not for the good of the community, but for malevolent ends. Witches were said to be in league with malignant water monsters or with the bad spirit they called "moyshee Monoetoo." In normal times the Shawnees did not regard their own shamans as witches; they cherished their medicine bundles and, despite their fear of witches, did not generally associate the bundles primarily with witchcraft. But however unlikely, the malevolent use of the power contained in the bundles was always a possibility.

It was this fear of such abuse of power that Tenskwatawa drew upon in his condemnation of the use of medicine bundles and of the shamanic practices associated with them. While he may have exempted the tribal bundles, which were regarded as special gifts of the Creator, the prophet called for the destruction of all other medicine bags. Like other eastern Indians, Shawnee hunters and ordinary warriors also relied on medicine bundles in their everyday work, believing that they conveyed power essential to the success of their ventures. Tenskwatawa, however, taught that those medicine bundles contained a dangerous and malevolent substance and for that reason must be destroyed. He drew on a long-standing belief—found among Delawares and other peoples as well as the Shawnees—that medicine bundles contained portions of the body of the Great Serpent. While the serpent was clearly malevolent, it was generally believed that, in the right hands, the power inherent in its preserved flesh could be employed to negate evil and protect the people. It was this belief in the potential benevolence of the bundles that Tenskwatawa disavowed. In dualistic terms, he identified serpent flesh and other objects of power in the bundles with evil.

In conversations with Trowbridge some years after the collapse of his movement, Tenskwatawa explained his case against the bundles by drawing upon the familiar story of the Great Serpent but finding in it a new meaning. Although the ancestors of the Shawnees had killed the Great Serpent, the author of evil, during their migration into their homeland, certain wicked individuals had preserved parts of its body. That body, the prophet explained, "was like that of a snake & he had the head, horns & neck of a large buck. His body was cut into small pieces, and every thing connected with it, even to the excrement, was carefully preserved. The head, horns, flesh, et. cetera was mixed with the heart & flesh of the animal [a crocodile] found on the seashore, and forms the medicine witches use. . . . It is still preserved, and the flesh, tho' many thousands of years old, is as fresh as if it had just been killed." Those pieces of serpent flesh, which possessed great power, were now being preserved in the sacred bundles. Periodically renewed by infusions of human flesh and blood, those bundles, according to Tenskwatawa, enabled their possessors to become invisible, fly through the air, change shape, and inflict illness and death. Social strife and disorder as well as sickness were the result of witchcraft made possible by the evil power in the bundles. Like the Delaware prophetess many years earlier, Tenskwatawa believed the destruction of medicine bundles to be essential to the restoration of both physical health and social harmony.[86]

The Witch Hunts

The Shawnee prophet, as one contemporary observer recorded, claimed to have been "endowed with supernatural powers that enable him to see every witch."[87] Rumors about his gifts as a witch finder spread throughout the Indian villages of the region. Two communities fearful of the activities of witches in their midst soon sought his aid. The first was Woapikamunk, one of six Delaware Indian villages located in the White River region of Indiana.[88] The first Delawares had settled in the White River country in the 1780s, driven westward by the pressure of white immigration into the Ohio valley and terrorized by incidents such as the notorious massacre of Moravian Delaware converts at Gnadenhutten in eastern Ohio in 1782. In 1799 the Moravians established a mission on the White River, but they found the Delawares highly resistant to their message. [89]

The impoverished and demoralized residents of the Delaware villages were distressed by the inability of the Moravian preachers to arrest the onslaughts of epidemic disease that periodically afflicted them. In 1802 some Delawares, as the mission's diarist related, "had come to the conclusion that perhaps the Christian Indians were the cause, for the reason that before the Word of God was preached here among them, not so many heathen Indians had died." The village leaders believed that witchcraft was responsible for the epidemic, but, uncertain about the identity of the malefactors, they resisted pressure to blame the handful of Delaware Christian converts living at Woapikamunk. Instead, in keeping with the general practice of attributing witchcraft to marginal people or outsiders, they accused two refugee women in their midst, one a Nanticoke, the other a Mingo. The chiefs declared that these women, new to the community, "had said that they wished to harm the Delaware nation." Carrying out that threat, the accused allegedly transformed themselves "into night owls, flew about at night over all the Indian towns, and brought them into a fatal malady." The two were put to death. [90]

Although the Delaware sachems had momentarily diverted suspicion from local Indian converts, animosity toward Christians continued to fester. The White River mission diary entry of May 19, 1803, complained that most of the Delawares not only refused to listen to the gospel message but also harassed the few who visited the mission. A family of converts who had apostatized accused the mission's interpreter, a Mahican Christian named Joshua, of killing "their child by means of witchcraft." "Such talk," the Moravian diarist noted prophetically, "cannot work anything but great harm to us." [91]

In the late spring of 1805, the missionaries at White River wrote that "a bilious fever was raging" in the Indian villages of the region. "Many died of it in a few days." Once again suspecting witchcraft, the Delawares undertook "a rigid investigation to find out who the Indians were who are making them sick and bringing about their death." Although the residents of Woapikamunk promptly denounced a number of their compatriots as witches, the village leaders, some of whom were themselves accused of witchcraft, were at a loss to know how to prove guilt or innocence. They relied initially on a local prophetess, a Munsee woman who had once associated with the Moravians and who is known only by her Christian baptismal name, Beata, given to her as a young woman when she had lived at a Moravian missionary community in eastern Ohio. The Moravians related that at the time of her emergence as a witch finder, Beata "had an extraordinary vision and swallowed three times a light that appeared to her." John Sugden writes that Beata taught that her people "had become degenerate—neglecting ancient ceremonies that propitiated the spirits, and drinking, fornicating, stealing, and abusing others. The Great Spirit was offended, and he intended sending a child, or perhaps a resurrected Delaware warrior who would show them the correct conduct. It was important that they listen, for an apocalypse was coming, a storm that would destroy all the world." Beata warned that witchcraft was rampant, but she soon found the task of witch detection far too trying and withdrew her services. But several prominent tribesmen, including two chiefs, Tetapach-sit and Hockingpompsga, remained under suspicion. Both were somewhat unpopular because of their earlier complicity in land sales to whites. Impressed by stories of a powerful prophet living at the Shawnee village recently established nearby at Greenville in western Ohio, the White River Delawares, after nearly a year of turmoil, sought his aid.[92]

Arriving at the Delaware settlement on March 15, 1806, the Shawnee prophet ordered that the suspects be brought before him. As the villagers encircled the accused, the prophet, after performing "many ceremonies" designed to deepen his insight into the spirit world, passed judgment. We will presently review the outcome of those judgments, but we should note at this point that, although the prophet's teachings on witchcraft appeared to be directed against traditionalist shamans, the victims of the witch hunts inspired by his message at White River and later in Wyandot country were most often highly acculturated Indians who advocated a policy of accommodation with the United States. Some were Christian converts. Even so, they were charged with possession of medicine bundles and with the malevolent use of those bundles, for the prophet's followers believed that the profession of Christianity and the practice of witchcraft often went hand in hand. Jay Miller notes that "on the White River of Indiana, Delaware anxiety crystallized around a belief that such bundles were being used to weaken, infect, and kill Delaware holding to their ancient religion." On the White River and elsewhere, the witch hunts were inextricably bound up in conflicts over acculturation.[93]

The first of the victims Tenskwatawa condemned was Coltos (sometimes called Kaltas, Caritas, or Anne Charity), an elderly Delaware woman who had been raised by Moravian missionaries in Pennsylvania. Shortly after the Gnadenhutten massacre in 1782, Coltos had left the Moravians and taken refuge, as one missionary noted, "with her heathen relations," who took her to "the White River, to be out of the way of the murdering gang of White people who had destroyed so many of their relations already." Although she was not regarded as one of the Christian Indians at White River and did not associate with the Moravian missionaries there, Coltos was nonetheless highly acculturated. Her neat and orderly household, we are told, reflected habits she had learned as a child growing up in the family of a Moravian minister named Youngman, and her mode of dress also set her apart.[94] We do not know if she also dabbled in the occult, although a medicine bundle that presumably belonged to her "was kept by her descendants until a decade ago."[95] It is likely that the case against her rested on nothing more substantial than her earlier connections with whites and her continuing emulation of certain white ways. Burned over a slow fire for four days, Coltos finally confessed her guilt. The executioners demanded that she tell them where to find her medicine bundle. She told her tormentors that she had given it to her grandson. Coltos was then put to death, and her grandson was apprehended and brought before the prophet. The young man confessed that he had used his grandmother's medicine bundle to fly through the air "over Kentucky, to the banks of the Mississippi and back again, between twilight and dinner." He insisted that he had returned the bundle to the old woman. Since he had harmed no one, the grandson was pardoned and released.[96]

The elderly chief Tetapachsit (sometimes identified as Tatapaxsit, Tatepocohse, or Teteboxti) was less fortunate. Accused of using a medicine bundle to bring about the "death of a large number of Indians," he was tied to a stake and tortured with firebrands. At first he refused to confess, but finally, to end his agony, he admitted his complicity in witchcraft and explained that he had hidden his bundle near the Moravian mission. He was then dragged to the spot where he claimed it had been secreted. After failing to produce it, Tetapachsit was tomahawked and his body burned in front of the mission.[97] The Moravians deeply regretted the chief's death, for he was an advocate of peace and accommodation, having been one of the signers two decades earlier of the Treaty of Greenville, which ceded much of Ohio to the United States. Missionary John Heckewelder, who knew Tetapachsit well, described him as "a quiet inoffensive and harmless man" friendly to those who professed the Christian gospel. But Tetapachsit was suspected of causing the death through witchcraft of Buckongahelas, a rival chief sympathetic to revitalization. Moreover, he was accused of selling alcohol, also a serious offense in the eyes of those who followed the prophets.[98]

The next to die was the Moravians' interpreter. Joshua, a sixty-five-year-old Mohegan from Connecticut, had originally been examined by a Delaware council, which, assisted by the prophetess Beata, declared that there was no evidence against him. But after Beata withdrew her services the council decided that all cases, including Joshua's, should be reexamined. Joshua was brought before the prophet, who agreed that he was not guilty of the original charge but found that Joshua nonetheless was dangerous, as he "possessed the power of sorcery, with which he could kill people." Joshua, he alleged, was the devotee of a cannibalistic guardian spirit shaped like a great bird that would eat his victims. The prophet's accusation was not as fanciful as some writers have suggested. Moravian minister John Luckenbach related that despite his Christian faith, Joshua "was never quite free of superstition, and in an hour of weakness, he boasted of a dream he had in his childhood. . . . [H]e told the Indians that if, after the heathen manner, he wanted to make use of the dream of his youth, he could also do evil, for in his vision a bird had appeared unto him and said, 'I am a man eater, and if you wish to feed me, you need but point out to me someone, and then I will put him out of the way.' " [99] No doubt informed of Joshua's unfortunate boast, the prophet used it as the basis of his judgment that Joshua was a witch. Alarmed by that finding, the villagers, as a Moravian minister who tried to negotiate for his release recalled, dragged Joshua to "a large fire" where "they insisted that he should confess how many people he had put to death" with the aid of his malevolent flying guardian. But Joshua protested his innocence. Since he refused to cooperate, one of his accusers "struck, from behind . . . [a] tomahawk-hatchet into Joshua's head. This action was repeated by the others, whereupon with heathenish yells, they threw his body onto the fire." [100]

After Joshua's death, two other converts were prepared for execution. One, Tetapachsit's nephew, a lesser chief named Billy Patterson, was burned at the stake. A tradition holds that Patterson died "Bible in hand, praying, chanting hymns, and defying the power of evil until his voice was stifled." [101] After Patterson was burned, the witch hunt was abruptly terminated. Anthony Shane, interviewed in 1821 by historian Benjamin Drake, claimed that as the next victim, the old chief's young widow, was about to be taken from the council meeting to the stake, her brother, a young man of twenty years, "arose, took her by the hand, and led her out of the council to the astonishment of others." He then returned and denounced the Shawnee prophet for bringing suspicion and strife to the community. His exclamation that "the devil has come among us and we are killing one another" allegedly broke the prophet's hold over the villagers and ended the witch hunt at Woapikamunk. [102] The Moravian missionaries, whose account is more authoritative, provide a different explanation. In their diary entries for April 9 and 10, 1806, they wrote that "we heard that the savages were about to put to death their last surviving chief, old Hockingpompsga beside the Chief of the Nanticokes and 6 other Indians of both sexes. Just as they laid hands on their unfortunate victim, the friends of the chief took their weapons, sprung into the midst of the people, and threatened to kill anyone who should take part in the murder. This put a check on further slaughter." Hockingpompsga, condemned to death as a witch by the Shawnee prophet, was restored to office. [103]

Despite the prophet's aid and encouragement, the witch-hunters at Woapickamunk had incurred the opposition not merely of acculturated Delawares who favored accommodation with whites but also of many traditionalists. It is significant that after the witch-hunters were ousted from power at Woapikamunk the tribal leaders did not reaffirm their previous friendly relations with the Moravian missionaries and instead embraced a nativist program. Chief Hockingpompsga, once sympathetic to Christianity, now took the lead in asking the Moravians to leave. The missionaries abandoned their White River mission before the year's end. [104]

Woapikamunk's leaders now reinstituted the great communal rituals—the Big House Ceremony and the Green Corn

Dance—which had lapsed during the year of the witch hunt. [105] Traditionalists feared the consequences of neglecting the ancient rites. Among the Mohawks a few years earlier, a visionary had proclaimed that the deity Thauloonghyauwangoo, the Upholder of the Skies, had revealed that he had inflicted the Iroquois with disease, war, and hunger because he was angry over their abandonment of the practice of offering a white dog in sacrifice. The traditionalist faction, led by Chief Blacksmith at Oneida, promptly restored the White Dog Ceremony, a decision later confirmed by the Seneca prophet Handsome Lake. [106] The Indiana Delawares felt similar anxiety about lapses in their ritual life. Telling evidence of the witch hunt's effect on religious practices in the Delaware villages at White River is the omission in the diary of the Moravian mission of any mention of the celebration of the great public rituals during the witch-hunt period. In previous years the missionaries had regularly recorded and deplored those events. Their restoration represented a determination on the part of traditionalist leaders to restore the unity that had been shattered not only by the witch hunt but by controversies over acceptance of the Moravians.

When Governor Harrison rebuked the Delawares at White River for their witch killings and their susceptibility to the "false" teachings of the prophet, the tribal leaders replied that "you white people also try your criminals, and when they are found guilty, you hang or kill them." But their rejection of the governor's admonition and their repudiation of the Moravians are best understood as expressions of resentment against white meddling in their affairs, not as affirmations of the witch-hunting methods of the Shawnee prophet. [107] Unfortunately, the White River Delaware community remained divided. Despite the efforts of their leaders to allay suspicions and heal wounds, a new witchcraft scare in 1809 led to the killing of "a dozen people within a year." The Shawnee prophet played no role in that witch hunt. [108]

In May 1806 the Shawnee prophet responded to an invitation

to assist in a witch purge mounted by some young Wyandots living on the Sandusky River in Ohio. After visiting several of their villages in the late spring of that year, the prophet condemned four women as witches. We know very little about the accused. A missionary, Joseph Badger, referred to them as the "best" women in their community. Given his biases, that comment has led some historians to conclude, probably correctly, that they, like their Delaware counterparts, were highly acculturated and that their accusers were young, disaffected Wyandots critical of the policy of accommodation then pursued by their elders. The Wyandot witch hunt was probably the outgrowth of a power struggle against the Wyandot accommodationists. But whatever the origin of the witch hunt, the Shawnee prophet's actions immediately engendered opposition. After he issued orders that the women be killed, one of his designated executioners called on Joseph Badger, protesting that "he had not consented" to the killings and did not know what to do. The missionary advised him to go to "the chiefs." Under the prodding of Tarhe, the principal chief, the leaders intervened to protect the accused, and the first Wyandot witch hunt claimed no victims.[109] A second witch hunt, in 1810, led to several killings. The most prominent of the victims was Shateyaronyah, a chief whom the Americans called Leatherlips. Although some white observers and many later historians charged the Shawnee prophet and Tecumseh with responsibility for those executions, the victims appear to have been supporters of the prophet. John Sugden has concluded that this witch hunt, as well as several witch killings among the Missouri Shawnees, were the work of Tenskwatawa's enemies.[110]

After receiving word of the witch burnings at White River in 1806, Governor Harrison had sent the Delawares a letter demanding that they reject the Shawnee prophet as an "imposter." "I charge you to stop your bloody career," the governor wrote. "Let your poor old men and women sleep in quietness, and banish from their minds the dreadful idea of being burnt alive by their own friends and countrymen." He suggested that Lalawethika be put to the test. "If he really is a prophet, ask him to cause the sun to stand still—the moon to alter its course-the rivers to cease to flow—or the dead to arise from their graves. If he does these things, you may then believe that he has been sent from God."[111] The prophet rose to the challenge by announcing at Greenville that the Master of Life would turn the sun black at his request on June 16, 1806.[112]

The eclipse of the sun, which did occur on that day, did much to enhance the prophet's prestige, but it did not bring him the power he sought. Lalawethika/Tenskwatawa never won the loyalty of the majority of the Shawnees. At one point he attempted to use witchcraft hysteria in his own bid for power among the Shawnees, but he failed completely in his efforts to unseat Black Hoof and several other accommodationist Shawnee chiefs whom he accused of witchcraft. Although, as Edmunds notes, "a fear of witches and their evil power permeated Shawnee culture," the prophet's particular brand of witch-hunting required not only abandonment of some of the most fundamental Shawnee beliefs relating to the use of medicine bundles and the efficacy of certain shamanic ritual but also the execution of esteemed tribal leaders. There was no large-scale witch hunt among the Shawnees comparable to the Delaware purge of 1806. The prophet's supporters in 1807 murdered two Shawnees on the ground that they were guilty of "bad medisin," but they never gained control of the major Shawnee villages in Ohio.[113] Elsewhere, the prophet's efforts to encourage witch killings were of little effect. He had few followers among the Miamis and other Ohio tribes. His message was received with more enthusiasm in the West, but we have only one other recorded instance of violence against suspected witches in that region. In 1809, Tenskwatawa's followers persuaded the Kickapoos, a group said to be particularly ardent in their support of the prophet, to burn an old man who had refused to relinquish his medicine bundle. But their efforts to secure the execution of several other Kickapoos whom they accused of witchcraft were unavailing. [114] Despite the exhortations of the Shawnee prophet and his disciples against the dangers of witchcraft during numerous visits to Indian villages throughout the Old Northwest, there is no record of any other killings. A significant but often overlooked fact about the prophet's witch hunts is that they encountered substantial resistance and yielded relatively few victims.

With the failure of the early witch-hunting campaigns, his spokesmen softened the prophet's message. John Tanner, a white captive among the Ojibwes of Lake Superior, reported that the first messenger of the prophet to visit the Ojibwes demanded drastic reforms in Indian life, including the destruction of medicine bundles. He won some adherents, but his exhortations did not lead to a witch hunt. A second messenger, sensitive to the resistance provoked by some of the prophet's more extreme demands (such as the proscription on the use of metal to make fire), offered an easier path to renewal. He taught that Indians must give up intertribal warfare, "no longer steal, defraud, nor lie," and eschew the use of alcohol and the consumption of hot food and drink. [115]

The Shawnee prophet himself on occasion soft-pedaled witch-hunting. John Heckewelder, who believed erroneously that the prophet's witch hunt claimed numerous victims, admitted that "he did not succeed in all his schemes and undertakings; for one day, when in the height of the exercise of his assumed power, he met with a spirited inferior chief, who defied him, boldly stepping up to him in a language, or expression he could not misunderstand, asked him if he dared to accuse him of witchcraft; he immediately became sensible that limits were set to his power and proceedings." Confronted with opposition, the prophet, as Heckewelder related, backed off and confined his remarks to a denunciation of "white people." [116] That exchange was far more characteristic of the prophet's witch-hunting campaign than Heckewelder realized. Although the witch hunts were originally used as a weapon in the struggle against established, pro-accommodationist village chiefs, they proved counterproductive. Shane claimed that the prophet was forced to give up witch-hunting by his more humane and chivalrous older brother. [117] As we will see, Shane is not entirely reliable, but Tecumseh's recent biographers, emphasizing his pragmatism and political sagacity, tend to accept his claim. It is clear that the witch hunts were divisive and served only as a hindrance to the pan-Indian unity the brothers hoped to forge. [118] In 1807, in an effort to heal the divisions among the Shawnee communities in Ohio, Tecumseh "publicly disavowed the Prophet's attempts to have the Wapakoneta chiefs assassinated as sorcerers." [119] There is no evidence that the prophet objected to his brother's action. Thereafter, witch killing played no part in the brothers' efforts to purify Native American communities.

3

Tenskwatawa, Tecumseh, and the Pan-Indian Movement

Despite the dissension that surrounded the Shawnee prophet's involvement in the Delaware and Wyandot witch hunts, Tenskwatawa's call to renewal soon won adherents throughout the Old Northwest as word spread of his remarkable powers, exemplified in miracles such as the eclipse of the sun allegedly commanded by the prophet on June 16, 1806. The prophet's followers would soon gather in a community of believers, diverse in tribal background but united in their dream of a divine restoration of the Indian world. At the time of his first vision, the prophet and his brother Tecumseh were living in the White River country of Indiana, near the present-day town of Anderson. Shortly thereafter they moved to Wapakoneta, where they challenged the leadership of the accommodationist chief Black Hoof and sought to convert the Shawnees there to the nativist gospel. They were unsuccessful. As members of the Kispoko band, the brothers lacked political stature, as leadership had traditionally been entrusted to the Mekoches. The Shawnee tribal council remained loyal to Black Hoof. Frustrated in their bid for power and embarrassed by the activities of a follower, an elderly prophetess who in the spring of 1806 had led a number of Wapakoneta Shawnees to assemble on the banks of the Miami River to sing the prophet's promised new world into being, the brothers established a new community at Greenville.[1]

The Sacred Community at Greenville

Built at the edge of a prairie three miles from the ruins of Gen. Anthony Wayne's Fort Greenville, the prophet's village was dominated by a council house 150 feet long and 34 feet wide situated on a hill. Nearby were some fifty-seven small houses built by the Shawnees. Further away visitors found an open-air meeting ground adjacent to the tent encampments of a group of Wyandots who, under the leadership of Roundhead, followed the prophet. In addition to listening regularly to the sermons and revelations of the prophet, the faithful offered prayers to the Great Spirit at sunrise and sunset in a ceremony described by white visitors as both solemn and dramatic.[2] The brothers hoped that Greenville would be recognized as the new center of Shawnee life, that Shawnees from all over the continent would gather there. In that expectation they were disappointed, but Greenville did attract visitors from numerous other Algonquian nations.[3] Shortly after the founding of the community at Greenville, a delegation of Kickapoos from the Illinois country visited Lalawethika, embraced his teachings, and returned to convert their people to the new faith. Despite the efforts of agents sent by Governor Harrison to warn against listening to the Shawnee prophet, "by the summer of 1807 the Kickapoo villages on the Sagamon had become seedbeds for the Prophet's influence in Illinois."[4]

From his base at Greenville, the prophet reached out to the west and to the north, sending messengers in the fall of 1806 with "invitations to a series of intertribal councils to be held on the Auglaize River the following summer." The messengers warned that soon "a great darkness would envelop the earth and that only the Prophet could save them from groping blindly in the forest."[5] Among those who responded were Potawatomis from Michigan, Illinois, and Wisconsin who were disaffected with the accommodationist policy of their eastern "annuity chiefs." These militant Potawatomis, led by the warrior-shaman Main Poc, who spent two months at Greenville, were captivated by the prophet's vision of a new world free of whites. Soon Potawatomi converts would help spread new gospel in the West, inviting Sacs, Winnebagos, and Menominees to a council at Crow Prairie on the Illinois River in the late fall of 1807.[6]

Among the northern nations, the prophet's most important convert was an Ottawa warrior known as Le Maigouis—in English, the Trout. Designating him as "his Herald," Lalawethika presented the Trout with a wampum belt and charged him with responsibility for carrying the message to the Ottawas and the Chippewas. In his travels to the northern villages, the Trout spoke of the anger and wrath of the Creator and warned that those who failed to obey the directives that the Great Spirit had revealed to the Shawnee prophet would be "cut off from the face of the earth" and denied, in the coming time of darkness, the light that only the prophet could provide. The Great Spirit had heeded the prophet's plea not to destroy the world just yet, giving his true people an opportunity to repent. All Indians must therefore heed the prophet's call for separation from whites. Particularly to be shunned were Americans, "the spawn of the Great Serpent." Henceforth, Indians were not to eat the white man's food or wear his clothing. Hats, in particular, were proscribed. Indians must also reform their religious practices, avoiding in particular the innovations of the Wabenos. The Trout revealed that he had also spoken with the Great Spirit, who had explained that the scarcity of game and the emaciated condition of the few animals remaining was the result of the Indians' emulation of whites. "You destroy them yourselves for their skins only, and leave their bodies to rot, or give the Best Pieces to the Whites. I am displeased when I see this, and take them back to the earth." The Great Spirit promised to reward Indian renunciation of contact with Anglo-Americans by restoring the game. To accelerate the rebirth of the world that had died when whites invaded their lands, the Trout taught his followers a new dance, based no doubt on the Shawnee prophet's, which would give them the power to "destroy every white man in America." He also encouraged the traditional lacrosse game. After summoning representatives of all the tribes in the region to his village, the Trout then revealed that the Great Spirit had declared that Indians must "never to go to war against each other, but to cultivate peace between your different Tribes, that they may become one great people." Despite the efforts of American agents in Michigan to discredit both the Trout and the prophet he heralded, hundreds of Ottawa and Chippewa villagers in the summer of 1807 destroyed their medicine bags and prepared to make the pilgrimage to Greenville. The Trout's followers thwarted the efforts of Michigan governor William Hull to secure more land cessions. In the summer of 1808, Ottawas and Chippewas joined with disaffected Wyandots and Potawatomis to repudiate those of their leaders who advocated the accommodation of American land demands, declaring it "a crime punishable by Death for any Indian to put his name on Paper for the purpose of parting with any of their lands."[7]

Greenville in 1806 and 1807 was a vital spiritual center, attracting Native Americans from throughout the Old Northwest. The prophet's village was crowded with visiting Kickapoos, Potawatomis, Ottawas, Chippewas, Sacs, Wyandots, Delawares, and Miamis as well as Shawnees disaffected with the accommodationist policies at Wapakoneta. As David Edmunds notes, the prophet "kept them in a state of religious exhilaration. On almost every evening they assembled in the council house to listen to the Prophet's new revelation and to dance and sing in celebration of their deliverance."[8] When whites visited Greenville, the prophet's spokesmen downplayed or concealed the anti-American aspects of his message. Leaders of an Ohio Shaker community who called on Lalawethika and listened to his teachings as explained by an interpreter were favorably impressed by the prophet's sincerity, moral rectitude, and peaceful intentions. "God," they declared, "in very deed was mightily at work among the Indians" who flocked to Greenville to hear the prophet. Comparing them to the tribes of Israel marching into Canaan, the Shakers praised "their simplicity and unaffected zeal for the increase of the work of the Good Spirit—their ardent desires for the salvation of their unbelieving kindred, with that of all mankind—their willingness to undergo fatigue, hard labor and sufferings, for the sake of those who came to learn the way of righteousness—and the high expectations they had of multitudes flocking down to hear the prophet . . . were considerations truly affecting." Pondering the meaning of all they had seen, the Shakers concluded: "Although these poor Shawnee have had no particular instruction but what they received by the outpouring of the Spirit, yet in point of real light and understanding, as well as behavior, they shame the Christian world." The Shakers provided substantial aid to the prophet's community, alleviating a serious food shortage in the early summer of 1807.[9]

Although a Quaker missionary who had made an earlier visit to the prophet also spoke well of him, whites living nearby were alarmed by the constant processions of unfamiliar Indians bound for Greenville. Rumors soon circulated that the prophet's followers were murdering white settlers and that the prophet himself was a British agent. Although those rumors were without foundation, they were encouraged by leaders of the rival Shawnee village at Wapakoneta, who feared the prophet's influence with dissident Shawnees and resented his efforts to gain access to American annuity payments. Lalawethika, Tecumseh, and the aging Shawnee war chief Blue Jacket, now a follower of the prophet, all sought to convince American authorities of their peaceful intentions. Blue Jacket, by persuading Governor Hull that the prophet "was a friend to the United States," obtained a substantial share of the federal annuities for Greenville.[10] But some federal officials were suspicious. The Indian agent at Fort Wayne, William Wells, informed the territorial governor that his Indian informants in the North had told him that "all the Indians in that quarter believe in what the Prophet tells them which is that the great spirit will in a few years destroy every white man in America. . . . [E]very Indian has made himself a war club." Wells, a former Miami captive and adoptee who had once fought for his father-in-law, Little Turtle, but had deserted to join Anthony Wayne's army, was convinced that the prophet was in the pay of the British. Wells clamored for the ejection of "the villain and his insolent band" from Ohio.[11] A man of questionable character who would be dismissed from his post for financial irregularities in 1808, Wells on one occasion had forged a document implicating the British in a plot to incite Indians. His superiors in Washington were inclined to dismiss his warnings about the Shawnee prophet.[12] Nonetheless, Wells proceeded with his campaign against the prophet. His accusations and his demand that the prophet vacate Greenville were conveyed directly to Lalawethika by a go-between, Anthony Shane, a man of mixed Shawnee and white parentage close to the agent.[13]

Despite Wells's questionable veracity, his condemnation of the prophet had the support not only of numerous white settlers in Ohio but also of Indiana's territorial governor, William Henry Harrison. In a letter to Secretary of War Henry Dearborn, Harrison reported that he had sent an agent to demand "the immediate removal of the Imposter from our Territory and the dispersion of the warriors he has collected around him." Harrison agreed with Wells that the prophet and his followers were instruments of "the British Indian agents" who awaited their "signal to commence the attack."[14] In a message to the Shawnees, Harrison deplored the "dark and bloody councils" allegedly held at Greenville under the aegis of the prophet, whom he characterized as "a fool who speaks not the words of the Great Spirit, but those of the Devil and of the British agents."[15] In the summer of 1807 some eighty white settlers in Ohio petitioned Wells for the dispersal of the prophet's community.[16] While the prophet and other Greenville leaders indignantly denied the charges leveled against them, they soon realized that their position in Ohio was untenable.

Prophetstown

Early in 1808, Tenskwatawa (as the prophet was now called), Tecumseh, and their followers accepted the invitation of the Potawatomi chief and shaman Main Poc to resettle in Indiana at the junction of the Wabash and Tippecanoe rivers. Writing of the strategic value of that site, Governor Harrison declared that "it is impossible that a more favorable location could have been chosen. . . . It is nearly central with regard to the tribes which he wishes to unite. . . . He has immediately in his rear a country that has been but little explored, consisting principally of barren thickets, interspersed with swamps and lakes, into which cavalry could not penetrate, and our infantry only by slow laborious efforts."[17] The new community was known to whites as Prophetstown. Of its prophet, one Euro-American observer later recalled that "the Indians flocked to him from every quarter; there was no name that carried such weight as his. They never ceased talking about his power, or expatiating on the miracles which he has wrought, and the more extraordinary the revelations he made, the more willingly were they believed and confided in."[18] Anthony Shane, no friend to the prophet, recalled that "an immense number of the lame, the halt, the blind" were attracted to the sacred community by Tenskwatawa's claim that he could "cure all diseases."[19] The inhabitants of Prophetstown were drawn from nations throughout the Old Northwest. Word of the prophet's miracles and of his teachings reached distant Indians on the Great Plains and would soon be carried by Tecumseh to the Deep South.

Agent Wells at Fort Wayne was alarmed by the reappearance of what he regarded as a nest of troublemakers. Well aware of the threat that the prophet and his brother might pose to American expansionism, Wells assured Secretary of War Dearborn that he would enlist "as more than a counter poise to the prophet" the Potawatomi chief Main Poc, "the greatest warrior in the west . . . the pivot on which the minds of all western Indians turned."[20] A tall, muscular man "of surly and brooding countenance" whose name meant "crippled hand," Main Poc, born without fingers or thumb on his left hand, was said to be a shaman of fearful prowess. He claimed not only communion with spirits and the ability to bewitch adversaries but told his followers that he could see, and avoid, bullets in flight. While we have little concrete information about his specific religious beliefs, some evidence points to Main Poc's adherence to the practices of the wabeno cult described by the Ojibway captive John Tanner. The wabenos, who walked on fire and handled red-hot coals, engaged in an archaic form of heroic shamanism that involved frenzied dancing to induce a trancelike state followed by spirit possession. Their rituals, according to Tanner, were extremely erotic, occasioning "much licentiousness and irregularity." Not only did Wabeno rites have little in common with Tenskwatawa's worship of the Master of Life; they also violated, in a spectacular manner, his exhortations against the medicine dance. The traditional medicine societies also opposed the wabenos, for the new cult stirred up old fears of spirit possession, which had come to be identified with both cannibalism and madness. During his two-month residence at Greenville in 1807, Main Poc had forged a close personal relationship with the Shawnee prophet. But, while agreeing that whites were the spawn of the evil Great Serpent, Main Poc found other aspects of the prophet's message uncongenial. He refused to give up alcohol, claiming that the Great Spirit ordered him to imbibe in order to enhance his powers (Main Poc was in fact an alcoholic, notorious for his violent behavior when in his cups). He rejected as well the call to Indian unity and brotherhood, "insisting that he would become weak and lose his medicine power if he were to give up warfare against the Osage and other enemies." As a wabeno, he also found Tenskwatawa's call for the abandonment of shamanistic practices incomprehensible and unacceptable. But despite those disagreements with the prophet, Main Poc was not about to become Wells's "counter poise" to the visionaries at Prophetstown. To win over the Potawatomi warrior and holy man, Wells gave him all the provisions he had in stock at the Fort Wayne Indian store. Main Poc accepted the agent's bribe but refused to do his bidding, proclaiming his independence as he departed from Fort Wayne. In 1811, defying the advice of the prophet, he attacked American settlers in the Illinois country, thereby triggering a series of events that would lead to the burning of Prophetstown.[21]

Tenskwatawa and Tecumseh both hoped to avert war. In the prophet's early revelations, the restoration of the land to its rightful owners would occur when the Great Spirit, persuaded that his true children had indeed embraced his commandments, chose to remove whites from the continent through miraculous means. In the meantime, Indians were to unite, resist further alienation of their land, and restore their cultural integrity, but they were to avoid violent confrontations with the intruders. Indian unification, the brothers believed, would lead finally to American respect for their land rights and thereby pave the way to a period of peace. To that end, every effort was made to persuade whites of the prophet's commitment to nonviolence. Summoned to a public meeting in Chillicothe in September 1807 by Ohio governor Thomas Kirker, the prophet's representatives carefully refuted allegations that their community at Greenville threatened white settlers. The aging yet still eloquent war chief Blue Jacket, a man greatly respected by his former white adversaries, declared that "we have laid down the tomahawk, never to take it up again. If it is offered to us by the French, English, Spaniards, or you, our white brethren, we will not take it." Tecumseh echoed these assurances. One white observer recorded that "from the confident manner he spoke of the intention to adhere to the treaty and live in peace and friendship with their white brethren, he dispelled as if by magic the apprehension of the whites."[22]

On several occasions over the next year, the prophet's representatives repeated these assurances. For his part, Tenskwatawa sought to conceal the anti-white thrust of his teachings. He urged Governor Harrison not to listen to the lies of "bad birds," explaining that "it is my determination to obey the voice of the great spirit and live in peace with you and your people. . . . We are all made by him, although we differ a little in colour. We are all his children and should live in peace and friendship with each other. . . . I had no intention but to introduce among the Indians, those good principles of religion which the white people profess. . . . The Great Spirit told me to tell the Indians, that he had made them and the world, that he had placed them on it to do good, and not evil." [23]

Harrison was not persuaded, but Pres. Thomas Jefferson, reviewing reports from Ohio, at first concluded that the prophet was harmless, "a visionary, enveloped in their antiquities, and vainly endeavoring to lead his brethren to the fancied beatitudes of their golden age." Jefferson believed that few Indians would be attracted to Tenskwatawa's message, as they had learned from whites how to live in comfort and would therefore not wish to return "to the hardships and privations of savagism." But during the war scare following the British boarding of the American warship *Chesapeake* later in 1807, Jefferson had second thoughts. He worried that the prophet might be used by the British to bring the Indians of the Old Northwest into an anti-American alliance. Could Harrison bribe him? The president also suggested that while the government could certainly not take direct action, it would be convenient if the prophet's Indian enemies dealt with him, perhaps through assassination. [24]

Despite the nativism at the core of the prophet's message, the founders of Prophetstown did not envisage an immediate break in relations with the United States. In 1807, while still at Greenville, Tecumseh had conveyed to Governor Kirker the hope that Wells would be replaced by an agent sympathetic to their aspiration to live in a community that was purified of corruption and culturally independent yet assisted by federal annuities and other aid. At Prophetstown the brothers understood that their vision of a new order free of all artifacts and practices of Euro-American origin could not be realized overnight. They were still dependent on whites for certain vital trade goods, for the repair of guns and metal implements, and, for a time, even for food. They did not call for the total rejection of all postcontact innovations. The prophet proscribed neither guns nor horses nor, for now, the commerce needed to acquire them.

Coexistence, however, was a temporary expedient. Tenskwatawa promised his followers that if Native American peoples obeyed his teachings he would soon be able to use his great powers to transform the world. Henry Aupaumut, a Mahican Christian convert living at White River, reported that early in 1808 the prophet told a visiting delegation of Sauk warriors that he "could destroy white people at any time," as the "great Creator" had given him power over "the whole world and all the creatures therein." While Aupaumut's account was somewhat garbled, it seems that Tenskwatawa threatened that those who failed to "believe his doctrine" would soon be "utterly destroyed by the spirits in the air, and great snakes under the earth," and that in the afterlife they would then be "tormented in darkness by the Devil, until they shall be burnt to ashes." The prophet claimed the power to "take down the sun and the moon," plunging the world "into great darkness," as "all the spirits [were] subject to him." He promised that, if Indians obeyed his commands, he would "cause the day of judgment to come" within four years. Its advent would be marked by the rising of "three suns at one instance, one from the North, the other from the West, the third from the South." [25]

Despite Tenskwatawa's boasts, his first year at Prophetstown was inauspicious. The community could not provide adequate food for all who responded to the prophet's call and gathered at the new center on the Wabash. By some estimates there were as many as three thousand pilgrims at Prophetstown. In the late spring of 1808 a visiting white fur trader, John Connor, found them "in a state of starvation, living on nothing but meat and roots." He predicted, accurately, that their summer corn crop would prove to be woefully inadequate.[26] In August, Tenskwatawa and several hundred of his followers called on Governor Harrison at Vincennes to ask for help. Harrison described them as "the most miserable set of starved wretches my eyes ever beheld," but he was favorably impressed by the Shawnee prophet, whom he characterized as "rather possessed of considerable talents . . . the art with which he manages the Indians is really astounding." The governor concluded that, contrary to earlier reports, Tenskwatawa might well be a peaceful reformer and, potentially, both a good influence on his people and a valuable ally. He therefore rejected Wells's advice to let the prophet and his followers starve and sent a shipment of food to Prophetstown. In response to a visit from Tecumseh, the British at Fort Malden also provided some help. It was far from adequate, however, and hundreds of Indians from many nations succumbed to famine or disease at Prophetstown in the hard winter of 1808–9.[27]

From the outset, Prophetstown's relationships with some of the Indian nations of the Midwest and Great Lakes were problematic. Little Turtle's Miamis immediately challenged the legitimacy of the settlement. Friendly to Black Hoof and the Wapakoneta Shawnees, the Miamis asserted that the prophet and his followers were poaching on their land. The White River Delawares, still angered by the prophet's role in their witch hunt, also made clear their displeasure with his return to Indiana.[28] The prophet brushed aside Miami and Delaware protests, proclaiming that the Great Spirit had ordained that he settle on the Wabash. But some of the pilgrims from the North were soon disillusioned. Disease at Prophetstown in 1808 and 1809 had claimed more than 160 Ottawas and Ojibwes but only 5 Shawnees—a strange contrast in the numbers of dead that suggested witchcraft to the survivors. To test the validity of the prophet's claim that the Great Spirit himself would destroy anyone who harmed a Prophetstown resident, several warriors killed two of Tenskwatawa's people—a woman and a child—just outside the gates of the sacred village. When nothing happened to the killers, skeptics concluded that the Shawnee prophet was indeed a fraud. Only through the intervention of Governor Hull were the Ottawas and Ojibwes dissuaded from sending war parties to destroy Prophetstown in 1809.[29] The prophet never fully regained his influence in the North. However, he soon won substantial support among the Kickapoos and Winnebagos. These western tribes saw in the prophet's movement their best hope for preserving that independence which so many other Indian nations had already lost.[30]

Despite the prophet's efforts to assure American officials of his pacifism, reports that he intended to make war on Americans persisted. In the spring of 1809, Governor Hull warned from Detroit that "the influence of the Prophet has been great, and his advice to the Indians injurious to them and to the United States." Tenskwatawa, Hull concluded, was under the sway of the British, who knew how to appeal to "the savage character."[31] For his part, Harrison reported to Washington on several occasions that visitors to Prophetstown had predicted that "the Prophet will attack our settlements." After meeting with Tenskwatawa early in the summer of 1809, he reversed his judgment of the previous year and wrote to the secretary of war that "I must confess that my suspicions of his guilt have been rather strengthened than diminished in every interview I have had with him since his arrival."[32] Rumors that the prophet and his warriors were planning to massacre all whites on the frontier were rampant over the next two years and were used very effectively by Harrison in 1811 to secure authorization for sending an armed force against Prophetstown.[33]

Those rumors were false. The Shawnee brothers had no immediate plans to attack the white settlements already established in Indiana and elsewhere in the West. To the contrary, they discouraged frontier raids. Stories about their malevolent intentions reflected, in part, confusion over their role in the war plans of some of the more militant Winnebagos and Sacs who lived west of the Mississippi. These Indians, who had signed no treaties with the United States, were enraged by the establishment of Fort Madison on the Mississippi's west bank in 1808, for they feared it presaged American occupation. Convinced that "the land devil has his mouth open again," some of their leaders proposed a preemptive attack on the American fort, and in April 1809 they sent representatives to ask aid from Prophetstown. Tecumseh and Tenskwatawa advised them not to initiate hostilities. The prophet assured Harrison that he had no part in "the late combination to attack our settlements" but had "prevailed upon . . . the Tribes on the Mississippi and Illinois River . . . to relinquish their intentions."[34]

But while the Shawnee brothers still hoped for peaceful coexistence with the United States, by the time of the founding of Prophetstown they had developed a political agenda that envisioned the possible use of force to prevent further losses of Indian land. In his reply to Little Turtle and the Miamis, who were seeking to bar him from settling on the Wabash in 1808, Tenskwatawa explained that under the guidance of the Great Spirit he would create a new "Boundary Line between the Indians and white people" defended by his warriors. [35] To secure that boundary, the brothers declared that only their Indian confederacy—led by Tecumseh as head chief and Tenskwatawa as spokesman of the Great Spirit—had the right to sell land, and they threatened to put to death any Indian who without their permission signed a paper granting land to whites. They sought and received both food and weapons from the British at Fort Malden.

In explaining Prophetstown's objectives to Francis Gore, the lieutenant governor of Upper Canada, Tecumseh declared that they hoped to "collect the different nations" on lands not yet occupied by the Americans "in order to preserve their country from all encroachments." They did not intend "to take part in the quarrels of white people," but "if the Americans encroach upon them they are resolved to strike." [36] Gore assured Tecumseh that His Majesty's government recognized the Indians' right to all of the Ohio country under the boundaries set in 1768 and suggested that, should Great Britain receive the aid of Indian allies in a future war with the United States, the Americans might well be forced to evacuate all of the lands whites had occupied after that date. Tecumseh was wary and reminded Gore that Indians had heard those promises before. They remembered that the British had abandoned their Indian friends in 1794, when the survivors of Fallen Timbers were barred from Fort Miami. Tecumseh declined to enter into a military alliance with the British, but he did accept their offer of aid for Prophetstown. [37]

Through that aid and through the industry of its inhabitants, the community at Prophetstown became not only viable but also prosperous, and once again it attracted new residents. The town contained more than two hundred houses covered in bark, a large guest lodge known as "the House of the Stranger," a substantial council hall, and a medicine lodge—a low, long structure where the prophet communed with the Great Spirit. The adjacent crop lands totaled around one hundred acres. Visitors found it an orderly and a sober place, despite the steady traffic of pilgrims who came to hear to the prophet. [38]

Despite Tecumseh's efforts to win recognition of Prophetstown as the capital city of an all-encompassing Indian confederation committed to the preservation of existing boundaries, the village chiefs of the various nations in Ohio, Indiana, Illinois, Michigan, and elsewhere generally rejected his claim. The prophet and his brother failed to block further white encroachments on Indian land. Following the cessions mandated in the Treaty of Greenville in 1795, new treaties signed in 1803, 1804, 1805, and 1807 had already resulted in the additional loss of hundreds of square miles in Ohio, Indiana, Illinois, and Michigan. In defiance of Tecumseh's declaration that Indian land belonged to all Indians and could not be sold by individual chiefs, at Fort Wayne on September 30, 1809, Miami, Delaware, and Potawatomi representatives, in exchange for some trade goods and some increases in their annuities, ceded more than three million additional acres in Indiana and Illinois. In his exhortation to the Indians assembled to consider the proposed land deal, Harrison had "urged the vast benefit" the chiefs would derive from an increase in "their annuities, without which they would be unable to clothe their women and children." Given the declining price for peltry on the world market and the great scarcity of game, he argued, "it was absolutely necessary that they should adopt some other plan for their support." The governor pointed out that the "the raising of Cattle and Hogs required little labor and would be the surest substitute for the wild animals which they had so unfortunately destroyed for the sake of their skins. . . . The proposed addition to their annuities would enable them to procure the Domestic Animals necessary to commence raising them on a large scale."[39]

As Harrison prepared his address, he was no doubt mindful of Jefferson's prediction that, as Indians became dependent on American goods to support the development of a Euro-American-style agricultural economy, they would be only too happy to sell more land. In a letter to Harrison in the winter of 1803, the president had written: "When they withdraw themselves to the culture of a small piece of land, they will perceive how useless to them are their extensive forests, and will be willing to pare them off from time to time in exchange for necessities for their farms and families." Jefferson outlined a strategy to accelerate that process: "To promote this disposition to exchange lands, which they have to spare and which we want, we shall push our trading uses, and be glad to see the good and influential individuals among them run in debt, because we observe that when their debts get beyond what individuals can pay, they become willing to lop them off by a cession of lands." Ultimately, Jefferson added, through that process Indian independence in the areas east of the Mississippi would be extinguished. Native Americans must ultimately be either incorporated within the states, subject to the laws and customs of their white neighbors, or be removed "beyond the Mississippi."[40]

Prophetstown's leaders did not accept Jefferson's analysis and threatened to kill the Indians who had signed the Treaty of Fort Wayne. The brothers dispatched agents to argue against the treaty and to undermine the authority of those who counseled acceptance. Tecumseh himself journeyed to Ohio to persuade Shawnee and Wyandot warriors to repudiate their accommodationist leaders, accept his authority, and regroup at Prophetstown to defend the new boundary the prophet had established against white expansion. His efforts fell short of his expectations. As Edmunds notes, "Tecumseh's efforts to destroy the position of the village chiefs and to become 'alone the acknowledged chief of all the Indians' (as he had boasted to Harrison at Vincennes) was a concept more alien to traditional Indian ways than any of the teachings of the Prophet."[41] It was extremely divisive. Among the Wyandots of Ohio, controversy over alienation of land and over Tecumseh's political claims led to the resumption of witch-hunting and to several vigilante-style witch killings later blamed on both supporters and enemies of the prophet. To the north, the Ottawas and Ojibwes resisted efforts to win them back to the prophet but decided not to negotiate any additional land sales. The Potawatomis remained divided, with the western tribesmen hostile to the accommodationist eastern chiefs who had signed the Fort Wayne treaty. Elsewhere, tensions between those who believed that the days of armed resistance were past and militants inspired by Tecumseh's call and the prophet's promise of divine aid engendered new rumors of war.[42]

Utilizing two French traders as spies at Prophetstown, Governor Harrison determined that the opposition of the prophet and his people to further American expansion was deep and intractable. Although he discounted the more extreme rumors and doubted that the prophet was really strong enough to attack Vincennes, Harrison was disturbed by the possibility of violent resistance to the establishment of new white settlements in Indiana. In a ten-day meeting with Tecumseh and a number of his warriors at Vincennes in August 1810, the governor sought to persuade Tecumseh to accept the Fort Wayne land cessions. Tecumseh remained adamant, telling Harrison: "You have taken our land from us and I do not see how we can remain at peace with you if you continue to do so." Renewing the threat to execute chiefs who sold land without his permission, he said of the territory signed away at Fort Wayne, "If you do take it you must blame yourself as the cause of trouble between us and the Tribes who sold it to you. I want the present boundary line to continue. Should you cross it, I assure you it will be productive of bad consequences." Invited, along with the prophet, to visit Washington DC to discuss the matter with the president, Tecumseh declined. Harrison, he charged, was working to prevent the unification of Indians into one people holding their lands in common. "You want by your distinctions of Indian tribes in allotting to each a particular track of land to make them go to war with each other. . . . [U]ntil our design is accomplished we do not wish to accept your invitation to go and visit the President." [43] Tecumseh's denunciation of the treaty had the support not only of the Prophetstown Shawnees but also of Wyandot, Kickapoo, Potawatomi, and Winnebago warriors who had accompanied him to Vincennes. Several of their leaders spoke in support of his position. The Indian signatories to the treaty present at the conference, though severely castigated in the speeches of Tecumseh and his followers, remained silent, clearly intimidated by the militants. [44]

After the conference adjourned, Tecumseh and Harrison met privately. Tecumseh, still seeking to avert war, told the governor that he did not trust the British and would prefer to work out an accommodation with the United States. But he warned that no peace with the Americans would be possible if the provisions of the Fort Wayne treaty were put into effect. Harrison promised to raise the matter with the president but doubted that the treaty could now be set aside. Tecumseh replied, "I hope the Great Spirit will put some sense into his head to induce him to direct you to give up this land. It is true; he is so far off. He will not be injured by the war. He may sit in his town, and drink his wine, whilst you and I will have to fight it out."[45]

Realizing that his efforts to secure acquiescence to the new land cessions had failed, Harrison reported to Secretary of War William Eustis that the prophet and Tecumseh were still determined "not to permit the lands lately purchased to be surveyed."[46] In his annual address to the territorial legislature in November, the governor warned of the threat of "hostilities by a combination formed under the auspices of a bold adventurer, who pretends to act under the immediate inspiration of the Deity." He added: "I accuse myself, indeed, of an error in the patronage and support which I offered him upon his first arrival on the Wabash, before his designs of hostility to the United States had been developed." The prophet, he charged, was unjustly stirring up "disaffection" against the treaty. Harrison denied that the Indians had any grounds for complaint, given the government's "liberality and its benevolence."[47] The future of Indiana, Harrison declared, required the elimination of Prophetstown. While the prophet was losing ground among the Indians at large and would probably never be able "to form a Confederacy strong enough to commence hostilities," he did pose an obstacle to economic growth. If not removed, he might well intimidate prospective white settlers by raising "those alarms which have so mischievous an effect in retarding the population of our country." The governor demanded to know if "one of the fairest portions of the Globe [is] to remain in a state of nature, the haunt of a few wretched savages, when it seems destined by the Creator to give support to a large population, and to be the seat of civilization, of science, and of true religion?"[48] The possibility, however remote, that that might prove to be the case, if the prophet remained influential, was very much on the governor's mind when he advised Eustis on December 24, 1810, that "the Indians appear to be more uneasy and dissatisfied than I ever before saw them, and I believe that the Prophet's principle, that their land be considered common property is either openly avowed or secretly favored by all the tribes west of the Wabash." Unless something was done to silence the prophet, his followers would soon "shut the door against any further extinguishments of Indian title upon the valuable tract of country south of the Wabash, which is embraced by our settlements upon three sides."[49]

Seeking to explain and justify in advance the hostilities he knew would be provoked by his efforts to eliminate the prophet as a factor in negotiations in Indiana, Harrison in an earlier letter had explained to Eustis that the Indians were incapable of keeping the peace. "The mind of a savage," he expatiated, "is so constructed that he cannot be at rest, he cannot be happy unless he is acted upon by some strong stimulus. That which is produced by war is the only one that is sufficiently powerful to fill up the intervals of the chase. If he hunts in the winter he must go to war in the summer, and you may rest assured Sir, that the establishment of tranquility between the neighboring tribes will always be a sure indication of war against us."[50]

Harrison's claim about the warlike nature of "savages" was, of course, a smoke screen to disguise his own provocation of hostilities. The prophet's case against the Fort Wayne treaty was compelling. Quite apart from Tecumseh's controversial claim, in earlier talks with the governor, that "the Great Spirit intended . . . [the land] as the common property of all the tribes," the treaty was suspect. Some of the village chiefs who affixed their signatures to the treaty had no claim whatsoever to the land in question, while others whose territory the treaty violated were not represented. Harrison's instructions from the secretary of war had stipulated that "to prevent any future dissatisfaction, chiefs of all the Nations who have or pretend right to these lands, should be present at the treaty." [51] Harrison on previous occasions had negotiated land treaties with leaders whose claims to authority to sell those lands were questionable at best. [52] His new instructions notwithstanding, the governor's conduct in these negotiations followed the old pattern.

A number of Harrison's contemporary critics describe his dealings with Indians as rapacious and corrupt. Harrison for his part complained that unnamed whites had undercut his position. Tecumseh, Harrison claimed, had declared before a large audience that several whites had "urged him to oppose the execution" of the Treaty of Fort Wayne. These unidentified foes of Harrison had assured Tecumseh that "his pretensions would be supported by a considerable portion of our citizens." The governor, enraged by this opposition, asked the legislature to pass a law punishing those who, in conversations with Indians, criticized the "intentions of the government." [53] But widespread reservations about Harrison's treaty making, expressed most forcefully by former Ohio governor Thomas Worthington, led instead to the appointment, in June 1812, of a federal commission to investigate Indian grievances. Unfortunately, the outbreak of war with England led to the abandonment of the inquiry. [54]

With the failure of the Vincennes conference, Tecumseh and the prophet were finally convinced that even a short-term accommodation with the United States was unlikely. They accordingly redoubled efforts to build a pan-Indian Confederacy. Its political leadership was entrusted to Tecumseh, who, accompanied by some of his closest supporters, undertook a series of visits to Indian nations from the western reaches of the Illinois country to the remaining Iroquois settlements in New York. Proclaiming the religion of the prophet as the true revelation of the will of the Great Spirit, he called for internal reform in the life of the people and for unity under his leadership in resisting further American

expansion. He asked that they repudiate past subservient relationships to the United States and express their rejection of
American land claims by refusing to accept annuity payments.
Conferring with the British at Fort Malden, Tecumseh now spoke
openly of making war on the United States and accepted the
alliance he had rejected two years earlier. British officials, now
alarmed lest they be dragged into war by their rash new ally,
advised caution and considered warning the Americans.[55]

The outcome of Tecumseh's mission was mixed. In the East
and North he encountered fairly solid opposition from established
leaders and won only a few converts with his appeal that believers
in the prophet seize power from local chiefs. In September 1810
some two thousand Indians—Wyandots, Delawares, Shawnees,
Munsees, Iroquois, Ottawas, Ojibwes, and others—gathered under the watchful eye of Governor Hull at the site of the conference
ground of Blue Jacket and Little Turtle's old confederacy to denounce Tecumseh's pretensions to leadership and to declare their
intention of remaining at peace. After Hull departed, however, the
assembly resolved not to consider further land sales.[56] Tecumseh was most successful in winning adherents among western
Potawatomis and among the Kickapoos and Winnebagos. His
protracted trip through the lower South in 1811 (to be discussed
in detail in the next chapter), although the source of numerous
stories, failed to produce much new support. While he attracted
some warriors in every area he visited, the overall strength of the
force Tecumseh recruited prior to the outbreak of the War of 1812,
as John Sugden notes, "fell short of the grand confederacy of the
1790's."[57]

Harrison, assessing the strength of the prophet in May 1810,
had estimated that he had around eight hundred followers. He
noted, correctly, that the Kickapoos were his strongest adherents,
along with a number of Potawatomis and Winnebagos. If the
prophet and Tecumseh succeeded in converting other Indians
"between the Illinois River and Lake Michigan," Harrison believed

that their forces then might be doubled in strength. "However contemptible this force may seem," he warned Secretary Eustis, "it is capable, from the nature of our frontier settlements, of spreading slaughter and devastation to an immense extent." For that reason, the governor was determined to "counteract the Prophet's design" and block the spread of his confederacy.[58]

Although Harrison's reputation as an unprincipled—indeed, somewhat ruthless—negotiator greedy for Indian land won him few real Indian friends, he had little difficulty prior to 1812 in thwarting the prophet's efforts within the Indiana Territory. Whatever their feelings about Harrison, the Great Father, Americans, or whites in general, many—probably most—village leaders in the Old Northwest doubted that they could defeat the United States. They now saw no alternative to compromise and coexistence. Blue Jacket and Little Turtle had fought in the 1790s to defend a land that contained only a few small white settlements on the borders. By 1810, by contrast, white settlers west of the Appalachians and east of the Mississippi outnumbered Indians by about four to one. Significantly, Tecumseh's strongest support came from the West, from regions not yet heavily settled by Euro-Americans. In the East, with game now scarce if not nearly extinct, Indian communities had long been economically dependent on whites. Without trade, they could not function. Without annuities, some would starve. They were, moreover, accustomed to a lifestyle that incorporated many material items obtainable only from whites. By the early nineteenth century, the restoration of the lost world of precontact America was hardly conceivable. Most of the Indian communities to whom Tecumseh appealed felt the need for alliance with a white trading partner and protector, a need that Tecumseh—a more skillful politician than his brother—sometimes addressed by stressing the prospect of a British alliance. Significantly, warriors from some of the groups who rebuffed Tecumseh in 1810, such as the Miamis and Delawares, would join him in fighting on the British side in 1812.

The opposition to the prophet and his brother reflected disagreements over strategies for dealing with the United States that were compounded by old tribal animosities and current political rivalries. More fundamentally, however, Native Americans differed in their responses to Tenskwatawa's spiritual claims. To those who truly believed in the prophet's promise of providential aid, the imbalance in power now so painfully apparent was of little concern, for they would soon be given new power by the Great Spirit. But it must be emphasized that in all areas Tecumseh encountered the opposition, not only of acculturated chiefs committed to coexistence through compromise, but also of religious traditionalists unimpressed by the prophet's claims. The traditionalists were often in the majority. To cite one example, while Tecumseh was visiting the Sacs, his demand that medicine bags be destroyed engendered strong opposition from many tribesmen who depended upon their power. They promptly issued a counterdemand that the prophet's representatives prove their claim to be agents of the Great Spirit by raising the dead. Tecumseh ignored the challenge and made few Sac converts.[59] Many years later, Black Hawk lamented the Sacs' failure to take Tecumseh seriously.[60] Others had no regrets. Several years after Tecumseh's death, the Wyandot chief John Hicks, in conversations with a missionary, described prophets such as Tenskwatawa as "deceivers" who had tried to lure Indians away from the "old religion." The chief found equally distasteful the Christianity preached by the missionaries and the new doctrines of the Shawnee prophet. Others shared that sentiment.[61]

Tippecanoe and Its Aftermath

In the late spring of 1811, Harrison decided to destroy Prophetstown. In seeking authorization for a preemptive strike, he informed Secretary of War Eustis that he had been warned by numerous informants that the prophet intended to march on Vincennes and demand abrogation of the Treaty of Fort Wayne as the price of peace. To protect that land cession, Harrison asked for military reinforcements. [62] "Unless some decisive and energetic measure is adopted to break up the combination formed by the Prophet," he protested in July, "we shall soon have every Indian tribe in this quarter allied against us." Echoing his earlier complaint to the legislature, he reported that some whites (whom he did not name) had encouraged the prophet's resistance by telling him that the United States would give up the contested land "rather than go to war with the Indians."[63] In correspondence with Washington DC, Harrison pointed to the prophet's seizure of part of a salt annuity intended for other tribes as further evidence of his implacable hostility. [64] To his distress, the War Department instructed him to negotiate in the hope of averting war. [65] Harrison now had no faith that he could win Prophetstown's acceptance of the Treaty of Fort Wayne through negotiations. Predictably, a new meeting between Harrison and Tecumseh that summer proved unproductive, as neither would budge on the issue of land cession. [66] Dismissing Tecumseh's claim that the alliance he sought to build was peaceful and defensive, Harrison warned that the Shawnee diplomat's trip to the South, begun soon after the conference, had been undertaken in order "to excite the southern Indians to war against us."[67]

Despite his efforts in correspondence with the War Department to blame Tecumseh, the prophet, and the British for frontier violence, Harrison on occasion had acknowledged that the root of the problem was white lawlessness. In 1807 he advised the territorial legislature that he would have little problem coping with foreign agitators if the courts would uphold the laws protecting Indians. He deplored the fact that they had not yet convicted "even one of the many people who have committed murder on their people." [68] The previous year he had urged the legislators "to lose no opportunity of inculcating, among your constituents, an abhorrence of that unchristian and detestable doctrine which would make a distinction of guilt between the murder of a white man and an Indian." [69] But it did not serve the governor's purposes in 1811 to deal with that aspect of the problem in his communications with the War Department.

The governor received from the nation's capital a somewhat equivocal response to his complaints about the futility of negotiations. In his instructions to Harrison that summer, Secretary of War Eustis had advised that President Monroe expected the governor to avoid the use of force if at all possible, but now Eustis did not rule out action against "the banditti under the prophet" if that were to prove "absolutely necessary." [70] Harrison made the most of that opening. On August 13 he informed the secretary that, although he would try to comply with earlier orders that he maintain peace with the Indians, he and his fellow western governors (Edwards of Illinois and Howard of Missouri) were agreed "on the necessity of breaking up the Prophet's establishment on the Wabash." [71] On August 22 the secretary authorized the assembling of a force of regular army and militia for use in occupying and protecting the contested land cession of 1809. [72] Several weeks later, Eustis informed Harrison that although the prophet's community should be dispersed peacefully if possible, force should indeed be used in the event of resistance. [73] In justifying his decision to attack Prophetstown, Harrison maintained that the prophet had already initiated hostilities. Beginning the previous spring, a series of Indian raids on the Illinois frontier—most carried out by warriors loyal to the Potawatomi chief Main Poc—had intensified American fears of a general Indian war orchestrated from Prophetstown. [74] In July, Gov. Ninian Edwards had written from Illinois Territory to declare peace "totally out of the question; we need not expect it until the Prophet's party is dispersed." [75]

The governors were mistaken. The prophet and Tecumseh were not responsible for those attacks on whites. In fact, they had urged restraint, hoping for time to build a larger coalition able to negotiate from strength or win a war. After conferring with a number of Shawnees, Wyandots, and Senecas at a conference at Piqua, Ohio, Indian agent John Johnston reported to a local newspaper on August 27 that the problem was limited to Potawatomis in the Illinois country, assuring his readers that none of the other Indian groups posed even the "smallest danger" to "frontier inhabitants." [76] But Harrison insisted that the prophet was planning to attack and must therefore be removed through a preemptive military strike. [77] He dismissed as "absolutely false" reports that Main Poc, not Tenskwatawa, was responsible for the attacks on whites in Illinois, assuring the secretary of war that "the truth is they were directed by the Prophet for the purpose of forcing the Indians of the Illinois River to unite with him. He has determined to commit to the flames the first of our men he can take in person." [78] The War Department, lacking firsthand knowledge of the situation, was in no position to argue with the governors.

Believing that the prophet lacked Tecumseh's skills as a leader, Harrison had earlier advised his superiors that "nothing but the great talents of Tecumseh could keep together the heterogeneous mass which comprises the Prophet's force." He proposed to take advantage of Tecumseh's long absence on his southern recruitment mission in the fall of 1811 and march on Prophetstown. [79] In order to disrupt the prophet's force, Harrison first put pressure on the Tenskwatawa's non-Shawnee followers, demanding that they leave Prophetstown and return to their home villages. Warning that he would "not suffer any more strange Indians to settle on the Wabash," he ordered all tribes "who have any warriors with the Prophet to withdraw them immediately" and threatened those who remained with "destruction." He demanded that the Miamis evict the prophet from their lands. Meeting with their chiefs, he enjoined them not to be afraid to oppose the prophet: "You shall be supported by my warriors. My warriors are getting ready and if it is necessary you shall see an army of them at your backs more numerous than the leaves of the trees." [80]

In a series of communications with Prophetstown in the late summer and early fall of 1811, Harrison charged the prophet with responsibility for the murder of whites on the Illinois frontier and demanded that the prophet surrender to white justice those responsible, several of whom, he declared, were known to be in residence at Prophetstown. The governor also repeated his demand that all of the residents who were not Shawnees be expelled from Prophetstown. He also complained that the Prophetstown Indians were stealing horses, and demanded their return. Tenskwatawa offered to restore the horses but equivocated on other matters.[81]

Dissatisfied with the prophet's responses and persuaded that any lack of firmness in dealing with his insubordination would embolden other, presently uncommitted Indians to join in resisting land cessions, Harrison mustered his forces and marched on Prophetstown. Tenskwatawa's response to Harrison's aggression does not corroborate the commonplace image in the historical literature of the prophet as blundering, inept fool unfit to lead. He first attempted to avert an attack through negotiation, sending a delegation of respected chiefs to Vincennes. His envoys repeated the earlier promise to return the stolen horses and offered assurances that the prophet would undertake a search to locate Indians guilty of killing settlers. Harrison rejected that overture, explaining to Washington that he had advised the chiefs that the evidence he had of the prophet's "designs against us" was so damning that nothing less than the immediate surrender of the "murderers" would dissuade him from attacking and destroying Prophetstown.[82]

Tenskwatawa then issued a call for the reinforcement of Prophetstown. Although most of the local Delawares, Miamis, and Weas remained neutral, several hundred Wyandots, Potawatomis, Piankeshaws, and Kickapoos rallied to his defense. Harrison's efforts to turn all of the tribes of the region against the prophet had failed. As preparations for the defense of the prophet's sanctuary proceeded, his warriors carefully tracked, and occasionally harassed, the governor's army. As the invading force drew near to Prophetstown, Tenskwatawa sent a delegation to Harrison with an offer to negotiate. Over the objections of some of his officers, who recommended an immediate attack, Harrison scheduled a conference for the next day. The governor and his men encamped about a mile from Prophetstown.[83]

Prior to his departure, Tecumseh had advised his brother to avoid hostilities, but Harrison's demands were extreme and provocative.[84] By early fall, the prophet understood that the governor intended to force him to disband the sacred community. If he accepted Harrison's terms, which required banning non-Shawnees from his village, his mission would be at an end. If we accept the premise that the prophet believed in his own message and was not, as his enemies charged, a charlatan, his resistance was neither irrational nor irresponsible. But, contrary to the impression given in most of the historical literature, we do not really know what action the prophet actually authorized on the eve of the battle. The deliberations within Prophetstown during the hours immediately before Tippecanoe are obscure. One version, generally accepted by historians, holds that, rather than meeting with the governor as he had promised on November 7, Tenskwatawa decided to strike the Americans before dawn at their encampment about a mile from Prophetstown. As Edmunds and others have told the story, the prophet, appearing before his warriors wearing a necklace of deer hooves, holding in his hands strings of sacred beans, revealed that the Master of Life had declared that Harrison must die. They were to attack before sunrise, for in the dark their enemies would be blinded and stupefied by the prophet's medicine, which would also provide brilliant light to guide the warriors. A hailstorm would spoil the Americans' gunpowder, but through the prophet's power his warriors' weapons would be unaffected. Their assault must first strike the governor's tent. Once he was dead, the American troops could easily be captured and enslaved. Having thus exhorted his people, Tenskwatawa withdrew to a nearby hillside to commune with the Great Spirit in order to guarantee victory.[85]

The evidence supporting that account is suspect. It rests for the most part on the secondhand stories of Indians and whites who were not present at Prophetstown when the attack was allegedly planned. Moreover, most if not all of these commentators were enemies of the prophet.[86] There is, however, another, and better-supported, account of the outbreak of hostilities that historians have generally overlooked. A few weeks after the battle, one of the prophet's adherents, a Kickapoo chief, told Matthew Elliott, the British Indian agent at Amherstburg in Upper Canada, that the prophet did not intend to attack Harrison's army but rather planned to fight only if the governor attacked. During the night, however, "two young Winnebagos" were shot and wounded by American sentinels. "This insult aroused the indignation of the Indians, and they determined to be revenged and accordingly commenced the attack at Cock crowing."[87] The Kickapoo chief's explanation was echoed several months later by Tecumseh, who declared at an intertribal assembly that the violence at Tippecanoe was "the work of a few of our younger men." He assured all present that "had I been at home there would have been no blood shed."[88] The account given by the Kickapoo chief and later by Tecumseh may have been mendacious, intended to divert attention from the prophet's role in the attack on Harrison's forces, but it is more likely that they were telling the truth. The decision to attack was probably a spur-of-the-moment response forced by a few young warriors, not the result of a premeditated plan. The prophet, if he ordered the attack at all, may have been swayed by the emotional pressures of the moment and by rash counsel.

This interpretation is given credibility by the fact that, in the weeks preceding the battle, the prophet's forces had mounted no full-scale attack on Harrison's very vulnerable army as it struggled through an unfamiliar wilderness. It may be that until the last moment the prophet hoped to abide by his agreement with Tecumseh to avoid an armed confrontation with the governor. It is worth noting that, in conversations with Michigan governor Lewis Cass in 1816, Tenskwatawa denied that he had ordered any hostile action against Harrison. "It is true," he conceded, "that the Winnebagoes with me at Tippecanoe struck your people. I was opposed to it but could not stop it." [89] Some years later, former Indian agent John Johnston also claimed that "the Winnebagoes forced on the battle of Tippecanoe." He concluded that the prophet lost control of the situation. [90]

The battle did not go well for the prophet's forces. American resistance was fierce, and the warriors did not prevail. Although the losses on the American side were heavier, the prophet's forces retreated when Harrison counterattacked. Miami chief Little Eyes claimed that the warriors then confronted the prophet, who at first "assured them that by the power of his art half the army was already dead and the other half bewildered or in a state of distraction." The warriors, he continued, should "rush into the [American] camp and complete the work of destruction with the tomahawk." One of the Winnebago warriors immediately shouted: "You are a liar . . . you told us that the white people were dead or crazy when they were all in their senses and fought like the devil." Tenskwatawa then "appeared much crestfallen . . . held his head between his knees," and blamed his wife for spoiling his medicine by touching his sacred objects while menstruating. The warriors, angry and now untrusting, refused his plea that they mount another attack. Whatever the circumstances leading to the attack, it is reasonable to assume that the prophet endeavored to invoke sacred power to secure victory once battle was joined. Before the conflict he had probably assured the warriors that through his magic they would enjoy the help of the Great Spirit. Little Eyes told one of Harrison's officers that after the retreat the Winnebagos seized the prophet and bound him with cords. The

Miami chief thought they would probably put him to death, but he was wrong. Instead, the prophet and some of his Shawnee followers encamped at Wildcat Creek, about twenty miles from the battle site. [91] In weighing Little Eyes's testimony, we need to remember that he was reputedly the prophet's ally, both before and after the battle. He may well have endeavored to mislead the Americans about the prophet's actual status after Tippecanoe. [92]

When American troops entered Prophetstown the day after the battle, they found only one elderly and infirm woman. The rest of the inhabitants had left, most of them returning to their villages in the West. Harrison's army burned the prophet's empty capital. In addition to wigwams and houses, more than five thousand pounds of food stores were put to the torch. In a bizarre act of desecration, the Americans dug up the graveyard at Prophetstown, leaving the corpses to rot above ground. Hearing rumors that Tecumseh was approaching from the south with a thousand warriors, the army retreated to Vincennes, where the militia disbanded. [93] One veteran later recalled: "after destroying our considerable baggage, in order to make room for the conveyance of the wounded we began our march to Vincennes expecting the Indians would follow and attack us. Such an event was greatly to be dreaded; as we were nearly out of provisions, and had upwards of a hundred and thirty wounded men to be attended to, who were painfully situated in the wagons, especially those who had broken limbs, by their continual jolting, on an unbeaten road through the wilderness." [94]

Shortly after the battle, a captured Potawatomi chief assured Harrison that his people now hated the prophet and would soon kill him. Several weeks later, two Kickapoo chiefs also informed the governor that they held Tenskwatawa responsible for their misfortunes and were now "desirous of making peace with the United States." In reporting those conversations to the secretary of war, Harrison expressed much uncertainty about their credibility. [95] His distrust of the chiefs who claimed that Tenskwatawa was now universally hated turned out to be well founded, as the chiefs were only telling the governor what they thought he wanted to hear. The facts do not support their claims. Although numerous historians have repeated stories about the prophet's disgrace after Tippecanoe, his retreat from Prophetstown proved to be temporary, and the disaffection of his followers was greatly exaggerated.[96]

After the destruction of Prophetstown, Tenskwatawa and about forty followers, primarily Shawnees, remained at Wildcat Creek for a time and then resettled briefly on the White River. Little Turtle assured Harrison that "all the Prophet's followers have left him," but Indian agent Joseph Lalime warned Governor Howard in February that "it is to be expected that they will gather again at his old place." Lalime was right. The gathering had already begun. When the prophet and his party returned to the site of Prophetstown, they found encampments of Kickapoos, Winnebagos, and Piankeshaws ready to undertake the task of rebuilding the sacred community.[97] On January 21, the acting governor of the Michigan Territory advised the secretary of war that Prophetstown had been reestablished, with some 550 residents from various tribes. He predicted that the prophet would soon send Harrison his peace terms, which would prove unacceptable. He would therefore probably go to war sometime in the spring.[98] Tecumseh returned from his southern mission several weeks later. Soon thereafter he sent Harrison word of the prophet's peaceful intentions.[99] According to a British intelligence report, Tecumseh was "much dissatisfied with his brother for engaging Governor Harrison, last fall, as their plans were not fully matured."[100]

In the writings of most Anglo-American historians, Tecumseh's dissatisfaction was transformed into fratricidal rage. The great warrior allegedly assaulted the prophet, screaming that he deserved to die for his bungling at Tippecanoe.[101] The British report is plausible. Tecumseh probably did express anger and disappointment with the prophet's loss of control. But the death threat story is suspect. The story of Tecumseh's alleged attempts to kill his brother originated in the testimony of Anthony Shane and his wife and was first recorded by Benjamin Drake. It is preserved in the great research collection of Lyman Draper at the Wisconsin State Historical Society, and it has been consulted by many generations of Tecumseh scholars. Although many writers have been impressed by the fact that Shane was married to a relative of Tecumseh's, he is not a reliable witness. The Shanes both harbored a deep dislike of the prophet. They claimed that Tecumseh never believed in his brother's religion but only went along "as a matter of policy" because "most of the Indians" did believe in him. On two occasions, the Shanes asserted, Tecumseh attempted to assault Tenskwatawa. The first incident allegedly occurred at Greenville, the second, and more serious, at Tippecanoe, where Tecumseh, believing his brother had run from the battle he so unwisely provoked, "was much angered and was with difficulty prevented from killing him for his false prophecies."[102]

The Shanes' story about Tecumseh's presumed disbelief in Tenskwatawa's teachings is contradicted by numerous other contemporary accounts, which consistently portray Tecumseh as a disciple of the prophet. All sources agree that he preached his brother's religion in his recruitment trips throughout the West and South.[103] Shane's claim that he did so cynically, in order to manipulate credulous Indians, itself lacks credibility. Nor is there any evidence to support Shane's charge that Tenskwatawa ran away from the battle at Tippecanoe. The sources agree that he was not part of the war party that attacked Harrison's encampment, but they also tell us that he sought to fulfill his role as a holy man by invoking the power of the Great Spirit from a vantage point near the battleground. Other than the Shanes' testimony, we have no evidence suggesting he behaved in a cowardly manner. He did not desert Prophetstown, but, as we have seen, urged the warriors to resume the attack. Tecumseh certainly understood his brother's role in the battle, even if Drake and other white historians have not. While it may well be that Tecumseh expressed some anger toward his brother immediately after learning of Tippecanoe, the evidence does not support the view that the setback there persuaded Tecumseh that his brother was a fraud. As we shall see, Tenskwatawa continued to play an important role in the leadership of the movement. We must remember that the story that Tecumseh had to be restrained from killing Tenskwatawa comes from a biased source.[104]

British Indian agent Matthew Elliott, in a dispatch to the British military commander, Gen. Isaac Brock, on January 12, 1812, reported that Harrison's raid had failed. Although the Americans burned Prophetstown, "the Prophet and his people do not appear as a vanquished enemy; they re-occupy their former ground." Elliott gave as his source "a Kickapoo Chief" who had been present at the battle. Indian losses at Tippecanoe, the chief reported, had been minimal, with no more than twenty dead. "From this man's report," Elliott wrote, "the Chiefs of these tribes have determined to come here early in the Spring and make a demand of ammunition and arms." [105] Elliott's assessment of the prophet's position after Tippecanoe reflected more than wishful thinking. Read carefully, Harrison's correspondence and other American reports offer confirmation. On December 11 the governor informed the secretary of war that the prophet was still dangerous. Skeptical that Tenskwatawa's Winnebago and Kickapoo followers had really deserted him, he predicted that when Tecumseh returned from the South they would see "other dispositions." Accordingly, Harrison recommended that "the Miamis, Potawatamis and Kickapoos be made to drive off the Prophet and all the strange Indians from the Wabash." Doubting, however, that Indians could be relied upon to do the job, he thought it might be "necessary to employ a respectable force to drive them back and prevent those Vagabonds from turning on our settlements." [106]

Late in January 1812, the governor, noting that the prophet

had been supported by a majority of the Potawatomis, Kickapoos, and Piankesaws, expressed renewed doubt about the accuracy of Indian reports concerning their disaffection. [107] He knew full well that he had not inflicted on the Indians of the Wabash the crushing defeat he claimed in his public pronouncements, and so did most of his contemporaries. Indian agent Wells, writing from Fort Wayne, reported that two Munsee envoys from Fort Malden were on their way to consult Tenskwatawa. He concluded that the British were arming the Potawatomis and assumed that the prophet was still very much a part of the war plan. [108] On January 18, 1812, Capt. Josiah Snelling of the U.S. Army informed Harrison of a rumor that Indians loyal to the prophet would go to war with the United States "as soon as the Spring corn was two feet high." [109] A month later, the territorial governors of Louisiana and Illinois as well as "Boilvin and Blondeau, Indian agents on the Mississippi," all warned that the prophet's Winnebago followers "intend to attack our settlements." [110] Listening to such reports, Harrison felt no confidence that the menace posed by the prophet and his brother had ended at Tippecanoe. Nor did other white settlers in the West. When an earthquake of massive proportions hit New Madrid, Missouri, on December 16, 1811, a local inhabitant wrote the *New York Herald* that "the Indians say that the Shawnee Prophet caused the earthquake to destroy the whites." [111] In January, at Fort Madison on the western frontier, Capt. Horatio Starks conjectured that the killing nearby of several Americans was the work of followers of the prophet. [112] In March, Governor Edwards of Illinois warned the secretary of war that "the Prophet is regaining his influence." [113] In June, Indian agent Thomas Forsyth reported from his post on the Mississippi that "the Prophet's party is increasing daily. . . . [T]he Indians of this country have news from the Prophet's town every week." [114] In July he added, "the Indians in this country sent word to the Prophet latterly that if he had asked them earlier last fall for assistance, they would have given him all in their power." [115]

In none of the contemporary reports from Indian agents, traders, and public officials on the aftermath of Tippecanoe can we find confirmation of the claim that Harrison had won a decisive victory. The governor's assertion that "the Indians have never sustained so severe a defeat since their acquaintance with white people" was accepted by few if any other participants in the engagement.[116] On the contrary, his political enemies and other critics charged that many of the American dead died needlessly because of Harrison's disregard of his officers' pleas to attack the prophet the day before the predawn assault on the American camp.[117] The governor and his friends therefore sought to protect Harrison's image and reputation, and in the process they created a myth of triumph in the wilderness that would later pay great political dividends.[118] Benjamin Drake's presidential campaign biography of Harrison—published in 1840, a year before his biography of Tecumseh—glorified the victory of "Old Tippecanoe."[119] In a typical restatement of the myth, one of Harrison's twentieth-century biographers declared that "the effect of Tippecanoe on the West was immense. It was not merely that Tecumseh's great confederation had been destroyed and the English had been checkmated. It was more than that," as Harrison's "triumph on the Wabash" finally opened all of the Old Northwest to white settlement.[120]

Some historians now recognize that while Tippecanoe was a setback for the prophet, it was not the disaster to the Indian cause commonly portrayed in the earlier historical literature. One recent writer, historian John Sugden, points out that, given the fact that they were outnumbered, the prophet's warriors did an admirable job of inflicting casualties on the invader.[121] Many of the prophet's supporters, as Harrison himself noted, soon returned to the Wabash. A large number had gathered there to await the prophet even before Tecumseh's arrival. Prophetstown was rebuilt on a new site near the ruins of the old less than three months after Harrison's raid. Historians commonly credit

Tecumseh with accomplishing that task in the face of suspicion, even hatred, of the prophet, but the process was well under way before he returned from the South. It appears that those later historians who accepted at face value stories about the prophet's disgrace were taken in by an elaborate deception that did not fool Harrison and his contemporaries. The latter had evidence indicating that disenchantment with the prophet and his teachings was largely feigned. That evidence was not restricted to reports of the reoccupation of the Prophetstown site. In a dispatch to the secretary of war dated January 7, 1812, Harrison noted that a Wea informant had warned that "the Disposition of the Kickapoos and the Winnebagos was by no means as they wished us to believe. . . . [M]any of them still retained their confidence in the Prophet." The informant concluded that the Kickapoos who had told him that they no longer believed in the prophet were "not sincere." [122]

While white commentators have ridiculed Tenskwatawa's claim that his menstruating wife had ruined his war medicine, often assuming that Tecumseh and other warriors shared their disdain for such "superstition," the fact is that, in its cultural context, Tenskwatawa's explanation was quite credible. The evidence available to us suggests that, for many of his followers, the momentary shock and anger of defeat at Tippecanoe was soon followed by acceptance of the prophet's explanation and renewed faith in his message. Other informants, as we have seen, add credibility to the Wea informant's account. On January 12, Harrison received orders from the War Department to negotiate a peace with all the Indians of the region, including the prophet and his followers. Peace terms were to include the requirement that "the Winebagoes, Potawatomis, and those of other tribes who joined, or have been connected with the prophet, must return to their respective tribes." [123] The government's objective was to prevent the rebuilding of Prophetstown. Harrison expressed doubt that "either the Prophet or Tecumseh can be prevailed upon to go" to any conference he might call and accordingly asked, in a letter to the secretary of war on February 19, if he should provide a hostage to guarantee their safety. He added: "I think it probable that the Prophet will wait until he hears what success Tecumseh has met with in raising the other Tribes before he will submit." Clearly, the governor still regarded the prophet as a powerful and dangerous leader, not as a discredited charlatan. His efforts to persuade Tecumseh and the prophet to take part in a peace delegation to Washington DC came to naught. The Shawnee brothers rejected all overtures. From Fort Wayne, Indian agent Benjamin Stickney reported on April 18 that "the Prophet and Tecumseh returned the wampum that had been sent to them, and of course refused to meet." [124] Hearing rumors that large numbers of Indians were making their way toward Vincennes, the governor expressed fear that they came not to negotiate but to attack. [125]

Harrison was not alone in his anxieties. On March 1, Agent Wells at Fort Wayne had reported that the prophet had sent the British a delegation of twenty-four Shawnees, Winnebagos, and Kickapoos to obtain munitions. Wells added that the prophet's brother, newly returned to the Wabash, "has determined to raise all the Indians he can, immediately, with an intention, no doubt, to attack our frontiers." [126] After a conference with Indian representatives in February, Harrison briefly entertained the hope that the local tribesmen had learned their lesson; they appeared "humble and submissive." [127] But the massacre, in early April, of a frontier family living some thirty-five miles from Vincennes convinced the governor that "the Prophet and his Brother were either altogether insincere in the professions which they made in February or they had been induced to adopt other politics in consequence of the probability of War between the United States and Britain." He warned the secretary of war that "they are again organizing a force for hostile purposes." Diplomatic efforts to avert bloodshed would probably fail, as "one of the most mischievous and successful of the Prophets schemes is that of destroying the influence of the Chiefs amongst the Pottawattimies and Kickapoos particularly. The young men are under no kind of control, each man does what he pleases, and we have in my opinion no alternative but War." [128] Hearing a rumor soon thereafter that the Delawares were responsible for an attack on Vallonia in southern Indiana, Harrison expressed doubt that he could maintain Delaware or Miami neutrality, as the Miami chief Little Eyes was working to ally his tribe with the prophet. [129] Another killing near Vincennes led the governor to suggest to Washington that negotiations were pointless. He recommended in their place a "war of extirpation." [130]

Violence escalated throughout the spring of 1812. In all some forty-six American settlers were killed by Indians in the western territories and in Ohio, and all but two of those incidents were the work of "warriors from groups which had fought at Tippecanoe. They were not the first blows of a full-scale onslaught on the frontiers, as some believed at the time. They were revenge slayings . . . the final accounting of the battle at Tippecanoe." [131] In May, alarmed that those killings would provoke a renewed attack on Prophetstown, Tecumseh joined delegates from other Indian nations at the Massassinway River in Indiana for a conference attended by both American and British observers. In attendance were representatives of the Shawnee, Kickapoo, Piankeshaw, Winnebago, Potawatomi, Delaware, Miami, Eel River, Wea, Ottawa, Wyandot, and Chippewa nations. Tecumseh spoke for the Prophetstown community. Without exception, the delegates deplored the recent attacks on whites. They were agreed also in holding the Potawatomis responsible for those attacks. They disagreed, however, on the role of the prophet. The Potawatomi chiefs declared the killers "a few Vagabonds" who had been misled by Tenskwatawa. Since the prophet had worked to "detach them from their own chiefs and attach them to himself," those warriors could no longer be considered as "belonging to our nation." The Potawatomis, they declared, "will be thankful to any people who will put them to death, wherever they are found." For his part, Tecumseh did his best to offer assurances that the prophet and his followers hoped to "live in peace" with the white people of Indiana, blaming the violence at Tippecanoe on "a few of our younger men" and castigating the Potawatomis for their continuing attacks on whites. In response to Potawatomi and Delaware spokesmen who blamed the prophet for provoking those incidents, Tecumseh replied: "We defy a living creature to say if we ever advised anyone, directly or indirectly, to make war on our white brothers. It has constantly been our misfortune to have our views misrepresented to our white brethren." He blamed "pretended chiefs" who "have been in the habit of selling land to white people that did not belong to them" for the campaign of calumny against the prophet. He added, however, a word of warning to the Americans: while his people would "never strike the first blow," they would resist any further efforts to drive them from the Wabash. "We will die like men," he vowed.[132]

Although all of the Indian delegates, including Tecumseh, had proclaimed their desire to live in peace with Indiana's white settlers, the governor had insisted that, as a condition of peace, they apprehend and surrender the warriors responsible for the recent attacks on white settlers. On that matter he received no satisfaction. Moreover, soon after the conference adjourned, informants warned that Tecumseh's professions of peaceful intent could not be trusted. On June 3, Harrison advised the secretary of war that "the major part of the Winnebago Tribe are at Tippecanoe with the Prophet and Tecumseh . . . they have been joined by many small bands from the Illinois River and the east of Lake Michigan, making a force at least equal to that which they commanded last summer. . . . [T]heir intentions . . . [are] entirely hostile." Harrison and Edwards believed that the activities at the rebuilt Prophetstown were part of a larger British scheme to incite Indian attacks on the United States.[133]

Tecumseh, the Prophet, and the Second Anglo-American War

Tecumseh was, in fact, soon in touch with the British. Their Indian agent at Fort Malden, Matthew Elliott, had repeatedly warned him that His Majesty's government expected their Indian friends to refrain from attacks on the Americans while England remained at peace with the United States. In a message to Elliott on June 8, Tecumseh cast the Americans in the role of aggressor, explaining the attack of the "Long Knives" at Tippecanoe as an unwarranted response to Potawatomi attacks on the frontier. Prophetstown was punished for crimes the people there had not committed. He reiterated his desire for peace but declared that he would lead a general Indian uprising if "we hear of any of our people being killed." [134] In preparation for making good on that threat, more than eight hundred warriors had already assembled at the rebuilt Prophetstown. Envoys had been dispatched to the West and to the North bearing black wampum and red-painted tobacco, both symbolic of war. They proclaimed Tenskwatawa the prophet of the Great Spirit and promised victory to those who rallied to the cause. [135] Not all responded favorably. The Otos of the Great Plains told the messenger of the "Shawnoe Prophet . . . that they could make more by trapping beaver than by making war against the Americans." [136] Even so, one recent estimate finds that by the summer of 1812 the prophet was supported by around thirty-five hundred warriors, centered primarily in Indiana, Illinois, and Wisconsin but including adherents from nations as distant as the Creeks of Alabama and the Sioux of the Great Plains. [137]

Most historians' accounts of this phase of the movement assume that after Tippecanoe "the Prophet lost influence, and the Shawnee revitalization quickly changed into a series of military alliances under the leadership of Tecumseh." [138] But there is no contemporary evidence to support the claim that the religion of the prophet ceased to be an important part of Tecumseh's appeal to prospective allies at this time. The notion that Tecumseh repudiated the prophet's religion or that he regarded his brother as a fool is found only in the highly suspect testimony of the Shanes and in a few other reminiscences that were also dictated, often secondhand, long after the event. Too much has been made of Tecumseh's visibility outside Prophetstown and of his brother's seclusion. Alliance building had been important to the brothers long before Tippecanoe. Diplomacy was Tecumseh's forte; Tenskwatawa generally remained at home to commune with the Great Spirit and preach to the faithful who flocked to Prophetstown. Even before Tippecanoe, Tecumseh, possessed as he was of skills as a diplomat and warrior the prophet lacked, had come to play a more prominent role than in the earlier days when the movement did not contemplate armed resistance. The change in emphasis, as we have noted, was forced upon the Shawnee brothers by Harrison's determination not only to annex additional land but to drive all non-Shawnees from Prophetstown. Those who maintain that Tenskwatawa played no significant role after Tippecanoe fail to account for the fact that during Tecumseh's absences he continued to serve not only as prophet but as civil head of the community. The sources agree that those arrangements continued after Tippecanoe. There is no contemporary document from any American or British official reporting that the prophet had been deposed or demoted from his religious or civil responsibilities; to the contrary, they all testify to his continued prominence. Whatever loss of influence Tenskwatawa may have suffered as a result of Tippecanoe (and most secondary accounts clearly have greatly exaggerated its impact), he remained a person to be reckoned with in the eyes of both foes and allies.

In June, Tecumseh led a delegation to Fort Malden.[139] Stopping briefly at Fort Wayne, he demonstrated his continued adherence to the prophet's teachings by refusing to eat any of the food offered him by the Americans except potatoes, which he considered an Indian food acceptable to the Great Spirit.[140] At the time news was received of the American declaration of war against

England, Tecumseh was in Upper Canada. He quickly emerged as the preeminent leader of England's Indian allies, rendering invaluable service in harassing the American forces, cutting the supply line to Detroit, and paving the way for Hull's disastrous capitulation in August 1812.[141] The prophet, in command on the Wabash, continued the campaign of deception, informing American officials that he distrusted the British and intended that Prophetstown remain at peace with the United States. In furtherance of that ruse, on July 12, less than a week after learning of the outbreak of the second Anglo-American war, Tenskwatawa appeared at Fort Wayne with around a hundred Winnebago and Kickapoo followers. He assured Indian agent Stickney that he and his brother were now prepared to accept all of the land-cession treaties they had previously challenged, claiming that only their resentment of Harrison's high-handed behavior had prevented an earlier agreement. The prophet, Stickney noted, made "strong professions of peace and friendship" with the United States and condemned the British for treating Indians like "dogs."[142] Former agent Wells warned Harrison that Stickney was being duped by the prophet, but in fact Stickney shared Wells's misgivings. Both warned that the prophet and Tecumseh were planning a general Indian uprising.[143] Stickney later determined that Tecumseh had urged the prophet to send the women and children at Prophetstown to safety in the West and then attack Vincennes.[144]

In contrast to later historians' image of Tenskwatawa as a bungling, rash, and inept civil leader, contemporary reports of Harrison, Wells, Stickney, and others portray a shrewd, resourceful, and manipulative politician whose continuing influence with the Indian tribes of the region was a matter of serious concern. In 1812, during the crucial first summer of the war, Tenskwatawa was in command at Prophetstown and maintained excellent discipline there despite the tensions generated by war rumors and by a food shortage. His followers avoided provoking the Americans in Indiana as Tecumseh rallied support for the cause abroad.

Harrison's and Wells's suspicions were, of course, correct. The prophet and his brother no longer believed that peace with the United States was a viable option and were only waiting for the right time to strike. As Tecumseh forged alliances with other tribes and with the British, Tenskwatawa summoned the western tribes to a meeting at Prophetstown late in the summer, "when the corn is made," to plan an attack on the Americans.[145]

On September 10, warriors from Prophetstown struck Fort Harrison.[146] Insurgent Indians, mostly Potawatomis, attacked Fort Wayne in September and again in October.[147] Neither fort was taken. Counterattacking American forces burned Indian villages and fields throughout the territory. The new Prophetstown was put to the torch in November.[148] In December, the prophet, accompanied by some of his followers, fled to Canada. In January he accompanied Tecumseh on a return to Indiana, where the brothers spent the next three months urging the scattered and demoralized Indian population to regroup in Canada and there join in the fight against the Long Knives.[149] On February 11, Harrison reported that he had learned from some Potawatomis "that the Prophet was in the neighborhood of his former residence with about 300 Winnebagoes and about 200 of the other Tribes and that he was daily gaining strength."[150]

In their travels in Indiana, the Shawnee brothers enlisted a number of Kickapoos, Winnebagos, Potawatomis, and some Miamis, Weas, and Delawares, providing Tecumseh with an aug-mented multinational army.[151] Also committed to the British cause were Indians from the northern Great Lakes region recruited by the charismatic Indian agent Robert Dickson. But Indian support for Great Britain in 1812 was by no means universal. The Indians of Ohio remained for the most part opposed to the insurgency. More Shawnees fought against Tecumseh than with him. Harrison and other American commanders were supported by Indian auxiliaries from several tribes. Nonetheless, in 1812 warriors from nations once committed to peace with the United States, including the

Miamis and Delawares, were persuaded by the force of events and by the eloquence of the Shawnee brothers to take up arms against the Americans. News of Hull's surrender to the British at Detroit on August 16, 1812, emboldened many who had earlier rejected their appeal. Although not all the Indians who rallied to the cause were converts to the religion of the prophet, for many it remained a powerful source of inspiration.

The Shawnee brothers' early skepticism about a British alliance proved well founded. In the spring and early summer, two British efforts to take Forts Meigs, although initially well supported by Indian warriors, ended in failure, as did an attack on Fort Stephenson on the Sandusky. British planning for those engagements was inept, particularly in the deployment of artillery. As their ally bungled, Indian forces melted away, leaving only Tecumseh and his most militant warriors on the field of battle. Learning of the American naval victory on Lake Erie in September, the British commanders decided to withdraw their forces from Upper Canada and regroup at Niagara. Spread too thin, they lacked the resources to pursue an aggressive war in the West. Tecumseh and the prophet, enraged by what they regarded as British duplicity and cowardice, confronted the ranking British officer, Gen. Henry Proctor, with the demand that his troops either fight or turn over their military supplies so that the Indians could defend themselves against an advancing American army. Stung by that reproach, Proctor, after a strategic retreat from Amherstburg, halfheartedly engaged the enemy at the Thames River on October 13, 1813. Encountering stiff opposition and greatly outnumbered, British forces retreated after firing the third volley. Left to battle the Long Knives alone, Tecumseh and his warriors fought valiantly but were vanquished. Tecumseh did not survive the Battle of the Thames. Several Americans later claimed the honor of having shot the great Shawnee war chief, some of whom also boasted of having skinned his corpse. Jacksonian political folklore accorded the honor to Martin Van Buren's vice president, Richard Mentor Johnson.

The Prophet's Later Years

Tenskwatawa, evacuated with Proctor's army, was now the sole leader of a pan-Indian coalition plagued with desertion and with defection to the American side. The British initially tried to ignore the prophet's claim to be the new war chief, but when efforts to replace him with the fallen warrior's son Pachetha failed to win the support of the former Prophetstown residents, they had no choice but to accept him in that role. The continued loyalty of his core community from the Wabash suggests once again the error of assuming that Tippecanoe had destroyed the prophet's credibility. In 1816, Michigan governor Cass noted that some two hundred warriors representing a number of nations "have adhered to him under all vicissitudes with unbroken fidelity." Although many of the warriors who had rallied to the cause in the summer of 1813 deserted even before Tecumseh's death, the prophet's influence still extended beyond his own immediate community. Cass reported that the British in Canada used him as "the principal instrument in their hands for acquiring and preserving their influence over the Indians." Tenskwatawa's influence remained so great that "no proposition is made except through him." [152] The British were never happy with the prophet, whom they described as querulous, egotistical, and demanding. He proved a poor replacement for Tecumseh on the battlefield. Not much of a warrior, the prophet made little real contribution to the British war effort. But given his stature among those who remained in Canada, the British had no choice. Much is made in the historical literature of the prophet's failure to hold the broader pan-Indian movement together after the loss of Tecumseh, but there is no reason to believe that Tecumseh would have succeeded where his brother failed. Tecumseh's reputation was preserved by his death. By the end of 1813, military defeat and the British retreat from Upper Canada had alienated most of the allies recruited by the Shawnee brothers the year before.

At peace negotiations in the late summer of 1815, American negotiators offered an amnesty and repatriation to all Indians who had fought on the British side. Uncharacteristically, the United States asked for no land cessions. But the Americans were not willing to recognize Tenskwatawa's status as head of a community. He was welcome to return so long as he placed himself under the jurisdiction of his old enemy, the Ohio Shawnee chief Black Hoof. Unwilling to accept subordinate status, the prophet refused to sign the peace agreement. British officials in Canada, now regarding their former Indian allies as an unwelcome drain on the public treasury, tried to force them to return to the United States by cutting their subsidies and rations. Humiliated and hungry, many left, returning to former homelands in the American Old Northwest. The prophet sought and failed to negotiate arrangements to relocate his community on the River Raisin in Michigan. Governor Cass warned his superiors in Washington DC that the prophet was still dangerous and advised that he not be permitted to bring his followers back to the United States. Many of his followers, in defiance of the wishes of the U.S. government, returned to the Wabash, hoping to rebuild the sacred community, but Tenskwatawa, fearful of being arrested or even killed if he crossed into the United States, did not join them. In the end, their faith in the prophet proved greater than his courage. His leadership effectively ceased not at the Battle of Tippecanoe, or at the Thames, but with his absence from the new Prophetstown.[153]

The prophet remained in Canada for more than a decade but found no real role there. In 1825, under the patronage of Governor Cass, he returned to the United States, where he served as a spokesman for Jacksonian Indian removal. Although his advocacy of abandonment of the lands Tecumseh had fought to preserve has raised eyebrows, it was not incompatible with his teaching that the Great Spirit had proscribed continued involvement with whites and their culture. The aging prophet settled with the Shawnees in Kansas, where he died in poverty in 1836. [154] Tenskwatawa was not destined to enjoy the sort of uncritical posthumous adulation, by whites and Indians alike, that would soon be lavished upon Tecumseh. His faults were all too obvious and all too easily exaggerated by writers preoccupied with stereotypes of noble savages (Tecumseh) and ignoble savages (Tenskwatawa). Although Tenskwatawa has fared poorly in histories, novels, and plays written by Euro-Americans, stories about his exploits have been passed down from generation to generation by Shawnees loyal to his memory and by others, such as Winnebagos and Kickapoos, who once shared a part of his dream and his vision. [155]

4

The Red Sticks

A Jacksonian-era Tennessee judge named Josephus Guild, fan-
cying himself an authority on the career of Tecumseh, loved
to relate the story of the great warrior's southern recruitment
journey. He drew a vivid word portrait of Tecumseh and the
prophet appearing before tribal councils "entirely naked, except
for flaps and ornaments; their faces painted black, and their
heads adorned with eagle plumes. White buffalo tails dangled
behind them, suspended from girdles that were adorned with
the scalps of pale faces." Tecumseh exhorted the tribesmen "to
return to their primitive customs, to abandon their agricultural
and other industrial pursuits," and to fight against the Americans,
"a grasping, unprincipled race" that intended to reduce them to
"African servitude." They must adhere to the teachings of the
prophet, use no arms and wear no clothes from the aliens, but,
"clad in the skins of beasts," carry once again "the war club and
the scalping knife." The king of England, he promised, would
aid their efforts. "This speech, delivered in town after town,"
was "enforced by that of the Prophet, in which he declared that
those who should join in the war party should be shielded from
all harm, none should be killed in battle . . . the Great Spirit
would surround them with quagmires, which would swallow the
Americans as they approached."[1]

   Judge Guild's story may have captured something of the spirit of Tecumseh's message, but like many other accounts of the warrior's southern mission, it was riddled with inaccuracies. Guild believed the trip was made in the fall of 1812, whereas it actually occurred a year earlier. It is unlikely that Tecumseh wore the scalps of "pale faces." His strategy at this point, as we have seen, required that whites not be alarmed by disclosure of war plans. He did not prohibit the use of firearms; eyewitness accounts agree that his party carried rifles. Nor was he accompanied by the prophet; his companion was a lesser-known Shawnee holy man named Seekaboo, who was either a Creek who had resettled among Tecumseh's Shawnees or a man of mixed Shawnee and Creek ancestry.

The judge was not alone in his embellishments of the story. His contemporaries invented recollections of southern trips both before and after 1811 that Tecumseh never made, and they placed him in the midst of peoples such as the Cherokees, Seminoles, and Osages whom he probably never visited. Tecumseh did visit the Chickasaws, the Choctaws, and the Creeks. In addition to Seekaboo, he was accompanied by twenty of the prophet's followers, of whom six were Shawnees, six Kickapoos, and six Winnebagos. Also in the party were two Indians of southern background who acted as guides and interpreters. The group found little support among either the Chickasaws or the Choctaws. The Chickasaws twenty years earlier had rejected the appeal of the Shawnee war chief Red Pole, who sought their support of the pan-Indian northern confederation. Chickasaw warriors joined Anthony Wayne's army and fought against the Shawnees and their allies in 1794. Chickasaw warriors would fight against Tecumseh in Canada in 1813. Their tribal leaders, many of them mixed-blood descendants of the Scots trader James Logan Colbert, profited personally from trade and alliance with the United States and were more than willing, in 1805, to sell Chickasaw lands north of the Tennessee River. The mixed-blood ruling elite embraced not only Euro-American agriculture but also the acquisitive entrepreneurial and individualistic values of their white forebears and American allies. The full-blood members of the Chickasaw nation did not as yet feel sufficiently threatened by white expansionism to challenge their leadership. Few foresaw the massive dispossession and removal that would be their lot in the decades to come. Passing through Chickasaw territory late in August 1811, Tecumseh made no effort to explain his intentions to the Chickasaw leadership. He expected no recruits there. [2]

Tecumseh did make a serious effort to win Choctaw support. Late in the nineteenth century, Henry S. Halbert interviewed a number of Choctaws who shared family recollections about Tecumseh's visit. They recalled that he called for peace among all Indian tribes and for armed resistance against those who were taking their land. Tecumseh also allegedly told the Choctaws that they must support Great Britain in the coming war with the United States. One informant added that he deplored the practice of killing women and children in warfare and demanded that they always be spared in future battles. Halbert's sources agreed that, after hearing Tecumseh's message, as translated by Seekaboo, Choctaw leaders declared their opposition to Tecumseh's pan-Indian confederation and argued for continued friendship with white Americans. The Choctaw chiefs were on the payroll of the United States. They profited from peace and were also realists about the prospects of success in war. Although the chiefs had signed away some Choctaw lands in 1805, their people generally did not yet feel threatened. Although Tecumseh's party visited a number of Choctaw villages, they were trailed by the chiefs and their representatives, who spoke against war and generally prevailed. The claim—found in the older literature—that Tecumseh recruited three hundred Choctaw warriors is not supported in the sources of the period. He may have won over a handful, but in the overall battle with the chiefs for the loyalty of the Choctaws, Tecumseh, concludes one leading authority, "had suffered a great defeat." [3]

Tecumseh and his party proceeded to Alabama, where, among the Creeks (now often called the Muskogees), they met with a far warmer reception. Inspired by Tecumseh and Seekaboo, some Muskogee chiefs and shamans would soon make a pilgrimage to Indiana, where, in the vicinity of the ruins of the old Prophetstown, they would confer with the Shawnee prophet himself. Muskogee support for Tecumseh has often been explained in terms of kinship. Contemporary sources relate that his mother was a Creek. The "Red Stick" movement has frequently been treated as an outgrowth of his visit to his kinfolk. But the Muskogee insurgency that would lead first to a bloody civil war and then to a disastrous conflict with the United States was not simply a response to Tecumseh and to his revelations of the teachings of the Shawnee prophet. It had deeper roots. To be sure, the Creek militants incorporated some of the dances and songs taught to them by Seekaboo, who remained among them after Tecumseh's departure, but their words and actions did not always reflect either the prophet's teachings or Tecumseh's political advice. The Muskogee world had its own prophets, and those prophets had their own agenda and their own timetable.

In September 1811, Tecumseh visited a large assembly of Muskogee tribesmen. A few representatives from other Indian nations, including Cherokees and Choctaws, were also present. The meeting had not been convened to hear the emissaries of the Shawnee prophet. The issue under discussion was a demand, presented by federal Indian agent Benjamin Hawkins, that the Muskogees agree to authorize the construction of a road through their territory to be used by white soldiers, traders, and settlers. Tribal leaders had earlier rejected a similar request from President Monroe. Chief Hoboithle Mico had replied to that overture by declaring that although God had created the land "for us to walk on," the Creeks now had barely enough left to survive and must not be subjected to further white intrusions. But Hawkins now told the Muskogees that they had no choice, as "white people must have roads to market and for travelling wherever they chose to go through the United States." Hoboithle Mico's refusal had the support of most of those present. Indians in the Southeast had many reasons to fear white road construction. At minimum, as one of the Choctaws noted, a road would facilitate a "trade of liquor amongst us" and "cause the death of many red people." [4] The Creek chiefs worried about clashes between white surveyors and some of their more militant younger warriors. Drawing on earlier experiences throughout the Southeast, they also feared that white travelers would soon be followed by white poachers who would attack Indians and seize more of their land. Even so, Hawkins soon prevailed. Offered lucrative rewards, key Creek leaders changed their minds and agreed to the construction of a road that would cut through the center of the nation's territory. [5]

We do not know exactly what Tecumseh, a silent observer through most of those proceedings, finally said to that assembly. The accounts of his exhortation that have filled most of the history books over the years are neither contemporary nor reliable. Their fanciful reconstructions of his "Speech to the Creeks," replete with overblown rhetoric and cries to kill all whites regardless of age or gender, are not consistent with contemporary reports of his strategy in 1811. [6] Even so, one recent historian of Jacksonian Indian policy repeats their claim that, looking upon his audience with a "murderous smile," Tecumseh ended his speech to the Creeks by ordering them to attack their white neighbors and "burn their dwellings—destroy their stock—slay their wives and children, that the very breed may perish!" [7] Tecumseh no doubt called for continued resistance to Hawkins's demands for a new road, but it would have been out of character for him to proclaim an immediate all-out war with the United States, let alone a program of genocide. As noted in the previous chapter, the testimony of contemporaries indicates that at this time Tecumseh and the prophet were advising the tribes they sought to bring into the pan-Indian confederation that violent confrontations with whites should be avoided until their union was strong enough to prevail. Hawkins, who had his own Indian allies and informants at the meeting, related that Tecumseh had "told the Creeks not to do any injury to the Americans; to be in peace and friendship with them, not to steal even a bell from any one of any color. Let the white people on the continent manage their affairs their own way. Let the red people manage their affairs their own way."[8] In a similar vein, Cherokee agent Return J. Meigs reported to the War Department that Cherokees present at the meeting told him that Tecumseh urged that Indians live in peace with the Americans. Meigs added, however, that Tecumseh had called for an end to land cessions to whites. After war broke out, Hawkins complained that he had been misled about Tecumseh's activities.[9]

In fact, the Creek agent had not been particularly observant. Although Tecumseh did not advocate an immediate attack on whites, he was never secretive about his hostility to white culture and to Indians who succumbed to its appeal. Numerous accounts verify that in his meetings with prospective allies, Tecumseh usually ridiculed or denounced those tribesmen who advocated cooperation with the federal government and its "civilization" program. One nineteenth-century writer, drawing on southern Indian informants, captured the nativist thrust of Tecumseh's message. In 1851, Albert Pickett recalled that Tecumseh "exhorted them to return to their primitive customs, to throw aside the plow and the loom, and to abandon an agricultural life, which was unbecoming to Indian warriors." They were not to emulate "the grasping, unprincipled race."[10] Other witnesses reported that to underscore the urgency of the cause, Tecumseh warned that just as the Euro-Americans enslaved and abused blacks, so, if unchecked, they would soon deprive Indian peoples of their freedom and dignity. "Do they not even now kick and strike us as they do their black faces?" asked Tecumseh. "How long will it be before they will tie us to a post and whip us?"[11] Only through unity and resistance could Indians save themselves from dispossession and enslavement.

A rich folklore came to surround Tecumseh's journey, including most notably the story that Tecumseh told doubters that when he returned to the North he would stamp his foot and shake the entire earth. A Creek informant who was hostile to the Red Sticks related some years later that "Tecumseh had said to many in private, and to the national council, that he was determined to war with the Americans." To signal the beginning of his campaign, "he would ascend to the top of a mountain about four moons from that time, and there he would whoop three unbounded loud whoops, slap his hands together three times, and raise his foot and stamp it on the ground. By these actions he could make the whole earth tremble, which would be a sign of the success of his undertaking. If such did not happen, they would know that he would fail in his enterprise." [12] It is likely that this story, so often retold in popular accounts of Tecumseh's life, originated after the great New Madrid earthquakes of 1811, which leveled forests and changed the course of the Mississippi River. But the first of the earthquakes struck before Tecumseh had returned to Tippecanoe, and thus natural events did not conform to the schedule specified in the story. [13]

Another tale connects the great Shawnee warrior with a comet, which presumably appeared when Tecumseh flung his arm to heaven. The comet story is probably also apocryphal. [14] But neither of these stories is particularly relevant to explaining the Red Stick prophetic movement and rebellion. Muskogee warriors in 1813–14 killed accommodationist chiefs and fought Andrew Jackson's army and his Indian allies not because Tecumseh preached resistance or worked miracles but because of conflicts within Muskogee society. While the spiritual leaders of the Red Sticks were familiar with Tecumseh's message—some had visited Tenskwatawa in Indiana—their teachings were shaped by their own religious traditions and immediate historical circumstances. Tecumseh and the Shawnee prophet offered inspiration and reinforcement of their nativist convictions, but the message of the Red Sticks was cast in their own distinctive idiom. The Creek prophets seized on Shawnee promises of supernatural aid from the Great Spirit, and they learned to do the Dance of the Lakes and sing new songs learned from members of Tecumseh's entourage. The Dance of the Lakes, an empowerment ritual, unlike traditional Creek war dances, was performed before, rather than after, engaging the enemy.[15] But other Creek ceremonial practices remained unchanged, despite the Shawnee prophet's strictures against the old shamanism. Notably, the Red Sticks failed to heed Tecumseh's advice on the importance of forging a powerful confederation before confronting the United States. Their insurgency cannot, therefore, be understood simply as an extension of the Shawnee prophet's revitalization movement.

The Muskogee Spiritual World

To place the Red Sticks' uprising in its proper context, we first must turn our attention to the belief system that nurtured and sustained their prophets. Sacred power suffused the traditional Muskogee world. Its presence, strange and potent, permeates their myths, their ceremonies, and their sense of past realities and future possibilities. Muskogee stories of creation utilized the ubiquitous Earth Diver motif but added elaborate and distinctive details. In some accounts, two pigeons used a blade of grass to force the waters to subside and expose the earth. Another holds that "The One Above, the Creator," was assisted in some mysterious way by two redheaded woodpeckers, the only beings that existed before the emergence of the earth from the waters. The land emerged from the spot where the birds' tails had touched the water. The One Above placed seven newly created beings on the new dry land, and they proceeded to shape the remainder of the present universe by the power of their thoughts. In yet another version, spirit beings debated whether "it would be best, to have some land, or to have all water." They asked Eagle to decide. He sent Dove to find land. When she failed, the task was entrusted to Crawfish. In the Yuchi variant of the epic, Crawfish dives into the primal water to bring up the mud from which the earth was fashioned. Hawk and Buzzard dried the mud by fanning it with their wings. The land initially is very dark, lit only by a single star, but soon the moon appears, then the sun. The sun's warmth and light nurture life. Human beings emerge when a drop of blood falls from the sun and mixes with the dirt. We are thus the children of both the sun and the earth.[16]

In Muskogee cosmology, the earth is not the only abode of life. The universe is divided into three realms: the upper world, the middle world, and the lower world. The upper world is the realm of "the Sun and the Moon, Thunder and other gigantic beings." This world "released the powers of purification, order, permanence, clarity, and periodicity. Individuals tapped these powers by wearing jewelry and gorgets etched with moon signs or emblazoned wit solar motifs."[17] They believed it to be a great solid vault soaring above the flat plane of the earth. That sky vault, informants told anthropologist John Swanton, "was supposed to rise and fall upon the earth at intervals so that, by watching his opportunity, a person could pass under its edge." Beyond that edge dwelt both departed souls and "many supernatural beings." The middle world, the earth, is the home of animals and of human beings. It was not, however, devoid of spirit power, for "something of the supernatural attached to every created thing, every animal, plant, stone, stick, body of water, geographical feature, and even to objects which man himself had made."[18] The lower world, beneath the earth, was a troubling yet essential "realm of reversals, madness, creativity, fertility, chaos." The spirits that inhabited this world were dangerous. They included shape shifters, who ate human souls; wrathful ghosts of unavenged warriors and of unhappy suicides, who inflicted illnesses on their living relatives; and a great water cannibal, who was responsible for various intestinal aliments.

The most fearful of the denizens of the Muskogee underworld was the Tie Snake, a huge, antlered water monster with iridescent scales on its body and a glowing crystal in its head. The Tie Snake not only attacked river travelers but also spread disease. Despite its fearful attributes it was beautiful to behold, irresistible in its radiance. But those who gazed upon it went mad or died. Scales and crystal from the Tie Snake were of great power and were "highly prized in divination." Thus shamans sought them for their medicine bundles, undergoing special rites of purification to gain immunity from the powers of the lower world.[19]

The Muskogee high god, known as the Maker of Breath, maintained the precarious balance between the forces of the upper and lower worlds upon which all life depended.[20] At one time this supreme being had instructed the Muskogees in the rituals they must observe in order to help sustain the harmony and equilibrium of the world through the balancing of contrary forces. But, having thus empowered human beings, the Creator now manifested himself to them directly only very briefly during the annual observance of Busk. He was present in the sacred fire, which, having been newly kindled immediately after elaborate ceremonies of purification, was totally free of pollution.[21] He was not available for help in everyday life; instead, the Creeks called upon a wide variety of gods and spirits. Of the numerous deities regularly accessible to them, two sky gods were of particular importance. Hayu-ya, "the thunderer," brought rain, and Yahola assisted shamans in healing and in childbirth. The Muskogees held both in high esteem as powerful spirit guardians, portraying them in their medicine songs as "perfect, clean, undefiled." Those fortunate enough to obtain their favor were blessed not only with physical strength but with "clearness of vision and of thought."[22]

Muskogee shamans, as naturalist William Bartram noted, obtained their power from "communion with powerful invisible spirits who have a share in the rule and government of human affairs." The French traveler Jean-Bernard Bossu described a Muskogee divination very similar to the Shaking Tent Ceremony found among some of the northern tribes. The shaman, he wrote, enters a hut made of skins "completely naked and utters words, understood by no one, in order to invoke the spirit. After that, apparently in a complete trance, he gets up, shouts, and moves about as the sweat pours from every part of his body. The hut shakes, and the spectators think this is evidence of the presence of the spirit." [23] Some shamanic rituals conferred spirit power on hunters. Others empowered shamans to cure the sick or foresee the future. The most powerful were members of an elite secret society that possessed esoteric knowledge. They were endowed with great powers not given to others and were called upon in time of war. Bartram learned that the Creeks "never determine on an expedition against their enemy" without the "council and assistance" of "the high priest." They believed that their greatest holy men, through "communion with powerful invisible spirits," could not only "predict the results of any expedition" but also use their special access to the spirit world "to stop, and turn back, an army, after a march of several hundred miles." [24] Unlike the followers of Neolin and Tenskwatawa, who were taught to regard their traditional shamans as witches, the Red Stick prophets sought to walk in their footsteps.

Muskogee religion was grounded in the premise that humans must constantly seek to live in harmony with spiritual forces. In that endeavor, certain rituals of purification and restoration were vital. Muskogee men assembled each day in the town square to drink a tea brewed from the leaves of the cassina bush which Europeans misnamed the Black Drink (the Muskogee word meant "White Drink" and connoted purity). One eighteenth-century Euro-American commentator explained that the Muskogees believed this beverage "purifies them from all sin, and leaves them in a state of perfect innocence, that it inspires them with an invincible prowess in war, and that it is the only solid cement of friendship, benevolence and hospitality." A sacred exclamation, known as the *yohullah*, accompanied the ingestion of Black Drink. The drink in larger quantities was also used as an emetic in special purification rituals. Our informant noted: "Their mode of disgorging, or spouting out, the black drink, is singular, and has not the most agreeable appearance. After drinking copiously, the warrior, by hugging his arms across his stomach, and leaning forward, disgorges all the liquor from his mouth, to the distance of six or eight feet." Upon the death of a warrior, the regular gatherings in the town square were suspended, and Black Drink was taken outside until the death was avenged. A death within the community led to a four-day suspension of the ceremony. [25] The beverage, although used as an emetic, was essentially a stimulant, high in caffeine content. Its use was restricted to "mature men." It was never drunk "by women or young boys." [26]

Of greatest importance to the well-being of the people was the annual observance of Busk, the most significant of the Muskogee public ceremonials. [27] In this ceremony, which was held near the end of the summer, celebrants retold the story of the sacred origin of corn, the gift of an earth goddess. But Busk was far more than a harvest celebration. Lasting several days, Busk, as historian Joel Martin explains, "emphasized collective renewal. Its intent was to rekindle a sense of the sacrality of life." [28] Purification through the ingestion of a powerful emetic was essential to the achievement of that renewal. George Stiggins, a mixed-blood Creek whose account of tribal customs and history is one of the more important contemporary sources, related that the men chosen to lead Busk observances did not "eat or drink anything but the consecrated emetic, which they take profusely every day of the festival. They neither speak to nor touch a woman during the time, as such procedure would inevitably ruin their thanksgiving song and incur destruction not only to him that does it but to the community at large. Nor will they shake hands with an unpurified friend during the time of their officiating."[29]

Busk culminated in the kindling of a new fire, unpolluted by the transgressions of the past and containing the presence of the Maker of Breath. The new fire was lit in an enclosure containing logs situated so that they pointed to the four cardinal points. The design invoked the fundamental structure of the universe. As the fire grew, corn and other foods and medicines essential to the people were offered to its flames so that they might be made sacred. Men and women were segregated and assigned different roles during Busk but were reunited symbolically at the end. An American officer who attended a Busk in 1791 reported that, until the last day of the four-day ceremony, no man was permitted to touch a woman "even with the tip of his finger." While the men partook of the Black Drink and kept within the village square, women and children remained outside the square, seeking purification through dancing and bathing. Both sexes fasted until the fourth day.[30] Then, "feasting together villagers returned to ordinary life with new zeal, new appreciation of the sacred community and its sacred foundations."[31]

The Troubled History of the Creek Nation

The communal harmony ideally achieved at Busk and renewed throughout the year in the Black Drink rituals brought unity to village communities. The entity whites called "the Creeks" was not as easily unified. Although Tecumseh in 1811 addressed an assembly of the "Creek nation," a polity presumably governed by a "national council," that nation was never truly cohesive. The phrase "Creek Indian" would have had no meaning to a Native inhabitant of the Southeast in the seventeenth century. Nor could one have found in any of their languages a single word to designate a "Creek nation." The terms Muskogee and Muscogulge, favored by many modern historians and anthropologists, are derived from a word of Algonquian origin that was used to designate swamp dwellers.[32] As for Creek, that name was first used in the late 1600s by British traders from South Carolina to designate Indian trading partners living in the vicinity of Ochese Creek in what is now Georgia.[33] The British over the next hundred years extended the term to include all of those Native peoples in western Georgia, Alabama, and Mississippi who were not Cherokees, Choctaws, or Chickasaws. According to one historian, the term encompassed between fifty and one hundred autonomous groups. In the eighteenth century there were around sixty towns classified as Creek. The British came to distinguish between the Upper Creeks and the Lower Creeks. The former were found in Alabama in the vicinity of the Coosa and Tallapoosa rivers; the latter were found further east in Georgia, along the Chattahoochee and Flint rivers. The two areas sometimes followed different policies. The Red Stick movement would find its strongest support among the Upper Creeks, who, by virtue of location, had less contact with Euro-Americans.

The Creeks were a diverse people. A majority spoke languages of the Muskogean family, which included Muskogee, Alabama, Hitchiti, Choctaw, and Chickasaw. But many Creek communities did not. Non-Muskogean speakers included, among others, the Yuchis, the Pakanas, the Okchais, and some Shawnees living in the lower South. Historian J. Leitch Wright uses the term Muscogulges to designate both the Muskogean speakers and the others who comprised the peoples historically called the Creek. They were, as Wright notes, "an assemblage of numerous peoples. Tribes had merged with and been absorbed by other tribes, a process that had often been repeated."[34] Out of a history that cannot be reconstructed in any detail or precision there emerged, not a unified nation in the European sense of the term, but a polyglot confederation whose members were united by a loose sense of collective identity, some common or at least similar myths and rituals, and a "network of related clans" that cut across tribal lines. The members of this Creek confederation, one recent

writer notes, "defended certain lands as their own. Headmen from
the various towns frequently met to discuss matters of mutual
concern." Those towns "possessed a distinctive world view."[35]

In their efforts to explain the origins of the Creeks, modern
scholars write of the migrations of various peoples coalescing
to form the modern Creeks. Migrations from the West may have
begun as early as 1200 A.D., with the newcomers and indigenous
populations presumably creating new communities. In historic
times, refugee bands—including Natchez attacked by the French
in Mississippi and Shawnees from the Ohio valley driven out by
the Iroquois—augmented the Creek population.[36] Eighteenth-
century British Indian agent James Adair related that the recent migrants were generally bilingual, speaking both their own
languages and Muskogee, and honored the laws, customs, and
traditions of the Muskogean peoples.[37]

Creek origin stories also spoke of migrations but described
their history in mythic terms. One of those stories, particularly
reflective of their underlying spiritual values, related that their
ancestors had migrated from the northwest after escaping from
the mouth of a great earth cannibal. Four different groups joined
in the migration, crossing a "red bloody river" and encountering
a white fire whose flames they mixed with red and yellow flames
they had carried with them on the journey. At the source of
the white fire they discovered war medicine (four herbs) and a
magical burning stick called Wooden Tomahawk, which became
their symbol of war. Warriors from each of the four groups took
the war medicine and scalped enemies encountered on their trek.
The Kasihtas, who told the story, claimed that they emerged as
the preeminent people by virtue of scalping more adversaries
than anyone else. Before finding a homeland in the East, the
travelers killed a blue bird said to be a man-eater and a lion
whose bones were red and blue. They also attacked and destroyed
a town whose leaders had rebuffed their peaceful overtures by
sending them red arrows. However, the Apalachicolas persuaded

the warlike Kasihtas to turn from Wooden Tomahawk, embrace peace, and live in harmony with other peoples. War, they taught, was not a natural state. Creek towns, clans, and chiefs were divided between red and white. While this story does not lend itself to factual, linear Western-style historical narrative, it does tell us much about the Creek sense of identity and about their values, which held in tension and balance both the red road of war and the white road of peace.[38]

From both archaeological and historical sources we know that at the time of the Spanish entrada into the Southeast in the sixteenth century, the Indians of the region, including the ancestors of the Creeks, were organized in powerful, warlike chiefdoms characterized by hierarchical social classes, authoritarian political rule, and fairly elaborate religious rites. But even before the appearance of the first white men in the interior of North America, the Mississippian "Temple Mound" cultures were in decline. Scholars differ as to the reasons for their ultimate disappearance: crop failure, climatic change, warfare, class antagonisms, and disease have all been proposed as explanations. But on one point there is agreement: the Spanish entrada was accompanied by unprecedented outbreaks of epidemic disease. Having no immunity to the microorganisms carried by the intruders, the indigenous peoples suffered mortalities so high that some areas were depopulated within a few decades. Later Spanish parties of exploration often found deserted towns and abandoned, overgrown fields in regions that only a few years earlier responded to the Spanish presence by mustering hundreds of aggressive, armed warriors equipped with huge war canoes. Within a century, the population reduction totaled at least 90 percent.

By the time the British first encountered the Creeks in the late seventeenth century, their political and social organization no longer resembled that of the peoples described by the first Spanish visitors more than a century earlier. The Spanish had encountered Indian rulers so exalted that they were carried everywhere by litter and were said to possess the power of gods. But the chiefs with whom the British dealt had little formal power and ruled not by fiat but by persuasion and consensus. Only among the Natchez (in the French sphere of influence in Mississippi) did European colonists find a rigidly hierarchical society with a divine king, a powerful priesthood, and a clear division of social classes. The Natchez would soon be virtually destroyed by their French and Indian enemies. Many of their survivors would join the Creeks and become part of a society that European observers agreed was essentially egalitarian, with status conferred not by pedigree but, among males, by accomplishment as warriors and hunters.

In the first decades of contact with Europeans, the Creeks, driven by that hunger for European trade goods that transformed the lives of Indian peoples throughout the continent in the first years of colonization, engaged in intensive commercial hunting. The primary commodity in which they traded was deerskin, although in the early years they also sold Indian captives to Carolina slavers, who shipped them primarily to the Caribbean but occasionally to the northern colonies. Creek slaving raids against the Choctaws, who were allied with the French, and against the pro-Spanish Indian peoples of the lower Gulf Coast and Florida peninsula not only provided access to a steady supply of British trade goods but also protected the vulnerable British trading posts in the Carolinas from England's enemies. [39] Throughout the first half of the eighteenth century, as Kathryn Braund notes, "the Creeks slowly enlarged their effective hunting territories via wars against the Florida tribes, the Cherokee and the Creek." [40]

Although the Creeks' economic life was now intermeshed with white traders, Creek society in some ways remained unchanged until the second half of the eighteenth century. Politically, the villages remained autonomous. Clan affiliation remained basic to the individual's sense of identity, and families remained matrilineal. Despite British efforts to promote political consolidation by designating a chief or "Emperor" of the Creeks, leadership remained local. (In 1752, when an Upper Creek by the name of Tunape announced that the British had named him "king" of all the Creeks, his "subjects" poisoned him, leaving the would-be monarch "totally crippled, unable to move.") The challenge of dealing with the colonizers did foster innovations in leadership, as some Creek headmen reportedly became adept at playing the British, the Spanish, and the French against one another. One local chief, Brims of Coweta, was so skillful that one observer declared him "as great a Politician as any Governor in America."[41]

A prime objective of the diplomacy of Brims and other Creek leaders was to maintain secure access to European trade goods at reasonable cost. Such goods were not only necessary for security against armed Indian rivals but were now part of the basic fabric of everyday life. Tools of wood and stone and clothing of animal hides for the most part were now used only in Creek sacred rituals. By the early eighteenth century, metal implements, glass beads, and woven textiles had been fully integrated into the Creek domestic economy. As Braund notes, "This replacement of Creek manufactures with the commensurate loss of native handicrafts was one of the most significant results of the deerskin trade, and lay at the heart of the Muscogulges' economic dependence on imported goods."[42] However astute they were as diplomats, though, none of the Creek headmen were able to curb the abuses that accompanied the deerskin trade. Those abuses were particularly acute after the British victory in the French and Indian War. Unregulated by either Crown or colonies, unscrupulous traders, "arrogant in the knowledge that they could not be stopped, undermined the authority of the Muscogulge town councils, disrupted family life, and transformed young hunters into drunks and debtors."[43]

The better-established traders did not personally mistreat their clients, but their influence on Creek society would nonetheless prove subversive, at least to those who prized certain Creek

values that had persisted despite the sometimes disruptive effects
of the deerskin trade. Throughout the eighteenth century, substantial numbers of traders, most often Scots, settled within Creek
territory and married Creek women. Their mestizo sons, and
sometimes their daughters, were usually conversant in English
and often literate. Although Creek by virtue of their mothers'
bloodline, they usually shared the economic values of their fathers. These acculturated mestizos were generally not interested
in the preservation of a society based on hunting and warfare
and informed by communal and egalitarian values. In a few
instances, their ideas about personal success, their concepts of
property, and their sense of the nature of the good life had been
shaped not only by the example of their fathers but by experience
in colonial schools and business firms. From their fathers they
inherited not only ideas profoundly subversive of the Creek way
of life but often land, wealth, and black slaves acquired with
the profits of the deerskin trade. Thus, in Creek country in the
latter eighteenth century a new class emerged that emulated the
white planter class. Unlike traditional Creeks, they aspired to
substantial individual wealth and, in defiance of Creek custom,
had little interest in sharing that wealth. Their ambition as well
as their belief that the old ways were no longer viable impelled
them to work for the creation of a new order, a Creek nation
grounded in concepts of law and property that remained alien to
most Creeks.[44]

The Indian policy of the United States during the Washington
administration supported their aspirations. Indian agent Benjamin Hawkins, a former federal senator from North Carolina
appointed in 1796, worked zealously to promote the transition
of the Indians of the Southeast from "savagery" to "civilization." Hawkins and other leaders of the new republic, believed
that coexistence with Indians would be possible only if Indians
embraced Euro-American agricultural and industrial techniques,
accepted the concept of individual land ownership, and relin-

quished to white settlers the vast hunting preserves that their new economy would render superfluous. Federal commissioners who negotiated a Choctaw land cession in 1801 expressed a common assumption about Indian policy when they reported that since the Choctaws were willing to learn to farm and surrender their hunting lands, "the United States may be saved the pain and expense of expelling or destroying them." [45] Hawkins for his part declared his intention "to lead the Indians from hunting to the pastoral life, to agriculture, household manufactures, to weights and measures" as well as "money and figures." Under his tutelage, favored Creeks flourished as ranchers, planters, slaveholders, and merchants. Gender roles were recast to conform to Anglo-American expectations. Men herded cattle and grew cotton, working in the fields or supervising black slaves, while Creek women learned to use the spinning wheel. Political life was transformed as well. Under the agent's guidance, acculturated Creeks and mestizos established a "national council," replaced clan law with a national police force, and undermined village traditional autonomy. [46]

Hawkins's "civilization" program encountered substantial opposition from those Creeks who believed that maintenance of the older ways was not only essential to their identity but necessary to enjoy the continued favor of the Maker of Breath. Hawkins complained to Secretary of War James McHenry that, although he warned the Creeks that "the game was gone" and promised that "cattle and hogs would replace it," many protested that his plan "did not comport with the ways of red people." [47] The issue was not, however, simply a matter of belief or tradition. The new elite personally controlled the lion's share of the assets of the emergent Creek nation and did not feel constrained to use those resources for the benefit of the community. Capitalist individualism replaced communalism. Historian Claudio Saunt estimates by the early nineteenth century a fifth of the population controlled 60 to 70 percent of the "accessible wealth in Creek country, goods such as cattle, cotton, and spinning wheels. The bottom 50 percent, in contrast, owned only between 8 and 15 percent of the wealth." Saunt concludes that "this astounding degree of inequality among a people who only thirty years earlier had disdained the accumulation of property and the centralization of power explains to a great extent why Red Sticks took up arms in 1813."[48]

For those Creeks who were not beneficiaries of this economic transformation, life grew harder by the year. The deerskin trade in the mid-eighteenth century, according to one recent estimate, resulted in the killing of around four hundred thousand deer a year, and the herds could not long sustain losses of that magnitude. By the end of the century, commercial overhunting had crippled the older economy, which had balanced the trade with Europeans in deerskins with reliance on traditional horticulture. Reports from traders and data from the records of several trading firms reveal a steady, irreversible decline.[49] Overhunting explains most of that decline. One scholar, however, has noted that "part of the problem also lay with the territorial nature of the white-tailed deer. If their food sources disappeared, as often happened when settlers moved in with their cattle and pigs, the deer would not move on to another range: they starved or were hunted out."[50] Scarcity of deer was not the only problem afflicting Creek hunters and their families in the late eighteenth century. Falling prices on the European market meant that the hides they could still bring to market bought far fewer trade goods than anticipated. Between 1775 and 1792 the price paid for deerskin fell by 50 percent. Moreover, the American Revolution disrupted commerce between the colonies and the Creeks as scores of pro-British traders were driven into exile.[51]

Creek horticulture faced a crisis as well. Herds of domesticated animals, owned by white traders and by acculturated Creeks, not only drove away the game; hogs also devoured the acorns Creek women relied upon as a foodstuff and, along with cattle, decimated cornfields. Between 1804 and 1812, crop failures and food shortages caused widespread misery, and the suffering was exacerbated by the refusal of the newly wealthy to follow the tradition of sharing resources in times of adversity. Hawkins reported to Secretary of War Dearborn in 1804 that, although Creek farmers and ranchers were still well fed, those who followed the older ways were not only hungry but beginning to starve to death. He warned the Creeks that by not collaborating with his economic reforms they were in effect refusing to save "many of your little ones" from bring murdered by "the enemy called hunger." Hawkins declared that he would "help all those who help themselves" but that he would not "tolerate or support sturdy beggars." The Creeks, he stated, must recognize that the only way they could now "clothe and feed themselves" is by "farming, spinning and stock raising."[52]

The leadership's cession of additional Creek land to the United States in 1802, 1804, 1805, and 1811 further embittered many of those Creeks who had been marginalized and impoverished by the advent of a new economic order. In addition to losing land through treaties signed by the elite, Creeks in several frontier regions were pushed aside by aggressive white squatters. Federal agents sometimes enforced treaty provisions by removing those whites who had seized Indian lands illegally, but they did so reluctantly and inefficiently. Cherokee agent Meigs, after ejecting several squatters, expressed the view of most federal officials when he complained that while "these people bear the appellation of intruders," it should be remembered that they were fellow countrymen with a role to play in building America. "In our new country, every man is an acquisition. We ought not to lose a white man, for want of land to work on."[53] Hawkins, who, unlike Meigs, was not sympathetic to white squatters, steadily lost influence over Indian policy during the Jefferson and Madison administrations.

In three separate incidents in 1812 and 1813, insurgent

Creeks, determined to end white incursions on their lands, attacked and killed American settlers. The most inflammatory of those attacks occurred at the mouth of the Ohio River in March 1813. The leader of the band responsible, Little Warrior, had lived among the Shawnees for several years and was a follower of the Shawnee prophet. Historian Frank Owsley Jr. writes: "This incident, which included murdering seven families, was accompanied by extreme brutality, doubtless aimed at terrorizing the whole population. In one case, a woman was cut open, and her unborn child taken out and stuck upon a post for all to see. This had the desired effect—panic on the frontier."[54] Even before the Ohio raid, some southern politicians and newspaper editors had clamored for a war of extermination against the Creeks. In response to reports from the Ohio valley, former Tennessee senator Andrew Jackson, now a militia general, wrote in horror of "beloved wives and little prattling infants, butchered, mangled, murdered and torn to pieces." Jackson declared that "we are ready for our part for vengeance." A newspaper in Jackson's hometown, Nashville, rejoiced that "the Creeks have supplied us with a pretext for dismemberment of their country."[55]

Seeking to avoid that dismemberment, the Creek national council asked for an explanation. Little Warrior, who recently had visited Tecumseh and the prophet in Canada, claimed that he had been told during his return journey that war had broken out between the Creeks and the United States. Learning that he was mistaken, he urged the council to declare war, but they refused and expelled him from their deliberations. Hawkins demanded that the Creeks take stronger measures against Little Warrior and other frontier raiders. Under pressure from the Indian agent, the Creek council reluctantly condemned to death all of the participants in attacks on whites and sent out execution parties. Little Warrior was among those they put to death. But attacks on white settlements continued despite the efforts of the council.

Hawkins had hoped that the Creeks themselves could restore order, but events would soon demonstrate that they could not.[56]

The Red Stick Prophets

Andrew Jackson was certain that he understood the causes of the Creek War. In a meeting with Creek chiefs after the fighting had ended, he declared that many of their friends and kinsmen had been made "crazy by the prophecies of your wicked prophets . . . the tools of Great Britain and Spain." [57] Jackson of course understood next to nothing about Muskogee culture. The prophets he condemned and, when possible, executed were not driven by either madness or European intrigue but rather by the conviction that the growing influence of Anglo-Americans, if not arrested, would soon lead to the spiritual and physical destruction of the Creek people. Their message had a particular appeal to those Creeks who had not benefited from the new economic order fostered by Hawkins. The Maker of Breath, they held, had never intended that Indian men be farmers, as power over plants was given only to women. Men were empowered as hunters and as warriors. To depart from that role was to transgress against the natural order and harmony of the universe and could only bring disaster to the Creek peoples.

The tensions and animosities that would lead early in the nineteenth century to the Red Stick civil war within the "Creek nation" reflected both internal conflicts and external pressure from encroaching white settlements. The former have sometimes been described as the outgrowth of ethnic and linguistic diversity, most specifically of rivalries between those who spoke Muskogean dialects and those who did not. Some scholars have also found the origins of the Creek insurgency in a conflict between old chiefs and young warriors. But while ethnic antagonisms and intergenerational tensions were by no means absent, resentment of the new economic elite and detestation of the values they espoused was the underlying source of Red Stick rage. The geographical division of pro–Red Stick Upper Creek towns against the more accommodationist Lower Creek towns reflected degrees of access to the benefits of the market.[58]

There is some controversy about the reason why the insurgents were called Red Sticks. One story, related by nineteenth-century historians, claims that the name came from bundles of red sticks used to coordinate the timing of their military operations. Each band was given a bundle of those sticks, with instructions to pull one out of the bundle every day. When the bundle was empty, they were to gather for the attack. Others, however, report that their warriors carried red wands that were symbolic of their nativist mission. Another version held that the name came from their painted war clubs.[59]

There is little disagreement, however, about the nature and objectives of the movement, even though the sources provide less detail than we would like about some of the prophets' teachings. Whites were seldom if ever present during their most ecstatic visionary revelations. In a report to Hawkins, Alexander Cornells, a mixed-blood interpreter and well-to-do planter whose work for the agent had earned him a place on the prophets' death list, characterized their exhortations as follows: "Kill the old chiefs, friends to peace; kill the cattle, the hogs, and the fowls; do not work; throw away your ploughs and everything used by Americans. Sing the song of the Indians of the northern lakes, and dance their dance. Shake your war clubs, shake yourselves; you will frighten the Americans, their arms will drop from their hands."[60] Allowing for Cornells's bias, his report is reliable and is verified both by other reports and by events. The prophets, intensely hostile to most manifestations of Euro-American culture, looked to the restoration, through prophetic power, of the precontact economy grounded in horticulture, hunting, and communal sharing and sustained by the proper balance and harmony among men, women, animals, and the spirits. They were committed to the violent punishment of those Creeks who rejected their vision and their demands.[61]

The Red Sticks adopted a mode of dress that affirmed their nativism. Archaeological evidence from the battle site at Horseshoe Bend reveals that they did not wear the silver and brass ornaments or the glass beads popular with acculturated Creeks.[62] They eschewed not only alcohol but also the use of salt. One contemporary report related that a Red Stick prophet who had touched a salt eater "instantly commenced trembling" because of the "defilement."[63] Red Stick beliefs drew heavily on the traditional Creek concern with purification. Their prophets taught that not only whites but also domesticated animals were unclean. For some time, Native Americans had occasionally suspected that cows and pigs were responsible for the epidemics that periodically afflicted their communities. For that reason, the Choctaws had slaughtered some of their cattle in 1767. The Red Stick assault on domestic animals was far more extensive. A white soldier testified after the war that "not a track of a cow or hog was to be seen in the Creek country; and I marched through the greater part of it."[64] In a memorable vignette of prophetic fervor, one nineteenth-century account of the Creek War describes a battle scene in which a prophet waves at the enemy two wands made of the tails of dead cows. The tails had been painted red. The prophet, as he waved those symbols of the triumph of his medicine over a hated and unnatural domestic animal, uttered what the narrator describes as the "most appalling yells."[65]

The prophets sought through ecstatic singing and dancing to summon up sacred power of such force that their enemies, intimidated by this new reality, would drop their weapons in fear. The songs and the dance rituals learned from Tecumseh and Seekaboo were added to their traditional means of seeking spirit power. The prophet Josiah Francis taught his followers a ritual handshake that ended in a visionary seizure. A Creek warrior described shaking hands with one of the prophets: "He shook hands with me and immediately began to tremble and jerk in every part of his frame, and the very calves of his legs would be convulsed, and he would get entirely out of breath with this agitation." The prophet claimed he had been "instructed by the Spirit" in that new sacred ritual.[66]

Francis, a mestizo whose Creek name was Hillis Hadjo (Crazy Medicine), was the most prominent of the Red Stick spiritual leaders. His father was white, probably of French ancestry, and reportedly either a blacksmith or silversmith by trade. Francis's life prior to his emergence as a prophet and warrior in 1812 is poorly documented. Although some claim he spoke English, Spanish, and several Indian languages fluently, that claim is suspect. The evidence indicates that Francis was illiterate and, unlike Tenskwatawa, made no use of a secretary to correspond with Euro-Americans. His one effort to write a letter to the Spanish governor of Florida proved embarrassing, as we shall see. Francis's teachings were not entirely in harmony with the message of the "Indians of the Lakes." There is no doubt that Francis supported Tecumseh's call for rejection of Euro-American culture and resistance to white expansionism. It also appears that, like other revitalization leaders, he invoked the power of the Great Spirit and claimed a close relationship with the Creator. But Tenskwatawa's message had demanded internal reforms as well as resistance to external forces and had condemned many traditional beliefs and practices. Moreover, Tecumseh called for the political unification, under his leadership, of all Indian nations. Contemporary reports of Francis's teachings and actions indicate that while he adopted some of the rituals taught by northern visitors, he operated largely within the framework of traditional Creek belief and practice. There is no evidence that Francis and the other Red Stick prophets ceased using the traditional shamanic practices that Tenskwatawa had condemned as diabolical. Nor did they proscribe and replace any of the rituals that Creeks had long believed essential to communal well-being.

The Red Stick prophets are probably best understood as traditional Muskogee sorcerer-shamans. Francis, for example, claimed that, through the aid of a spirit helper, he could kill his enemies by willing their deaths. He also stated that he could fly through the air or remain underwater for indefinite periods of time. He provided some demonstrations of that latter feat which greatly enhanced his reputation. Those exploits would have been familiar to any Muskogee shaman. His invocations of the Creator, compared to Tenskwatawa's, were quite superficial. Francis claimed that "the Maker of Breath" had taught him to write Spanish, but when he dispatched a letter to the governor of Florida, presumably asking for guns and ammunition, the governor told his messenger that the paper contained meaningless markings. That episode undermined his standing with some of his supporters. To regain support, Francis assured his followers that through his shamanism he could make them bulletproof. Determined to protect Muskogees who were faithful to his message from the malice of the white man, he undertook construction of a "Holy Ground" in southern Alabama that would be surrounded by a magic barrier. Any non-Indian who tried to enter would be struck dead. Through his assertions of access to miraculous power comparable to that wielded by the greatest of the Muskogee shamans, Francis laid claim to a prime leadership position in the Red Stick movement.[67]

Francis did not, however, enjoy the sort of primacy accorded to Tenskwatawa. A number of other Creek nativist prophets also promised to summon the power of the spirit world to secure the restoration and preservation of their way of life. These visionaries joined with Francis in the support of the insurgency. Among them were Cussetaw Haujo (High Headed Jim), Tuskegee Hopie Tustanugga (Far-Off Warrior), Menawa, Yahoola Chapco, Peter McQueen, and Paddy Walsh. Of these, Walsh stands as a near equal to Francis. Indeed, some have seen him as the preeminent Red Stick holy man. Walsh was a full-blood who, as a child, had been adopted by a South Carolina Tory who had taken refuge among the Creek after the Revolution. He was rather short, probably about five feet, six inches in height, with a low forehead and a wide mouth. One contemporary described him as "inhumanly ugly." An audacious leader, Walsh was an exceptionally gifted orator said to be fluent in most of the Indian dialects of the region.[68]

Peter McQueen, like Francis, was a mestizo, son of a Scots trader. His commitment to the Red Stick cause is somewhat puzzling, as Hawkins reported that he had "a valuable property in negroes and stock."[69] We can only speculate about the appeal of the Red Stick movement to people of mixed ancestry such as Francis and McQueen. Their nativism may well have been the outgrowth of racial slights and of resentment over the inferior position to which they knew they would be consigned in a society dominated by Anglo-Americans. Reasons for supporting the uprising were, predictably, varied. Most were no doubt drawn to it out of their anger against the emergent economic elite, but some, paradoxically, may have joined to protect their own assets. One of the most effective of the Red Stick military leaders, William Weatherford (Red Eagle), was an affluent mixed-blood who never subscribed to the religion of the prophets. He was apparently coerced into joining the movement by his neighbors. Two of the daughters of Alexander McGillivray also became Red Sticks in order to protect their lives and property.[70]

One notable medicine man refused to support the insurgency. Captain Sam Isaacs claimed to have received, from many days underwater in communion with the great Tie Snake, both an infallible vision of the future and the gift of unlimited power. He later deepened his prophetic insights by visiting the Shawnee prophet at Prophetstown. For a time he commanded a large following in the Upper Creek towns, but for reasons not explained in the sources he led a war party that executed men accused of murdering white settlers near the mouth of the Ohio River. Among the eight Creeks they put to death was a fellow prophet,

Oostanaunaulah Kecoh Tustkey, a man who also had visited
Tenskwatawa. Pointing to Captain Isaacs's claim of association
with the dreaded Tie Snake as evidence of witchcraft, Francis and
other nativist prophets demanded that the community be purified
and spared impending disaster through his death.[71] When some
of the leaders of the Upper Creek villages rejected that demand,
Francis and his warriors first killed the messenger who conveyed
the chiefs' reply, then hunted down and slaughtered Captain
Isaacs, his nephew, and three of his followers.[72]

The Creek War
Francis and his fellow prophets now called for the death of all of
the Muskogee collaborators who had authorized or participated in
the execution of Indians whom Hawkins accused of killing whites.
They also declared that Hawkins and his interpreter must be
killed. A full-scale civil war broke out within and among the Creek
villages in the summer of 1813, a war that would soon involve
the United States in the suppression of the prophetic movement.
The Red Stick prophets' war parties terrorized the countryside,
burning the farms and plantations of mestizos and their Creek
emulators, killing and often mutilating those who had not fled.
Red Stick warriors visited their wrath on all symbols of white
influence—spinning wheels, mills, cotton gins, and domestic
animals—as well as acculturated Creek women whose modes
of life departed from their sense of tradition. As historian John
Buchanan relates, "everywhere dead livestock rotted. In the cattle
range of Tuckabatchee the stench continued for fifteen miles.
Towns were destroyed, people slaughtered."[73]

A Red Stick attack on the village of Okfuskee ended in the
killing of five chiefs and the slaughter of all their domesticated
animals. At Coosa a small band led by the nineteen-year-old
prophet Letecau invited the local chiefs to watch them perform
the Dance of the Lakes. After the chiefs were seated on the ground,
Letecau gave a war cry and his dancing followers struck the chiefs

with clubs and shot them with arrows. Nine were killed as others fled into the woods. Letecau declared the execution of those who were in league with evil spirits and with the white man an act of spiritual purification. Hawkins reported that in further acts of purification Red Sticks "destroyed, in several places of the Upper towns, all the cattle, hogs, and fowls." But the chiefs who had escaped from the killing at Coosa formed a war party and pursued Letecau and his seven companions. They found them in a remote wilderness area performing their dance. After killing all of them with clubs and arrows, the chiefs "scalped the prophet."[74]

Most of the Upper Creek towns rallied to the support of the Red Sticks. Hawkins's informants estimated that between twenty-five hundred and three thousand Upper Creek warriors were active supporters of the insurgency in the summer of 1813.[75] Claiming supernatural powers, the Red Sticks, according to Alexander Cornells, warned that "if any Indian towns refused their aid to the prophets, they should be sunk under earthquakes, or the hills turned over on them." After killing those who collaborated with Hawkins, "they would be ready for the white people, who could do them no injury, if they came among them, as the prophets would draw circles around their abode, and render the earth quaggy and impassible." The prophets' magic, they warned, had already killed several hostile chiefs who had stepped into a circle reserved for a prophet "and were immediately seized by madness, and died."[76]

In July, Red Sticks besieged Tuckabatchee, the village of the pro-American chief Big Warrior.[77] However, they were unable to break through its defenses, as they had few firearms. A war party of anti–Red Stick Creeks from Kasihta and Coweta dispersed the besiegers and evacuated the inhabitants. Red Sticks returned and burned the deserted village. Although they had destroyed several towns, wrecked a number of plantations, and killed a number of affluent pro-American Creek farmers, the Red Sticks were acutely aware that they lacked the firepower for a sustained war. Messages from the Spanish governor and from Tecumseh, then fighting for the British in Canada, had led them to believe that guns, powder, and shot would be made available to them at Pensacola in Spanish Florida. Accordingly, Peter McQueen, accompanied by several other prophets and three hundred warriors, set off for Spanish Florida. Upon arriving, they were rebuffed by the agents of the John Forbes Company, the British trading firm. The Spanish governor, who earlier had invited them to come to Pensacola to confer, also failed to meet their expectations. He gave them gunpowder, some lead, food, and blankets, but no guns. British and Spanish authorities would decide some months later to supply the insurgent Creeks with firearms, but by then it would be too late. In the decisive battles with Andrew Jackson and the Americans, it is estimated that not one Red Stick warrior in three had a gun.[78]

On July 27, 1813, while returning with the gunpowder, lead, and other provisions they had been given by the Spanish governor, McQueen's party encountered a band of 180 white and mixed-blood militiamen commanded by Col. James Caller. In the ensuing battle at Burnt Corn Creek, McQueen's poorly armed warriors drove off Caller's poorly disciplined militia. In the ensuing rout, Caller deserted his men. He remained in hiding for some two weeks after the battle.[79] Although there were few casualties on either side (only two of Caller's men were killed), the Indians upon returning to their villages "showed the scalps they had taken and claimed to have routed completely an enormous American army." To believers, the battle's outcome "proved they had supernatural power and could not be defeated."[80]

Emboldened by their success at Burnt Corn, the insurgents planned an offensive against Fort Mims, a stockaded enclosure surrounding the home of Samuel Mims to the north of Mobile. Maj. Daniel Beasley, the commander there, had sufficient men and resources to defend the fort and the three hundred or so whites, mestizos, blacks, and Indians who had taken refuge within the stockade. Many were residents of the Creek town of Tensaw, a nearby village dominated by well-to-do acculturated mestizos who feared the wrath of the nativists. Beasley, however, refused to take the Red Stick threat seriously. There had been a number of reports of sightings of Indian parties in the area, but the major discounted their significance, as he believed "savages" incapable of overrunning a fortified position. He dismissed Gen. Ferdinand Claiborne's warning that an attack was imminent. Had Beasley employed competent scouts, he would have learned that the day before the attack more than seven hundred insurgent Creeks had gathered about six miles from Fort Mims. But the two men he did send out to look for Indians paid little attention and saw nothing (even though they passed within a few yards of an advance party of Red Sticks), so Beasley chose to disregard the warnings he had received. When two young black slaves reported that there were many Indians in the nearby woods, he ordered them flogged for raising a false alarm. One was spared temporarily by the objections of his owner, who believed his story. On the morning of August 30, shortly before the attack, however, a friendly Creek named Jim Cornells also tried to warn Beasley that there were Red Sticks near the fort. Enraged, Beasley had the second slave flogged and tried to arrest Cornells, who escaped. Cornells later claimed that the major was drunk that morning.[81]

The insurgents struck Fort Mims at noon, while Beasley, after the flogging, was engrossed in a card game. The night before, Red Stick scouts had walked right up to the stockade walls and had found the east gate partly open, jammed by a pile of sand. It was still open at noon, as Beasley had dismissed warnings from those who had wanted the two gates to the stockade secured. The attackers rushed into the stockade, killed its startled defenders, and besieged the buildings in which many noncombatants had taken cover. A number of women and children were burned alive when the house and nearby sheds were put to the torch. Others who tried to flee were captured and scalped or disemboweled by the attackers. At least 90 percent of those who had taken refuge at Fort Mims died at the hands of attackers that afternoon. Major Beasley lost both his life and his reputation. The total death toll was estimated at 247.[82]

Red Stick losses, although not as heavy, were by no means insubstantial. Among the first to fall was a prophet richly clad in feathers. Despite the prophets' assurance that their magic would protect warriors from the white man's bullets, Capt. Joseph Kennedy of the U.S. Army reported finding one hundred Indian corpses in the vicinity of Fort Mims.[83] George Stiggins claimed that after the battle the Red Sticks "found that of their men who went into action fully half were killed or disabled or wounded." Those losses were unexpected and caused much dissension among the victors. Paddy Walsh had promised the warriors that before they engaged the soldiers in the fort he would run three times around its walls. The result of that maneuver, he explained, would be to "paralyze" the bullets in the guns wielded by the defenders. Walsh, as promised, ran around the fort, but he was shot down before he could complete the final circle. Nonetheless, from his prone position outside the walls "he kept encouraging his men to throw down their firearms and enter the fort with war clubs and scalping knives in hand." Once the battle was over, the Red Stick warriors, as Stiggins relates, "rose in fury against the prophet and leading man, Paddy Walsh, for losing so many men to death and wounds." The wounded prophet was forced to flee and seek refuge at Towassee, his home village.[84]

Although war hysteria spread throughout the white settlements on the Gulf frontier, there were no new attacks on major forts or settlements in the weeks and months after the raid on Fort Mims. The earlier failure of the Red Sticks to obtain the munitions they needed from the Spanish undermined their ability to wage war against the United States. Too many were armed only with bows and arrows, and many of the guns they had needed repairs that the Spanish at Pensacola had refused to provide. Moreover, the attack on Fort Mims had severely depleted their stock of gunpowder. Nonetheless, occasional Red Stick raids on minor settlements, and the few white casualties they inflicted, were sufficient to keep American war sentiment at a fever pitch. Ironically, most Americans believed the Red Sticks had been armed to the teeth by the Spanish in Florida. Military and civil officials alike were persuaded that the Fort Mims raid had been either commanded or advised by a Spanish or British officer. Some saw the inciting of a slave insurrection as their purpose. When a militia raid on the Red Sticks' Holy Ground produced some recent correspondence from the Spanish governor of Florida, Gonzalez Manrique, the frontier's worst suspicions were confirmed. The governor had congratulated the prophets on their victory at Fort Mims. His letter held out the prospect that Spanish aid would soon be forthcoming. While Manrique had rejected the insurgents' offer to assist in a Spanish attack on Mobile and advised that Spain preferred negotiation to war, American readers were alarmed by the Spanish governor's statement of support of the insurgents.[85]

The Red Sticks were now in a very vulnerable position. Late in 1813, General Claiborne and his Mississippi militia destroyed Ekonachaka. That town, located fifteen miles from the modern city of Montgomery, Alabama, was the "Holy Ground" the prophet Francis had declared invulnerable. The prophet had erected a magic barrier that was supposed to kill any white person who tried to enter the town. When the magic failed, Francis and many other Red Sticks fled in disarray. Only a small band led by Chief William Weatherford, who had never believed the prophets' boasting about their spirit power, fought the American intruders. But Weatherford was badly outnumbered. He made a spectacular escape from Holy Ground by leaping, mounted on his horse, off a high cliff into the Alabama River. Claiborne burned the town and its fields; then, a day later, he put to the torch another Red Stick village located eight miles upriver. Among the Indians killed in that engagement were three prophets. Many of the insurgents regrouped at a place whites would call "Horseshoe Bend."[86]

Although Claiborne's militiamen were disbanded at the expiration of their enlistments in January 1814, the campaign on the Alabama River had exposed the military weakness of the Red Sticks. Their political vulnerability was apparent when their efforts to recruit Choctaw and Chickasaw allies ended in abject failure. By contrast, the small regular army unit commanded by Col. Gilbert Russell that replaced Claiborne was amply supported by Choctaw and Chickasaw scouts. When the United States mounted its major offensive against the Red Sticks, the forces sent into southern Alabama would enjoy ample Indian support. Cherokees among others rallied to the American standard. Anti–Red Stick Creeks continued to fight the prophets. In October 1813, Creeks from Coweta attacked a band of the prophets' warriors and then devastated several villages sympathetic to the prophets and burned their fields. The insurgents retaliated by besieging Coweta.[87]

Claiborne's army was not the only militia unit fighting the Red Sticks in the fall and early winter of 1813. In November, 950 Georgia militiamen, commanded by John Floyd and aided by around four hundred Indians, including a small Creek force under the command of William McIntosh, had marched into Alabama. They struck the Red Stick stronghold at Autosse, near the juncture of the Tallapoosa River and Calabee Creek, and raised the siege at Coweta. Floyd was not, however, able to destroy the Red Stick fighting force, which retreated from the field at Autosse. But the insurgents were now out of gunpowder. A new visit to Pensacola proved disappointing. Despite earlier promises, Spanish aid was not forthcoming, as Governor Manrique now pleaded poverty. The British did send a small supply of powder. On February 27, 1814, the Red Stick leaders mounted a surprise attack on Floyd's force encamped near Fort Hull deep in Creek territory. While disagreements over tactics may have cost them a clear victory, the Red Sticks' raid stunned the Georgians. Plagued by declining morale and dissension over terms of enlistment, Floyd, who had been wounded during the battle at Autosse, resigned his command. Gen. Thomas Pinckney, in overall command of American forces in the district, ordered his successor to prepare supplies and offer support to Tennessee militia general Andrew Jackson. Bedeviled by the same difficulties that had dogged Floyd's campaign, Jackson, a stern disciplinarian, browbeat and cashiered uncooperative officers, executed a deserter, and drove his men relentlessly by example as well as words.[88]

Arriving in Creek country late in October 1813, Jackson had dispatched a detachment of nine hundred men under the command of Gen. John Coffee to attack the pro–Red Stick village at Tallushatchee. Coffee's men killed nearly two hundred insurgent warriors. "We shot them like dogs," Davy Crockett later boasted. A number of women and children also died. One of Coffee's officers related: "We found as many as eight or ten bodies in a single cabin. Some of the cabins had taken fire, and half consumed human bodies were seen amidst the smoking ruins. In other instances dogs had torn and feasted on the mangled bodies of their masters. Heart sick I turned from the scene." Coffee was also dismayed by the killing of noncombatants. His own losses had been modest in comparison to the punishment visited upon the Creeks: five American dead, forty-one wounded. Jackson declared that Coffee had executed his orders in "elegant style." Sharing Coffee's feelings about the sufferings of Indian noncombatants. Jackson rescued and adopted an Indian orphan whose parents had been killed in the burning of their village. Responding to an appeal from friendly Creeks besieged by Red Sticks, Old Hickory then marched on the village of Talladega. The failure of his suppliers to send provisions and the refusal of a rival general to permit reinforcements to join Jackson's army led some to doubt the wisdom of his action, but Jackson prevailed. His attack on the insurgents at Talladega (his first actual battle) ended in the death of 299 of the prophets' warriors, while Jackson's troops suffered 15 dead in battle and 80 wounded, some mortally. The victory was marred by the escape of the bulk of the Red Stick fighting force, which made its way through a gap in Jackson's line.[89]

The prophets' luck soon ran out. Their assaults on Jackson's forces at Emuckfau Creek and at Enitachopko Creek in January ended in failure and disarray. The decisive battle of Jackson's Creek campaign occurred at Horseshoe Bend on the Tallapoosa River in March 1814. Roughly a thousand Red Stick warriors had built an impressive breastwork wooden fortification at the neck of the river. As Jackson's army approached, three prophets, their bodies painted black and wearing red—dyed cow tails on their arms, danced the Dance of the Lakes to summon the power of the Great Spirit. They were in great need of such assistance, since they were badly outnumbered and short of guns and shot. Jackson's forces, including regular army (attached to his command by order of General Pinckney), white militia, and Indian allies, totaled around four thousand men. Jackson's artillery bombarded the Red Stick breastworks, at first to little effect. Then, in an unplanned and stunning maneuver, Indians swam the river and took the village from the rear. Jackson's men, emboldened by the audacity of their Indian allies, then stormed the breastworks in a bloody frontal assault. In the carnage that ensued, eight hundred of the prophets' supporters, including women, children, and aged men who had taken refuge in the village, were put to death. Anti–Red Stick Creeks "settled old scores and militiamen proudly took home reins for their horses that had been skinned from red-stick bodies on the field."[90] Jackson's militia lost only forty-nine dead; his Indian allies lost less than a dozen. As to overall insurgent losses during the war, it is estimated that of a population of twelve thousand in the Upper creek towns sympathetic to the insurgents, at least fifteen hundred were killed by American troops and their Indian supporters.[91]

Although one Red Stick leader, the wealthy mestizo planter William Weatherford, was treated with courtesy and magnanimity when he surrendered to Old Hickory, most fared poorly in the hands of the Americans and their Indian allies. Jackson was gratified after the battle by the sight of the dead body of the prophet Monahoee, whose jaw had been torn off by a blast of grapeshot. "Heaven," the general declared, "designed to chastise his impostures by a proper judgment." [92] For his part, Hawkins sought to disabuse the Creek chiefs of the notion that "the white people" wanted the Indians to spare the surviving prophets. He advised that although women, children, and some of the men should be "forgiven," the chiefs should hunt down the leaders of the insurgency "and put them to death." [93]

American military commanders matched Hawkins's vindictiveness. Paddy Walsh was taken prisoner by forces under the command of Gen. George S. Gaines. After an escape, Walsh was recaptured and put on trial. George Stiggins, no friend of the Red Sticks, described the proceedings as a travesty of justice. Walsh, Stiggins related, was "convicted of crimes without any evidence for or against him. A lying interpreter, who gave false answers to the court, said that Paddy, acknowledging the deed, gave himself great credit for it, and vowed that it was no more than he intended doing again." No one exposed the interpreter's deceit, and Walsh was found guilty and hanged at Fort Claiborne. [94]

A number of Red Stick survivors (probably as many as a thousand) found refuge in Spanish Florida, where they joined their relatives the Seminoles and were also for a time encouraged and armed by British agents there. Later efforts by Jackson and others to root them out would lead to the First Seminole War. Peter McQueen eluded capture and led raids against American intruders from his new bases in Florida. His colleague the prophet Francis was less fortunate. After the defeat at Holy Ground, Francis had fled to Pensacola, where he joined British forces commanded by Maj. Edward Nicoll. At the end of the second Anglo-American war he accompanied Nicoll to England, where he was made a colonel in the British army and given a diamond-studded snuffbox and a tomahawk edged in silver and gold.

But as the war with the United States was now over, the British government had no interest in offering further support to the Red Sticks. Nicoll's plea for intervention in Florida went unheeded. Francis made his way back to Florida via Nassau (where his host robbed him of his gilded tomahawk), finally settling in the Red Stick village on the Wakulla River. Visiting the Spanish at St. Marks in April 1818, the prophet saw a ship flying the British flag make its way into the harbor. Thinking that the British had finally returned to aid the Red Stick cause, Francis, in company with Homathlemico, a war chief, clambered into a canoe and paddled out to the vessel. Onboard they discovered it was an American ship, flying, in defiance of international law, a false flag. Francis and Homathlemico were turned over to Jackson, who had recently invaded Florida and seized the Spanish fort at St. Marks. Jackson ordered both captives executed, refusing to meet with the prophet or to honor his request for a firing squad. Both were hanged the morning after their capture.[95]

Aftermath

Contrary to the hopes and expectations of the Creek elite, the defeat of the Red Sticks did not win for the Creek nation the favor and protection of the United States. Jackson would soon reward his Creek allies by forcing the cession of half their land, and later he would mount a sustained campaign against the continuing Indian presence in the Southeast that would culminate in the Indian removal program associated with his presidency. At the end of the Creek War, however, Jackson and a few of the more prominent Creek chiefs had one common, ongoing concern: the protection of the South's "peculiar institution." Fear of independent, nativist Indian nations on the borders of the United States fueled much of the fervor of the southern advocates of Indian war, as such enclaves could and did serve as refuges for runaway slaves. Some of the anti–Red Stick Creek leaders were closely identified with the white slaveholding elite, as they personally held substantial numbers of slaves. Some took advantage of the continuing conflict to enhance those holdings. To cite a prominent example, William McIntosh, the Creek warrior whom Jackson described as "the bravest man I ever knew," was an affluent mestizo plantation owner and slave dealer who used military expeditions against the Red Sticks and Seminoles in Florida as opportunities to capture and enslave scores of blacks and sambas (Indians of partially black ancestry). McIntosh led Creek warriors into battle in support of the American invaders of Florida and profited greatly from the First Seminole War.[96] A few of Jackson's other Creek allies, most of them mestizos, received special federal land grants or "reservations" in Alabama after Jackson forced both loyal Creeks and Red Sticks to cede most of their land in that state to the United States in the Treaty of Fort Jackson. Those privileged Creek landowners, no more than thirty in number, were later exempted from the Indian removal program during Jackson's presidency. Some intermarried with whites, flourished as slaveholding planters, and soon became part of Alabama's white elite. A smaller number retained their Indian identity, ultimately reemerging as the Poarch band of Creek Indians.[97]

For most of Jackson's Creek allies and other Native American supporters, however, there were few favors, for Old Hickory felt little need to reward Indians. In his pre-presidential correspondence he regularly invoked crude stereotypes about "savages," writing of the "depravity, intrigue, cunning, and native cruelty of the Indians." Jackson's anti-Indian statements are striking in their intensity, their use of hyperbole, and their undercurrent of violence. Indians were irrational and treacherous by nature, Jackson maintained. He advised one correspondent that because "the Treachery of the Indian character will never justify the reposing of confidence in their professions, [one must] be always prepared for defense, and ready to inflict exemplary punishment on the offenders when necessary."[98] Because of their presumed unreliability, Indians, Jackson believed, were dangerous neighbors and, as potential allies of Great Britain in a future war, a grave threat to American security. [99] In the recent war, Cherokees, Choctaws, and Chickasaws had actually been allies of the United States, but Jackson expressed not only distrust but disdain for Indian allies, complaining that "you cannot keep them in the field; as soon as they perform an excursion and take a scalp, they must go home and dance." [100]

In his zeal to clear Indians out of the Southeast, Jackson as a treaty commissioner disregarded instructions from his superiors concerning the peace settlement that explicitly required protection of Indian allies. He also refused to honor promises made to the Creeks by Hawkins, whom he scorned as an Indian sympathizer. Jackson instead violated the territorial rights of his own Indian allies. Rather than negotiating a treaty that recognized and protected the landholdings of Creeks and Cherokees who had fought for the United States, Jackson forced both his allies and his enemies to accept a document that deprived the Creeks of half of their territory. He also demanded and obtained the cession of Cherokee lands guaranteed by previous treaties, justifying those demands by the claim that white occupation of the lands in question was essential to national security. [101] In a reply to protests from the Creek chief Big Warrior, Jackson, as one historian relates, declared that "he could by rights take every acre of Creek land if he wanted to because the Creeks had been deceitful." [102] Jackson thus held all Creeks responsible for the Red Stick uprising, regardless of their behavior during the Creek War. Another Creek chief who had fought against the Red Sticks declared in shock that Jackson "threatened us and made us comply with his talk." The chief worried about Jackson's "great power to destroy me" and with a heavy heart yielded to the general's demands. [103]

Cherokee leaders were also astounded by Jackson's conduct, as none of their warriors had fought against the United States and a number had served as volunteers in the war against the

Red Sticks. So was the Madison administration, which accepted the seizure of Creek lands but negotiated the return of the Cherokee territory taken by Jackson. But "Jackson and the frontier whites were furious." By means of a new treaty, secured by "intimidation and bribes" and signed by "a tiny minority of Cherokee chiefs," Jackson recaptured those Cherokee lands. While some protested his methods, the federal government did not challenge the outcome. It was a harbinger of many more treaties to come and an expression of popular commitment to expansion at the expense of Indians that would help propel Old Hickory into the presidency a decade later. At the time of the Red Stick prophecies among the Creeks, Cherokee dreamers who communed with ghostly sky spirits warned against emulating or trusting whites. But the leaders of the Cherokee nation, not facing armed opposition from the nativists in their midst, and even less trustful of Creeks than they were of the Americans, had declared their neutrality in the Creek civil war. They would continue to lead the Cherokee nation down the path of acculturation but would discover that embracing "civilization" would save neither their independence nor their homeland. [104]

5

The Seneca Prophet

The once powerful members of the League of the Iroquois (Haudenosaunee) were also victims of white land seizures disguised as treaties. Confined by the early nineteenth century to small tracts of land in western New York, the Iroquois, in the memorable words of Anthony Wallace, were now denizens of "slums in the wilderness."[1] Not long before, they had been a force feared by Europeans and Native Americans alike, their support eagerly sought by both the French and the British throughout much of the eighteenth century. Their diplomats had skillfully played off European rivals and thereby secured continuing Iroquois influence and independence. The defeat of France in the Seven Years' War and the consequent French loss of Canada confirmed in the Treaty of Paris of 1763 had unfortunate repercussions for Native Americans generally, as it eliminated an important constraint on British expansionism. But although they lost some land in the years immediately following the French capitulation, the Haudenosaunee were able to preserve much of their territorial integrity and political influence through a close alliance with the British, whom they placated in the 1768 Treaty of Fort Stanwix by ceding vast tracts of land claimed by the Delawares, Shawnees, and others. The Six Nations—Senecas, Oneidas, Onondagas, Cayugas, Mohawks, and Tuscaroras—remained prosperous, their rich granaries and lush orchards the envy of their neighbors.

The poverty and despair that marked Iroquois life at the end of the eighteenth century had its roots in the American Revolution. The members of the league had responded to the rebellion against Great Britain in diverse ways. Most Iroquois initially heeded early appeals from the revolutionaries calling upon them to remain neutral, but the Oneidas, after a period of neutrality, yielded to the importunities of Rev. Samuel Kirkland and contributed warriors to the war against the British. They were joined by some Tuscaroras. Most other Iroquois, discovering that neutrality was not really possible as "patriots" attacked their villages, joined the pro-British Mohawks and the Onondagas in sending raiders to terrorize American frontier settlements. For that they paid a high price, as American armies beginning in 1779 systematically burned their villages and fields, sometimes slaughtering the inhabitants and mutilating their corpses.[2] Mary Jemison, a white captive and adoptee who spent most of her life among the Genesee Senecas, recalled many years after the war that Gen. John Sullivan's men "burnt our houses, killed what cattle and horses they could find, and left nothing but bare soil and timber." After Sullivan departed, "We found there was not a mouthful of any kind of sustenance left, not even enough to keep a child one day from perishing with hunger."[3] Jemison did not exaggerate. A later analysis of documentary evidence revealed that a single raid on the Senecas destroyed "16,000 bushels of corn and extensive orchards of apples, pears, peaches, and plums, one of which contained fifteen hundred trees."[4] Barbara Mann, a scholar of Iroquoian ancestry, writes of the horrors of those years: "George Washington made a deliberate attempt to starve the Haudensaunee to death during the Revolution. Towards this end, he authorized massive, coordinated attacks on the women's harvests and surplus granaries. . . . In addition to being starved and exterminated between 1779 and 1783, Haudensaunee casualties were skinned, sometimes before they were quite dead, their hides tanned, cut into strips and fashioned into strops for sale as souvenirs."[5] An earlier Iroquoian scholar, writing in 1926, called that time in his people's history "the holocaust."[6] But despite their losses, the Iroquois were not defeated, and they remained in control of their lands when the war ended in 1783.[7] However, to resist the new republic's expansionism, they needed a European ally to supply trade goods and arms. The British were no longer willing to play that role, and they made no provision for the Six Nations—or any other Native American power—in the Treaty of Paris of 1783, which recognized the independence of the United States.

The peace which followed that treaty was a bitter one for the Iroquois nations. Most of the Mohawks and Cayugas relocated in Canada. Many other Iroquois also left New York. Those who remained were forced to cede or lease most of their homelands to the victors. Their power and influence gone, the Six Nations were now plagued by idleness, hunger, and alcoholism. The league no longer functioned. The council fire at Onondaga had been extinguished during the Revolution. When a reconstituted great council refused to ratify a treaty dictated by the victors at Fort Stanwix in 1784, it was ignored both by the chiefs who had agreed to give up millions of acres of land in exchange for peace and trade goods and by American officials and land speculators who promptly took possession. After the second treaty of Fort Stanwix, both Pennsylvania and New York exacted substantial additional land cessions. Among those forced to give up much of their territory were the Oneidas and Tuscaroras who had supported the Americans during the Revolution. Although some Iroquois lands were restored in the Treaty of Canandagua in 1794, a treaty negotiated while the Indian insurgency in the Ohio country and Great Lakes remained of deep concern to the United States, those areas were soon lost. To cite one example, in the Treaty of Big Tree in 1797, the Senecas gave up 95 percent of their remaining territory.[8]

Treaty negotiators at Big Tree who bribed Seneca chiefs, including Red Jacket and Cornplanter, also misled the clan mothers, assuring them that the Senecas could live in comfort on the annuities that would be paid in exchange for their land. That was not true. The Seneca annuity payment in 1799 amounted to "a paltry $3.40 per person per year." [9] Loss of land deprived the peoples of the Longhouse of many of the hunting preserves upon which they had so long depended. White expansion into the territories adjacent to Iroquois reservations drove away much of the remaining game. As hunters, Iroquoian men could still provide some food, but they could no longer obtain in quantity the surplus deer hides and other peltry needed to purchase goods from Euro-Americans. Nor could they any longer win distinction as warriors. They were now marginalized. As William Fenton writes, "persons of both sexes suffered from depression. Warriors, unable to validate their manhood by hunting and fighting, drank to excess. Suspicion of witchcraft reached paranoid proportions, and some individuals resorted to the 'fatal root,' the traditional means of committing suicide by ingesting water hemlock." [10]

Spokesmen for the United States warned the Iroquois that to survive they must abandon their traditional economy. In 1796, Secretary of War Timothy Pickering advised them that they should cultivate "the ground as the white people do" and thereby "get food and clothing without hunting." From Philadelphia, Quakers wrote to offer them instruction "in cultivating your land, and in the method which white people take to live plentifully." Only the Oneidas accepted that offer, and the Quaker mission that was sent to teach them to farm in the Euro-American manner lasted less than three years, withdrawn in response to growing Oneida misgivings about Quaker intentions. [11]

Distrust of whites was widespread in the Six Nations. Nativists warned of the moral corruption of the white race. A prominent Seneca leader named Farmer's Brother summarized the case against "civilization" by relating that "he had sent one of his grandsons to Philadelphia to be educated. But on a visit to the city he found his grandson successively in a tavern, in a brothel, and dancing." [12] Nativists spoke also of white greed and rapacity. Their best-known spokesman was Red Jacket, leader of the Seneca community at Buffalo Creek and speaker of the clan mothers council. Responding to a visiting white preacher in 1805, Red Jacket declared: "Your forefathers crossed the great water and landed on this island. Their numbers were small; they found friends and not enemies. They told us they had fled their own country for fear of wicked men, and had come here to enjoy their own religion. They asked for a small seat; we took pity on them and granted their request and they sat down amongst us. We gave them corn and meat, they gave us poison in return." The outcome was one that the Indians, well meaning and innocent, could not have foreseen. "At length their numbers had greatly increased; they wanted more land; they wanted our country. Our eyes were opened; our mind became uneasy. War took place; Indians were hired to fight against Indians; and many of our people were destroyed. They also brought strong liquor amongst us; it was strong and powerful and it has slain thousands." [13] In a more jocular vein, Red Jacket frequently told a story about an Indian sitting on a log. A white man came up and asked if he could sit down; he said he needed only a little space. The Indian slid over to make room for him. Soon another white man came with the same request. Again, the Indian made room. But white men kept coming, each asking for a little space on that log. Each time, the Indian made room, and he was finally pushed off the log. [14] Red Jacket had long opposed those who argued that the Iroquois must emulate Euro-Americans. He appealed to memory of the past to support his claim that whites had nothing good to offer in the present. Remembrance of past sufferings at the hands of whites, Red Jacket hoped, would inspire the Haudenosaunee to hold fast to their old religion and observe its rituals, preserve their beliefs and customs, protect their communal identity, and resist those who would send children to the whites for education.

Cornplanter and the Quakers

Not all Iroquois agreed with Red Jacket's particular brand of nativism. The four-hundred-member Allegany Seneca band, who lived on a strip of land about a mile wide and thirty miles long straddling the border between New York and Pennsylvania, followed their chief, Cornplanter, in developing a mixed economy that blended traditional reliance on hunting and horticulture with new innovations that incorporated Euro-American agricultural and industrial technologies. The Allegany Seneca land was not, strictly speaking, a reservation, as it had been granted as a private holding to Cornplanter by the state of Pennsylvania. [15] Located in an isolated frontier area, Allegany was less impoverished than most other remaining Iroquoian lands. Game was still available, although Cornplanter and his followers realized that there could be no long-term reliance on hunting as the main source of animal protein and trade commodities. The son of a Seneca woman and a Dutch trader, Cornplanter had fought on the British side during the Revolution. After the war he generally advocated friendship with Euro-Americans, but at one point he threatened to join the western resistance movement led by Blue Jacket and Little Turtle if the United States did not recognize his people's need for land. Cornplanter was a realist and a pragmatist. While he was by no means an uncritical admirer of either white "civilization" or Christianity, he harbored no illusions about the future. Located in a remote area, Cornplanter's village was more prosperous than most. But Cornplanter realized that the game upon which they still subsisted would not last long. [16] To survive, he declared, the Senecas must "till the ground with the plow, as white people do," and also learn to "grind corn." In negotiations with federal officials, Cornplanter sought assistance in constructing sawmills and gristmills and asked that the government "send a blacksmith to settle among us." He therefore welcomed overtures from the Quakers. At his invitation, three members of the Society of Friends, sponsored by the Philadelphia Yearly Meeting, came to the Allegany Senecas in the late spring of 1799. Two of those missionaries, Halliday Jackson and Joel Swayne, established a model farm and made plans to build a gristmill. Their objective was to teach the Senecas how to produce a surplus for the market. To expedite the process, they paid Senecas cash incentives not only for food crops but for the textiles the women under their supervision would learn to weave. The third of the missionaries, Henry Simmons, was a schoolteacher who had served briefly at the Oneida mission. His plan was to teach the Seneca children English, thereby (in Simmons's words) enabling them "to read the great good book for themselves."[17]

Although Simmons was free of much of the virulent anti-Indian prejudice characteristic of white Americans in the early nineteenth century, he had little understanding and less respect for traditional Seneca customs. He later related to Gov. Joseph Heister of Pennsylvania that shortly after his arrival he had de-livered a speech, through an interpreter, in which he warned the Allegany Senecas of "the evil of many customs prevailing among them, particularly of dancing and shouting in such a hideous manner." In a confrontation with Cornplanter at around the same time, the missionary declared that Seneca dances "were certainly the devil's works." "I further told him," Simmons recorded in his journal, "that what made it more painful to me was that they collected the innocent children and were bringing them up in their footsteps, in doing that which was very wicked, when it ought to be otherwise." Simmons hinted that if those diabolical "frolics" did not cease, he would withdraw his services. Cornplanter took the matter up with the village council and informed Simmons that they would curtail social dancing, which he claimed they had learned from the whites, but would continue to hold two annual festivals "of their own productions." Later, responding to questions from the council, Simmons, in refutation of suggestion that the Christian religion was not intended for Indians, affirmed that after death Indians and whites go to the same heaven (or are consigned to the same hell) and that they speak a common language in the afterlife. In response to a question about the propriety of intermarriage in this life, however, Simmons gave an equivocal answer. Cornplanter then reaffirmed his support for Simmons but warned the missionary that "some of his people did not see and think as he did." While Cornplanter could not agree with Simmons that traditional Seneca religious rituals should be suppressed, he did share the missionary's aversion to drunkenness. Shortly after Simmons preached on the subject, Cornplanter and his council banned alcohol.[18]

In March 1799, Cornplanter received from the Senecas at Buffalo Creek a message warning, as Simmons related in his journal, that a girl had recently "dreamed that the devil was in all white people alike, and that the Quakers were doing no good among us, but otherwise. She had also revealed that it was not right for Indian children to learn to read and write." As the Iroquois placed great stock in dreams, believing that some contained messages and warnings from powerful spirits intended for all the Haudenosaunee, Cornplanter had no choice but to put the matter before the council. He himself discounted the story. The dream, he argued, was false. The girl had probably been told to say those things by enemies of the Quakers. But Cornplanter told Simmons that "many of his people were so foolish as to believe the dream was true." A few weeks later, a young man in Cornplanter's village had a dream that anticipated the more elaborate visions of Handsome Lake. He was led to hell by supernatural guides and saw torments inflicted upon drunkards, adulterers, and wife beaters. As he tearfully related the experience, the youth told the council that he would not only "try to do better than he had done," and cease drinking and abusing women, but also that he "intended to learn to read and write." To many Senecas, those dreams revealed that the great spirit beings supported Cornplanter's work and Simmons's school after all.[19]

Handsome Lake's First Vision

Both dreamers were soon eclipsed by a far more dramatic and compelling visionary. In the spring of 1799, Cornplanter's half brother, a sachem who bore the title Handsome Lake (a traditional name given to one of the league councillors), lay dying. His immediate malady was probably alcohol poisoning, although he had been in poor health, perhaps even bedridden, for about four years. Some years later, in a powerful retelling of the epiphany of Handsome Lake, Edward Cornplanter, a noted *gaiwiio* preacher, re-created for his spellbound listeners the scene in the humble cabin where the founder of the Longhouse religion received his first vision on April 15, 1799. Listeners frequently wept as they heard the story, which was narrated in the present tense and often in the words of Handsome Lake himself.[20] In his waking moments, the sick man reflects on his life. He is consumed by feelings of guilt. He realizes that by constantly "doing evil" he has made himself "loathsome" to the "Great Ruler of the Universe." Still half drunk, Handsome Lake then, in violation of sacred custom, begins to sing the Death Song and other sacred chants. He is not at peace. He wants another drink. But even more, he longs to "rise again and walk on the earth." He vows that if he is spared he will never take another drink. Reflecting on "the beauty of creation," he implores the Creator to allow him to "survive the night to see the sunlight again."

Believing that the Creator has heard his prayer, the sick man rises from his bed and walks through the cabin door into the sunlight. But he collapses and quickly loses consciousness. His daughter and son-in-law, working in a shed nearby, had heard him call out "So be it!" a moment before. They rush to his aid. When they reach his body, they find that Handsome Lake, ravaged by sickness, "is but yellow skin and dried bones." He is no longer breathing. His body grows cold. Certain that he has died, they call upon his relations for help. A nephew feels a small warm spot on Handsome Lake's body. Chief Cornplanter arrives and also feels the warm spot. Several hours pass. Finally, around noon, the spot begins to spread. Handsome Lake's nephew "feels the warm blood pulsing in his veins. Now his breath comes, and he opens his eyes." Handsome Lake exclaims, "Never have I seen such visions."

As his relatives gather around him, Handsome Lake explains that after he had awakened in his sickbed that morning he heard a voice saying "Come out awhile!" When he stepped through the doorway, he saw "three men clothed in fine clean raiment." With cheeks painted red, a few feathers in their hair, the men, all middle aged, each carried a bow and arrow in one hand and huckleberry bushes and several kinds of berries in the other. "Never before," Handsome Lake testified, "have I seen such handsome commanding men." The visitors, carrying objects that proclaimed their affinity for Iroquois tradition, explained that they had been sent to him by the Creator, who had been deeply moved by the sick man's expression of gratitude for the beauties of creation. Their mission was to "help him recover." Accordingly, they gave Handsome Lake berries to eat and advised that he would find "a fire in the bushes and a medicine steeped to give you strength." There he would also find "two medicine people" who would administer the medicine. They promised Handsome Lake that he would be well and told him that he must then celebrate with his relatives "a strawberry feast" at which everyone would "drink the juice of the berry and thank the creator for your recovery."

He had been spared for a reason. Handsome Lake, the messengers revealed, was to serve as an emissary to inform the people of the wishes of the Creator. His first charge was to tell the Senecas that they must continue to celebrate the strawberry festival. When "the strawberries were ripe, thanks must be given to the Creator, and the juice must be drunk by the children and the aged and all the people," because "strawberries were a great medicine" essential to human well-being. The messengers "bade me to tell this story to my people when I move upon the earth again." They informed Handsome Lake that they would visit him again and would bring further instructions from "the one who made us." Meanwhile, he must continue to reflect on "the evil things" he had done in his life and repent.

To impress upon him the true gravity of his situation, the messengers, before leaving, ordered him to "look through the valley between two hills. Look between the sunrise and the noon. And so I looked, and in the valley there was a deep hollow from which smoke was arising and steam as if a hot place were beneath. Then spoke the messengers saying 'What do you see?' I answered 'I see a place in the valley from which smoke is arising and it is also steaming as a hot place beneath.' Then said the beings, 'Truly you have spoken. It is the truth. In that place a man is buried. He lies between the two hills in the hollow and a great message is buried with him. Once we commanded the man to proclaim that message to the world but he refused to obey. So now he will never rise from that spot for he refused to obey. So now to you, therefore, we say, proclaim the message that we give you and tell it truly before all the people.' "

The "great message," as it was then given to Handsome Lake in his first vision, embraced more than a call to preserve certain ritual practices. After conveying the warning related above, the messengers disclosed that Handsome Lake's mission was to explain to his people that "evil upon the earth" emanated from four practices loathsome to the Creator who "made man a living creature." Those could be understood by reflecting upon "four words [that] tell a great story of wrong." The first of the evil words was *alcohol*, "a great and monstrous evil" that "has raised a high mound of bones." The Creator called upon the people "never to use it again." The second word was *witchcraft*. The messengers explained that "witches are people without their right minds. They make disease and spread sickness to make the living die." Handsome Lake was ordered to call upon witches to repent, confess, and seek forgiveness. Lesser malefactors were to confess in public, more serious offenders should confess to Handsome Lake privately, and the worst offenders should confess secretly to the Creator. The third word, denoting "the secret poisons in little pouches," is sometimes translated as *love charms*, but it really referred to a number of objects and materials used in the improper manipulation of spirit power to coerce the unwilling. Among them were charms used by warriors and hunters, as well as love potions. "A great pile of human bodies lies dead because of this word," the messengers declared, adding assurances of mercy for those who repented of the use of such things. "It matters not how much destruction they have wrought—let them repent and not fail for fear that the Creator will not accept them as his own." The fourth word, *yondwi'nias swa'yas*, best translated as "abortifacient," referred to herbs used to induce abortions. The Creator, the messenger explained to Handsome Lake, "created life to live and wishes such evils to cease. He wishes those who employ such medicines to cease such practices forevermore."[21]

Handsome Lake ended his recounting of his meeting with the messengers with a request that Chief Cornplanter call the council together and explain the message from the Creator. The gathering was attended by most of the members of the Allegany Seneca community. Also present was Simmons, was so impressed by Cornplanter's speech that he recorded in his journal that he "felt the love of God flowing forcefully amongst us." He was so moved, in fact, that he spoke to the council in affirmation of Handsome Lake's vision. Unlike missionaries of other denominations, Simmons as a Quaker could entertain the possibility that God had spoken to a unconverted, unlettered Indian. It is doubtful, however, that Simmons had a very clear understanding of the nativist thrust of Handsome Lake's message.[22]

Handsome Lake's Sky Journey and the Apocalyptic Gospel

The Seneca prophet's rejection of the Euro-American values that Simmons hoped the Senecas would emulate was fully revealed in his second vision. On August 7, 1799, Handsome Lake fell into a deep trance that lasted some seven hours. Led on a tour of heaven and hell by a guide dressed in sky-blue clothing and bearing a bow and arrow (the "fourth messenger"), he "was told the moral plan of the cosmos. This second vision would become the core of the new religion's theology." [23] We follow again Edward Cornplanter's narration, which quotes extensively from Handsome Lake's description of his journey. It is a story filled with vivid and disturbing images.[24] Among the most powerful were those that warned against embracing the teachings of those who hoped to "civilize" Native American peoples. Walking up the Milky Way, which had suddenly descended from heaven to receive them, Handsome Lake and his guide passed a jail. Looking inside, they saw handcuffs, a whip, and a hangman's rope, all symbolizing the severity of the white man's law. Even the Great Spirit was said to be "frightened" at the prospect that such judgments might be inflicted upon his Indian children. They came upon a church without doors or windows. The building was hot, and the people confined within were crying in distress. That image conveyed Handsome Lake's rejection of the severe discipline of those who would impose narrow and rigid constraints of Christianity on Indians. Earlier the travelers had passed a woman so fat that she could no longer stand, her condition symbolizing the misery to be inflicted on those who emulated whites in their greed and gluttony. Now, further up the road, they met Jesus, who showed them the nail scars in his hands and feet and his bloody spear wound. Whites did this to me, Jesus cried, and then warned Handsome Lake that Indians must not trust white people. He added that he would not return to help those people until the earth itself passed away.

The end of the world might well be immanent, Handsome Lake warned. He had seen in the sky two huge drops of liquid hanging above the horizon in the East. One was red, the other yellow. Both were lethal, and should they fall from the sky all living creatures would be in danger. The messengers assured him that they were working very hard to keep the drops suspended. He saw also in the West, near the setting sun, a large, rotating white object that kept the air in motion and sustained life. Its proper operation also depended upon the work of the messengers.

Many of the images Handsome Lake related as he told the Allegany Senecas about his sky journey were intended to warn the Iroquois of the danger of damnation in the life to come. After passing the home of George Washington—a good white man in Handsome Lake's judgment, as he had helped the Iroquois retain some of their independence after the Revolution—the prophet and his guide see a chief who had sold land to the whites. He is now forced to carry huge loads of dirt in a wheelbarrow. The messengers explain that because of his betrayal of his people, he would be forced to do that "laborious task" for the rest of eternity. [25]

The travelers soon came to a fork in the road. At that point the dead were examined by judges who admitted them to the road to heaven or consigned them to hell. Most adults were condemned. But as Handsome Lake watched a woman gain admission to the heavenly road, he learned that everyone would be given three opportunities to repent and embrace the way of life he would be proclaiming to the people. The road to hell was marked by a grisly human chest punctured by a bullet hole and hung on a post. It had been placed there to greet a murderer who was still alive and had not faced his final damnation. Handsome Lake followed that wide road into the domain of the Punisher. The Punisher was a shape-shifter who appeared in many manifestations, but he sometimes resembled the Christian Devil, replete with horns, tail, and cloven hooves. Looking down into hell through a magnifying crystal, Handsome Lake saw an enormous iron lodge extending to the far horizon. As he approached the lodge, he was buffeted by hot winds and almost overcome by intense heat.

Handsome Lake looked into the iron lodge. It was filled with fire pits and crowded with condemned sinners crying out in pain. The Punisher inflicted upon each sinner a torment appropriate to his or her offense. A drunkard was forced to drink from a goblet filled with molten metal. "The man pleaded but the Punisher compelled him to swallow the molten metal. Then the man screamed in a loud voice and fell prone upon the ground with vapor streaming from his throat." A witch was plunged into a boiling cauldron. "Suddenly she shot to the surface crying in a strange voice like some unknown animal." After the sufferer complained that the cauldron was too hot, the Punisher "flung her to one side. But the woman screeched in agony, 'O it is too cold' and she was thrust back into the boiling cauldron." A woman who had used charms to seduce men was infested with serpents that writhed in her body hairs as her flesh decayed. An "immoral woman" was penetrated repeatedly by red-hot penises. A man who had beaten his wife now struck a red-hot woman and suffered severe burns. "The man fell in agony, prostrate upon the floor screaming." A husband and wife who had quarreled excessively in life were now forced to scream at one another until their eyes and tongues bulged out of their bodies and flames leapt from their sexual organs. Two gamblers were punished by being forced to play with red-hot cards "until their flesh was eaten away and the meat fell off." Handsome Lake, who disliked the white man's music, also saw a violin player forced to draw a red-hot bow across his arm. "So in great agony he cried and screamed until he fell."

Leaving the Punisher, the travelers now entered a road where "a far more brilliant light appeared. It was then they smelled the fragrant odor of flowers along the road. Delicious looking fruits were growing on the wayside and every kind of bird flew in the air above them. The most marvelous and beautiful things were on every hand." They passed a spring of clear, bubbling water. A bottle filled from that spring constantly replenished itself. Arriving in heaven, Handsome Lake was greeted by his dog, sacrificed a year before in the White Dog Ceremony.[26] He met his dead son as well as the niece who had died, allegedly because of witchcraft, a year before. Other relatives and friends were there. They spoke of the importance of family and communal harmony and of the deference due to fathers (a theme the prophet would later develop in a rather radical way). His surviving son was criticized for lack of concern for his father, and his nephew Henry O'Bail, an outspoken critic of the old ways, was faulted for his lack of deference to his father, Chief Cornplanter. Handsome Lake's guide warned that if the people failed to heed the message he brought from the Great Spirit they would be devastated by "a great sickness." As a first step to avert that catastrophe, they must conduct the White Dog Ceremony as soon as possible.

Awakening from his trance, Handsome Lake told his brother about this new vision. Cornplanter summoned the council once again to hear the prophet's story. He invited Simmons to attend. When the headmen asked Simmons if he thought Handsome Lake's vision truly came from God, the missionary hedged. It was possible, he granted, but perhaps the prophet's recollection of it was not entirely accurate. Later, in response to a question from Simmons, Cornplanter declared that Handsome Lake's revelations had confirmed him in the belief that the Senecas must maintain "their worship dance, which they hold twice a year"—a "pagan" rite that Simmons had earlier asked them to give up. As to Jesus, the chief, echoing Handsome Lake's account of his latest vision, observed that the white people had killed him, so why should Indians follow the Christian religion? Simmons replied sharply that Christ had been murdered by the Jews, who were possibly ancestors of the Indians. Cornplanter declined to debate the matter any further, but the missionary was beginning to sense that Handsome Lake posed an obstacle to his hope that the Senecas would abandon their old pagan practices and embrace Christianity.

Simmons left Allegany in the early fall of 1799. Prior to his departure, he noted in his journal that he had warned the Senecas about "their vain and idolatrous way of worshipping the Great Spirit" and added that he "fully believed the manner in which they acted was displeasing to him even though it was their forefather's custom." [27] Other Quakers remained and, for a time, gained influence. As we will see, several years later some of them would clash with the prophet over the organization of Indian villages. By the end of the decade, their insistence that the Senecas abandon most of their traditional ways would alienate even Cornplanter. [28]

Six months after the second vision, on February 5, 1800, the messengers returned to Handsome Lake. The people, he was warned, had not yet appeased the Great Spirit. The teachings he had received from them must be written down in a book so that they would be remembered. Children must be taught to obey the *gaiwiio*, the good message brought by Handsome Lake. They must not fall under the influence of those who followed the Christian Bible. The prophet himself must devote half of his time to teaching. The villages must not quarrel; instead, they must be unified and obedient to the will of the Great Spirit. They must resist further loss of land to whites. Above all, there must be a religious reformation. Certain traditional practices should be continued, but others must be set aside. The custom of calling a "dance in honor of some totem animal" in order to enable an individual to gain "favor or power" was "very wrong, for you do not know what injury it may work upon other people." The Creator did sanction several major thanksgiving festivals conducted in his honor. "When the time for dancing comes," Handsome Lake declared, "you must wash your faces, paint your face with red spots and with a thankful heart go to the ceremony." But ritual was not enough. The people must obey the Creator's teachings as related by Handsome Lake and repent their many sins. "When you are preaching repentance," the messenger told the prophet, "explain that the Creator will not give up hope of them until they pass from the earth. It is only then that they can lose their souls if they have not repented." Handsome Lake was to assure the faithful that "the Creator always hopes for repentance." In recognition that life is eternal, the people were also to be told that they must curtail their mourning of the dead and abandon entirely the practice of observing an annual ritual to mark the anniversary of each bereavement.[29]

According to Seneca tradition, Handsome Lake received a number of other messages from the Great Spirit in addition to the three visions. Other than attributing them to the early years of his mission we cannot date those additions, but together they came to make up what Wallace has termed the "Apocalyptic gospel." He describes this aspect of the prophet's teachings as follows. "Signs of the coming apocalypse would be disagreements among the civil chiefs, among faith keepers, and even among the headmen. False prophets would arise. Crops would fail, and an inexplicable plague would kill many people. Witch women would boldly perform their spells in broad day light and boast openly of how many they had slain. The poisonous creatures from the underworld would be released to seize and kill those who did not believe in *Gaiwiio*." Individuals could escape the inferno through following the teachings of Handsome Lake. "The true believers would be spared the final catastrophe, simply by lying down to sleep and being taken up to heaven by the Creator. At the last, the Creator would suspend the powers of nature, and the earth would be engulfed in flames; the wicked would perish in the fire."[30]

Although Handsome Lake's rejection of Christianity as a religion for Indians was unequivocal, his own teachings, with their emphasis on the crucial importance of proper belief, on salvation through repentance, on avoidance of hell, and on the fiery end of the world, owed far more to Christian teachings than to traditional Iroquois religion. Handsome Lake's early visions were permeated with an obsession with sin and with personal redemption that had little counterpart in past Iroquois belief and practice. Although he affirmed the continuing importance of some of the great rituals in protecting the community from misfortune, the images in his sky journey were reminiscent of Dante. The great figures that played a dominant role in the traditional Iroquois story of creation— Sky Woman, the Earth Diver, Flint, Sapling, and others—were all absent in the *gaiwiio*.[31]

Witch Killings

Over the years, Handsome Lake has gained a reputation as a "notorious witch hunter."[32] That reputation is not entirely warranted. In seeing in witchcraft a prime cause of evil and suffering in the world, he reflected a commonplace Iroquois conviction. In his belief that witches threatened not only individuals but the survival of the people the prophet drew on a wealth of traditional lore, some perhaps of Christian origin but most indigenous. Iroquois society had long been pervaded by a fear of witchcraft, which was particularly acute in times of crisis or demoralization. Illness, death, accidental injuries, and other misfortunes were often blamed on witches. Most Iroquois believed that witches commonly used poisons, charms, and spells in their malevolent work.[33] Among their most feared means of killing was the shooting of a dangerous object into the victim's body, sometimes from a great distance. A seventeenth-century Jesuit missionary reported that the Hurons, a people closely related to the New York Iroquois, believed that witches made use of pieces of the flesh of a huge, dead serpent "which brings with it disease, death, and almost every misfortune in the world." He related that they would rub the flesh of that accursed serpent against some object, such as "a blade of corn, a tuft of hair, a piece of leather or wood, the claw of an animal or some similar thing." Use of such objects gave witches "a malignant efficiency, that causes them to penetrate into a man's entrails, into his most vital parts, and into the very marrow of his bones, carrying with them disease and suffering." The witches' victims soon died in agony.[34]

The Iroquois in Cornplanter's day believed that witches were initiated in secret rituals that "required the neophytes to swallow

a certain kind of snake and sacrifice a close relative or friend."
Witches gathered after dark and, having the power to shift shapes,
usually took the form of animals or birds. As John Swatzler writes,
witches "occasionally . . . kept their human form at night, and
lighted their way through the blackness by shooting flames out of
their mouths. The mere sight of mysterious lights moving through
the darkened woods or the sound of howling dogs or hooting owls,
were fraught, in some minds, with ominous connotations."[35]

Throughout the late eighteenth century and the early years of
the nineteenth, Iroquois communities were tormented by rumors
of witchcraft. Although some of the great rituals were designed
to counteract witchcraft, only two were certain to protect the
lives of people targeted by witches. One was to force witches
to confess and thereby lose their power. But if that was not
possible, the malefactors must be identified and put to death.
Mary Jemison claimed that the Genesee band killed at least
one witch a year.[36] We cannot confirm that claim, but we do
know that at Allegany on June 13, 1799, Cornplanter, as Simmons
recorded, ordered the killing of a woman whom he suspected of
having caused the recent death of his daughter. Rumor had it
that "she had poisoned others" and had threatened to continue
killing those who displeased her.[37] During the following year, Jiiwi,
another of Cornplanter's daughters, fell ill following childbirth. As
Handsome Lake had recently announced that spirit messengers
had promised to endow him with the power to diagnose and cure
illnesses, Cornplanter appealed to the prophet for help. At first
Handsome Lake protested that he had not received permission
as yet to use his new powers, but he was pressed by the chief
and finally agreed to undertake Jiiwi's cure. After going into a
trance, aided by inhaling tobacco smoke, he declared that the
community should perform the chants for the dead in order to
placate the restless spirit of Jiiwi's deceased sister. But the chants
had no effect, and Jiiwi's condition worsened. Handsome Lake at
first declared that the chants had not been performed properly,

but after examining the young woman he declared that she was the victim of witchcraft. [38]

Suspicion fell on a band of Munsees who had hunted in Seneca territory the year before. Some claimed that the Munsee chief, Silver Heels, had seduced Cornplanter's daughter, was the father of her child, and now sought to evade responsibility by killing her through witchcraft. Whether Silver Heels or someone else was the object of Cornplanter's suspicion is not clear, but Cornplanter seized the Munsee chief and held him hostage. Those who believed Handsome Lake's claim of witchcraft declared that the hostage should die if Jiiwi did not recover, but several hundred Munsee warriors massed near the border and threatened war. Cornplanter and his council then sought the advice of white friends in a nearby Pennsylvania settlement. They were told that under no circumstances should they execute Silver Heels. Fortunately, Jiiwi unexpectedly recovered, and the Munsee chief was released. Handsome Lake, however, used the episode to underscore the dangers of witchcraft. In a meeting of Seneca chiefs at Buffalo Creek in June 1801 he charged that the Delawares (of whom the Munsees were one branch) harbored many witches and that a few Senecas were also guilty. He implied that his political rival and nephew Red Jacket, speaker of the Seneca nation, was one of them. The council exonerated Red Jacket but agreed that witches must be exposed and persuaded, under threat of death, to confess and give up their evil practices. [39]

In their ongoing struggle against witchcraft, the Iroquois had long relied on the work of secret medicine societies, the most prominent of which was the Society of Faces. The Quaker Halliday Jackson related that the members of this society were "covered with bear skin, and a bag of ashes tied round their middle, with a hole to suffer the ashes to fly about as they moved. Their faces are covered with a large painted mask, having a high mane in the crown, made of coarse hair standing almost erect, and with large eyes encircled with a flame colored ring. Their mouth is open and shows their own teeth with which they grin in a terrific manner, and their hands are blackened so as to leave marks on every person they lay hands on." Carrying a rattle made of the shell of a snapping turtle, the masked men would rub it against the doorposts of the houses they visited to protect the inhabitants from misfortune.[40]

The False Faces were believed to have the power to command the services of Tawiskaron, one of the twins who had played a major role in the creation of the world of the Iroquois. To understand the function of the False Faces, we must relate a part of the Iroquois creation epic.[41] Before the formation of the earth, a pregnant woman fell from the sky world. Birds gently lowered her onto the back of a turtle floating on the waters that covered the lower world. She had become pregnant while in the sky world, but, under circumstances about which the tellers of the creation story do not agree, her husband had pushed her (or she had fallen) through a hole that appeared after the uprooting of a great light-giving tree. From the roots of the tree, she grasped in her right hand the Three Sisters, corn, beans, and squash, and in her left, tobacco. Those would be her gifts to the world that was about to come into being. The birds and sea animals that witnessed her fall had conferred and decided not only to save her but to form the earth for her and her unborn child. Several animals tried to bring mud up from the bottom of the sea, but they failed. Finally, Muskrat succeeded. From the mud the little animal placed on the back of the turtle the present earth grew.

Sky Woman soon gave birth to a daughter. Together mother and daughter roamed the new world, sowing seeds and creating new plants. Some years later, the girl was impregnated by the spirit of the turtle on which the world rests (in some versions described as North Wind) and bore twins, children of both sky and earth. One twin, Tharonhiawagon, upholder of the heavens (sometimes called Sapling), was born by the normal means, but the other, Tawiskaron (Flint), broke through his mother's side, killing her. Nonetheless, in some versions of the epic he became the favorite of his grandmother Sky Woman, who, after transforming her dead daughter's body and head into the sun and the moon, drove Sapling away.[42] Sapling, with the support of his father, the turtle spirit, then devoted himself to the completion of the work of creation, placing both animals and human beings upon the earth and filling it with good plants and running waters. However, he was hindered in that enterprise by his twin brother, who added thorns, snakes, rocks, and other things that made life difficult. When Sapling created streams that flowed both ways, Flint partially undid his work, so humans would have to paddle upstream. He imprisoned animals Sapling had created as food for the people in a cave and turned some of them into vicious predators. Both acted in extreme ways. Sapling made a world without obstacles or challenges. Flint's work as a creator not only made life more difficult but sometimes brought death.

In a fight at the western edge of the turtle island, Sapling through trickery defeated Flint, slamming him against the Rocky Mountains. But rather than killing his twin, he enlisted his aid in the ongoing work of sustaining life. As historian David Swatzler relates, "Flint could not repair the harm he had already done to creation, but he promised to become a benefactor to the Indians, if they would but remember him by wearing masks to represent his battered face, burning tobacco to honor him, and offering him an occasional bowl of corn meal mush. In return, he would protect the Indians against the evils he had introduced into the world: pestilence, natural disaster, and witches." Through their access to Tawiskaron and his power, the False Faces could "cure disease, restrain the destructive forces of nature, and counter the effects of witchcraft."[43]

In understanding the contest between Sapling and Flint at the far rim of the earth, it is important to bear in mind, as Barbara Mann has written, that dualistic Western concepts of good and evil do not apply here. The twins, she writes "were collaborators who, between them, brought forth the exhilarating and fruitful mixtures of the benign and the dangerous, the funny and the grave, the frightening and the comforting, that constitute the human world." "The point of the Twins tale," she notes, "is obviously the sacred role of cosmic equilibrium, a steady principle guiding most of the social inventions of Iroquoian peoples."[44]

Handsome Lake, in agreement with Neolin, Tenskwatawa, and Christian missionaries, believed in a devil who brought evil into the world and opposed the good work of the Creator. Handsome Lake's view of the world, like theirs, was rigidly dualistic. Iroquois lore about Sapling and Flint represented a more subtle, nuanced view of the spirit forces that sustain and threaten life. To Handsome Lake, however, Flint was not symbolic of that balance between creation and destruction that underlies reality; he was rather the evil twin, a being to be feared and execrated. He was, in fact, the Punisher. The prophet therefore demanded the suppression of the secret medicine societies on the ground that in calling on Flint they were engaging in devil worship. He encountered sharp opposition from those who considered their ministrations, and the intercession of Tawiskaron, essential to their health and well-being. His critics charged that people were dying of disease because of neglect of the work of the medicine societies. Their good offices, they believed, were essential to protect the people from witches. Handsome Lake at first insisted that illness had spread because the rituals he had prescribed for closing down the secret societies had not been observed properly, but he was ultimately forced to compromise, finally ruling that the secret societies could continue if their members refrained from the use of alcohol and scheduled their activities to coincide with the great religious festivals.[45]

Handsome Lake's exhortations against witches did not usually lead to violence. The *gaiwiio* stressed confession, repentance, and reconciliation, not vengeance.[46] However, there was an unfortunate incident approximately six years after the beginning of his mission. Handsome Lake, then in residence at Cold Spring, was concluding a sermon when a man standing in the doorway of the longhouse expressed his contempt by farting loudly. He then fled from the village. He was soon found in a nearby swamp seated on a pile of branches eating snakes. Brought back to Cold Spring, the man, obviously deranged, suddenly died. Handsome Lake suspected that he was the victim of witchcraft. By some means not explained in the sources, the prophet determined that two women—a mother and a daughter—had used a witch powder to deprive him of his senses. The Cold Spring council, ruling on Handsome Lake's accusation, concurred that the women were guilty of witchcraft and sentenced them to a flogging. Both women died from the whipping, which was administered by the headmen. In the Code of Handsome Lake, compiled after the prophet's death, we are assured that he did not foresee that the women would not survive their punishment. "This," the prophet presumably declared, "must never happen again because the Creator has not privileged men to punish one another." Several years later, however, Handsome Lake himself ordered the execution of a woman from Onondaga who had been brought to Cold Spring for trial as a witch. That killing disturbed the Quakers and angered Cornplanter. The chief raised pointed questions about the prophet's ability to determine guilt or innocence in witchcraft cases. After that, Handsome Lake condemned no more witches to death. The Code of Handsome Lake, as taught by gaiwiio preachers after his death, condemned witchcraft but declared that the punishment of witches must be left to the Creator. Handsome Lake's enemies charged, correctly, that he used witchcraft accusations as a means of discrediting those who did not accept his teachings, but almost all of the stories they spread about his witch killings were false. Nonetheless, rumors that Handsome Lake sent out "death squads" to execute women opponents whom he charged with witchcraft have persisted in some Iroquoian oral traditions down to the present.[47]

Handsome Lake and Acculturation

Although Handsome Lake's early visions appeared to support traditionalists who opposed the acculturation program offered by the Quakers and partially endorsed by Cornplanter, his revelations from 1802 onward would take on a somewhat more progressive cast. Cornplanter's son Henry O'Bail, an aggressive advocate of change, had complained that Handsome Lake, at the Buffalo Creek conference in June 1801, had declared that the Senecas "should not allow their children to learn to read and write" and should resist pressure to abandon the old ways. The prophet on that occasion had rejected the idea of producing a surplus for market. Although he allowed that the Senecas "might farm a little and make houses"—that is, live in Euro-American-style dwellings—he insisted that they "must not sell anything they raised off the ground" but rather "give it away to one another, to the old people in particular; in short, they must possess everything in common." O'Bail ridiculed his uncle's preoccupation with "witchcraft & dances and such things." [48] But Handsome Lake soon softened his opposition to economic modernization. While he never accepted his nephew's radical rejection of the traditional Seneca ways, he came to support some aspects of Cornplanter's more moderate program of partial acculturation. The chief and his sister, the powerful medicine woman Gayantgogwus, had given strong support to the prophet's religious reformation. After a brief period of opposition, Handsome Lake reciprocated by endorsing key aspects of his brother's social program. He now related that in one of his visions the Creator had declared that the time was drawing near when "the people will raise cattle and swine for feast food at the thanksgivings" because of the extinction of wild animals. [49]

Most aspects of the agenda of Cornplanter and Handsome Lake were not particularly controversial. The prophet's belated endorsement of some schooling in English, for example, seemed eminently sensible. Surely the Iroquois now must learn the white man's language and gain real skills in its use if they were to protect their interests. Handsome Lake now declared that the Great Spirit had told him that each of the Iroquois nations should send two children to white schools to become literate in English, explaining that "so many white people are about you that you must study to know their ways." [50] It is noteworthy that the prophet did not advocate educating all children in English and that he never favored their indoctrination in Euro-American values. The Quaker school established at Cornplanter's town soon closed its doors. There was little if any schooling in English in the Seneca villages during Handsome Lake's lifetime. Instead, in obedience to the command of the Great Spirit as revealed through Handsome Lake, a few Iroquois children were sent to Philadelphia each year to acquire those skills (such as a good command of the English language) that would be needed in dealings with whites in the future.

At home, the prophet urged that the Senecas learn whatever practical things the Quakers could teach them about farming and the industrial arts. But as we shall see, Handsome Lake also continued to preach against the sort of capitalist individualism the Quakers sought to inculcate in their Seneca charges. They sometimes had reason to deplore Handsome Lake's growing influence, as the prophet's vision of the good society did not basically agree with their own. The Quakers, determined to put Seneca men to work plowing the fields and cultivating cash crops, advised that women should no longer do agricultural work. [51] By tradition, however, Iroquois men did not cultivate the fields, although they were responsible for clearing them. Their primary roles were to hunt (thereby supplying animal protein and peltry for trade with Europeans), wage war, and conduct diplomacy and trade. Women were the cultivators and the heads of extended families. Traditional Iroquois believed that "the bond between women and the crop was so close that only women could make it grow." [52] While some Senecas were willing to put men to work on the cultivation of new crops such as wheat and oats, they refused to relegate women to the kitchen and the spinning wheel. The women, for their part, continued to ridicule men who took up the hoe. A Quaker missionary in 1809 related that they "laugh & say such a warrior is a timid woman." [53] The evidence suggests that very few Seneca men became farmers. During Handsome Lake's lifetime, lumbering provided the main source of cash income, although deer hides were still sold to whites. Reports of visitors to Allegany and other Iroquoian communities in the early nineteenth century make it clear that women still cultivated the cornfields and vegetable plots. [54] The Code of Handsome Lake contains no strictures against that custom.

In the late winter of 1802, Handsome Lake led a Seneca delegation that visited Washington DC. The Senecas, along with representatives of other Iroquoian nations, sought federal assistance in the form of livestock, farming implements, and carding and looming equipment. In response to their visit, Congress approved an appropriation of fifteen thousand dollars a year in technical aid. Handsome Lake, however, also used the visit as an occasion to lay claim to special status as the earthly representative of the Great Spirit. In a letter to Thomas Jefferson (whom he met during an audience granted to the delegation), the prophet explained that "the Great Spirit appointed me to guide my people and give them knowledge, good from bad," and had also charged him with improving relations between whites and Indians. The Indians, he acknowledged, were guilty of "drunken quarreling," but whites were not only responsible for corrupting them through the liquor traffic but, driven by their unrighteous greed, had seized most of the Indians' land. Handsome Lake appealed to the president to curb both abuses, warning that if those problems persisted "the Great Spirit will send a Great Sickness among us all." He asked Jefferson to acknowledge his status as one of the five special messengers ("angels") of the Great Spirit and his representative on earth. His message must be heeded by whites as well as

Indians. Both peoples suffered because "they do not think on the Great Spirit." But, the prophet assured Jefferson, the angels with whom he communed "tell me that if any man, whoever he may be, will look on the Great Being above us and do his will, when his days are out and the angels find he is a good man they will grant him more days to live in the world and if he lives a good man doing no evil in those days, when those days are over, he will take him to himself." Having thus held out the promise of redemption, Handsome Lake closed by advising the president to disregard rumors circulated by the drunken sachems of Buffalo Creek (his rival Red Jacket was the leader of that group) and work instead with Cornplanter and other true followers of the Great Spirit. If Jefferson heeded his advice, "we will be good friends here and when we meet with the Great Being above we shall have bright and happier days." [55]

Replying through Secretary of War Henry Dearborn, Jefferson commended Handsome Lake on his efforts to make Indians "sober, honest, industrious and good." As to the prophet's requests, Jefferson promised that the federal government would honor and protect the Indian land boundaries specified in treaties with the United States. He also informed the prophet that Congress was considering legislation to ban Indian use of alcohol. Handsome Lake replied with a new expression of concern about the security of Seneca lands, adding a specific request that he be granted a personal deed to a ten-mile-square tract at the Oil Spring Reservation. Jefferson promised to look into the matter. Handsome Lake wrote again to complain about some recent sales of Iroquois land to white purchasers. This time Jefferson, responding directly to the prophet on November 3, 1802, repeated his pledge that treaty rights would be respected, but he added the hope that Handsome Lake would reconsider his opposition to voluntary land sales. The sales in question, he maintained, had been approved by the chiefs, who had received a "satisfactory price." "The right to sell," the president admonished, "is one of the rights of property. To forbid you the exercise of that right would be wrong to your nation. Nor do I think, brother, that the sale of lands is, under all circumstances, injurious to your people; while they depended on hunting, the more extensive forests around them, the more game it would yield. But, by going into a state of agriculture, it may be advantageous to a society as it is to an individual who has more land than he can improve, to sell a part and lay out the money in stocks and implements of agriculture for the better improvement of the residue. A little land, well stocked and improved, will yield a great deal more [than] without stock or improvement. I hope, therefore, that on further reflection, you will see this transaction in a more favorable light, both as it concerns the interests of your nation, and the exercising of the superintending care which I am sincerely anxious to employ for their subsistence and happiness." [56]

Handsome Lake did not heed Jefferson's admonition to see land sales "in a more favorable light." Although he had agreed to the boundary adjustment negotiations of 1802, his social program affirmed the importance of maintaining a communal land base and rejected the philosophy of individual property rights implicit in the president's pronouncement. Cessions of land to whites, he told his followers, must not result in any further large-scale losses and should be limited to circumstances in which they made it possible to consolidate holdings and thereby promote communal life. He shared Jefferson's belief that agricultural reform was essential to Indian prosperity. The Code of Handsome Lake "unambiguously praised the abundant harvests, animal labor, and warm houses that white people could provide and urged the people to learn the white man's ways in these matters." [57] But the prophet never embraced the values of the capitalist market economy. Preaching against greed and deploring selfish individualism, Handsome Lake warned that the favor of the Great Spirit would be granted only to those who shared. His visions of hell continued to include torments for gluttons and hoarders. "The Creator," the messengers told the prophet, "made food for all creatures, and it must be free for all." Herbalists were not to charge for their cures, but patients instead were to offer tobacco to the Great Spirit. The Code of Handsome Lake stressed the importance of providing for the needs of all, and most particularly of the aged, who were entitled to the greatest respect. Moreover, the Creator demanded that his people be not only generous but also modest. They should never be proud of personal accomplishments, but always thank the Creator for whatever personal skills they might possess. The messengers warned Handsome Lake: "Your people must cease their boasting."[58]

While an affirmation of communalism underscored the persistent nativist strain in the teachings of Handsome Lake, his efforts to redefine family relationships were both radical and disruptive. Some have argued that he was driven by the need to integrate men as workers in the new agricultural economy.[59] But the prophet's criticisms of traditional gender roles went beyond the needs of economic modernization and probably reflect a political power struggle with conservative clan mothers. Persistent Quaker criticism of the role of women in Seneca society may have influenced Handsome Lake. Although the possibility of a pathological misogyny cannot be ruled out, it must remain purely speculative. Lack of information about his life before 1799 makes it impossible to probe his inner feelings. But in his visions, women were frequently portrayed as particularly offensive sinners worthy of truly sadistic punishments in the hereafter. In the sky journey, some of the Punisher's worst torments were reserved for women guilty of either witchcraft or sexual indiscretions. Since witches were not believed to be exclusively female in traditional Iroquois witchcraft lore, it is quite telling that both of the sinners punished for misuse of charms and spells in Handsome Lake's vision of hell were women. The extreme torment inflicted on two women guilty of sexual excesses is rather remarkable as well, as the Iroquois generally were not particularly puritanical about such matters.[60]

In other visions, the messengers revealed to Handsome Lake that the Creator was deeply offended by the current state of family life. Women, Handsome Lake declared, bore much of the responsibility for the moral decay he found rampant among the Iroquois. To be sure, men were not blameless. Some had deserted their children; others were unfaithful to their wives. Family obligations, the prophet declared, must be honored. The Creator deplored adultery, divorce, wife beating, and abortion. All couples must remain married and raise children. If they were unable to conceive, then they should adopt and rear the children of siblings. But in Handsome Lake's visions, women were the source of dissension within families and within the community. The Great Spirit, he reported, was grieved that all too often mothers resented the happiness of their daughters and did everything they could to disrupt their marriages. They taught young wives to treat their husbands harshly, holding that if they did not do so it would only prove that they were dull and stupid. In essence, Handsome Lake declared it was God's will that the Senecas live in nuclear families subject to the authority of the husband. A wife must now obey her husband, even if it meant disregarding the counsel of her mother. The prophet often portrayed women as liars and gossips spreading dissension and hatred among families. The "evil story teller" in one of his visions was a woman. Because of the sins of women, "the Creator is very sad." In a visionary pronouncement that occasioned great rage and controversy, the prophet reported that the Great Spirit deplored "the tendency of old women to do mischief."[61]

Traditional Iroquois society had not only honored "old women" but empowered them. Mann reminds us that the association of women with "sexuality, weakness, evil, inferiority" was alien to the traditional Iroquois, who conferred "high status "on the *gantowisas* (clan mothers) and revered them for their "ability, goodness, intelligence." [62] The most authoritative traditions regarding the founding of the League of the Iroquois assigned a crucial role to clan mothers, who instructed men on the necessity of embracing the Great Law of Peace. Indeed, in some versions of the foundation story, the league's founders—the Peacemaker Deganawidah and the reformed cannibal warrior Ayonwantha (Hiawatha)—succeeded in their mission only through the aid of the Jigonsaseh (a reincarnation, perhaps, of the daughter of Sky Woman), through whose good offices the powerful cannibal chief Adodaroh, leader of the Onondagas, "a terrifying shaman who wore live and writhing snakes in his hair and the severed heads of snakes on his finger tips," was transformed into a peace leader. She taught Ayonwantha how to cure Adodaroh of his madness by combing the snakes out of his hair. In all the villages that would become part of the Great League, clan mothers thereafter exhorted "the warriors to lay down their arms and take up peace."[63]

The clan mothers played a vital role in the ongoing politics of the league, as they had the power to nominate league councillors and bring impeachment proceedings against those whom they deemed incompetent or irresponsible.[64] In the villages, women's councils shared power with their male counterparts. As heads of clans, Iroquois women everywhere exercised substantial influence over male officeholders.[65] Policy decisions, including war making, required their consent. Power sharing, balance, and reciprocity informed gender relations in Iroquoian communities. Iroquois society was matrilineal and matrilocal: descent was reckoned through the female line, and a married man lived in the home of his wife's mother. Relationships between mother and daughter, uncle and nephew, and brother and sister were of far more significance than they were in the patrilineal, nuclear Euro-American family. As to the role of older women, Mann tells us that the wife's mother had the power to terminate marriages and "could do so unilaterally, regardless of her daughter's opinion, if she felt her new son-in-law was a slacker. Unless another elder woman in the Longhouse defended him, he was gone. In such a case, the ex-wife retained all the marital possessions, returning only wedding gifts to her ex-husband's mother." [66] It is perhaps indicative of the high status of women that polyandry—among the Senecas and perhaps some other Iroquoian peoples—was sometimes practiced. Some women also selected "hunting wives" to accompany their husbands on extended travels when duties at the home village made it inadvisable for them to travel. The key role played by women in Iroquois society is perhaps most clearly revealed in their control of property. While the Iroquois did not have private land ownership in the European sense, land-usage assignments to family lineages were granted to women by women. The forest was the domain of males, but the village and its fields were not. Again, gender roles were marked by balance and reciprocity.

It is a stunning indication of a severe social crisis that Hand-some Lake's vision included warnings against the physical abuse of women. In traditional Iroquois society, such abuse was un-thinkable. Rape, for example, was unknown. The prophet's stric-tures against wife beating are no less telling than his shocking characterizations of the Great Spirit's presumed anger against "meddling" mothers. [67]

Handsome Lake's Struggle for Power

The opposition of clan mothers and of chiefs loyal to and depen-dent on them would prove to be a major obstacle to Handsome Lake's political aspirations. He sought to convince Indians and whites alike that the Great Spirit intended that he not only be a teacher but also serve him as the ruler of a unified Iroquois nation. He portrayed the Creator as deeply saddened by strife and bickering among the Iroquoian peoples and warned that continued dissension would lead to unimaginable catastrophes. In 1801, with the news of his visions still fresh, the Buffalo Creek conference declared Handsome Lake "supreme leader of the Six

Nations." Two years later, Seneca leaders loyal to the prophet announced the transfer of the Great Council Fire of the league to Cornplanter's town on the Allegheny. However, many other Iroquois refused to acknowledge that transfer, instead recognizing the continued authority of the council fire that had been established after the American Revolution at Buffalo Creek, where Handsome Lake's rival Red Jacket was the dominant sachem. For a time neither council fire enjoyed anything more than local support, but in a gathering of New York Iroquois chiefs in 1807 formally proclaimed the reestablishment of the Great League and recognized the primacy of Buffalo Creek as the site of the Great Council Fire.[68]

By the time that decision was made, Handsome Lake had lost much of his earlier political power. In 1803 he quarreled with Cornplanter, ostensibly over the chief's operation of a privately owned sawmill on Seneca lands. The underlying cause, however, was the resentment the prophet and many of his followers felt over the chief's autocratic and domineering ways. Cornplanter was often less than deferential to the prophet. When Cornplanter in a fit of pique ordered his critics to leave his private lands at Allegany, Handsome Lake and many of his supporters reestablished their community at Cold Spring on the New York Seneca reservation. But soon after their relocation, Handsome Lake quarreled with the Quakers over his plans to build a traditional village there. As Wallace explains, the missionaries "wanted the Indians to give up the old way of living in small villages and to disperse among the fields in settlement patterns typical of rural white America, with houses built up a mile apart, each surrounded by its own fenced field and lanes." That proposal offended the prophet, who cherished a vision of communal harmony and felt that the people must live close together in order to maintain the sacred rituals ordained by the Creator. The issue divided the Cold Spring Senecas, with some supporting the Quakers against Handsome Lake.[69]

The prophet's problems with Cornplanter and with Quaker-influenced progressives were minor compared to the opposition from Buffalo Creek. Red Jacket and his supporters were indefatigable in their efforts to undermine Handsome Lake's claims to prophetic authority. They were motivated in part by personal jealousy but also by ideology. The prophet's religious reforms worried some traditionalists, who feared the consequences of abandoning or modifying any of the old rituals. And his dualistic monotheism offended those who still revered the true Iroquois creators, Sky Woman and her daughter, the Fat Faced Lynx, and the brothers Sapling and Flint, none of whom played any role in the *gaiwiio*. To many, the Great Spirit remained an improbable, alien god. Moreover, the prophet's statements about the proper roles of men and women angered not only clan mothers but also chiefs beholden to them. The campaign that Red Jacket, the clan mothers, and their supporters waged against the prophet was clever and effective. Describing him as a former drunk, a man of no consequence, and "an ignorant, idle, worthless fellow," detractors charged that Handsome Lake was so stupid that he sometimes could not recall his own revelations. He was not his own man, they warned, but rather the tool of Cornplanter, who was working to grab power by claiming the support of the Great Spirit. (These slurs, of course, disregarded the prophet's former status as a league councillor and his current falling out with his half brother.) Red Jacket's followers mocked Handsome Lake's pretensions to personal authority and thereby appealed to the Iroquois concept of leadership, which had no place for a single "ruler." But their most effective ploy was to exploit Handsome Lake's reckless and indiscreet remarks about witchcraft.[70]

As noted earlier, rumors that Handsome Lake had used witchcraft accusations to secure the execution of scores of people who refused to accept his revelations or his leadership were false. But the prophet's own sometimes frantic warnings that he was about to become the victim of a witches' conspiracy and his penchant in his sermons for placing in hell those who did not follow the *gaiwiio* lent credibility to the whispering campaign. Then, in 1809, Handsome Lake authorized the execution of the woman brought to Cold Spring from Onondaga for trial as a witch. That killing undermined most of the prophet's remaining support among the Seneca power brokers. Cornplanter announced his disapproval, and his council condemned witch killing. His son Henry O'Bail ridiculed Handsome Lake as a superstitious old fool and described his devotion to the White Dog Ceremony as barbaric. The outcry was so great that Handsome Lake, accompanied by a few followers, fled Cold Spring and took up residence for a time at Tonawanda. His exile was brief, but when he returned Cornplanter was firmly in control. Handsome Lake was again made a member of the council, but he no longer played a dominant role.[71]

Handsome Lake consistently preached peaceful coexistence with whites. He held that the Christian gospel, although not intended for Indians, was divinely inspired. In a conversation with Doctor Peter, an Oneida assistant to the missionary Samuel Kirkland, he declared that the Holy Bible and his own revelations came from the same source. The Great Spirit wanted his children "to live in peace and love all mankind." In the Code of Handsome Lake the Creator declared that Indians should give up "the constant fear that the white race would exterminate you," since all people, whatever their race, were under his protection. Handsome Lake joined with Cornplanter and other Seneca leaders in opposing the Shawnee prophet's call for armed resistance. When war came, however, Handsome Lake called for neutrality rather than support of the foes of Tecumseh and the British. When the league councillors refused to prohibit Iroquois enlistments in the armed forces of the United States, Handsome Lake called his own council, which did so. His bid to thereby regain his status as the preeminent league spokesman failed, but his campaign against the war was not entirely unsuccessful. Federal agents noted with some irritation that the prophet was instrumental in hindering their recruitment efforts among the Iroquois.[72]

At the time of his death at the age of eighty in 1815, Handsome Lake's dream of a unified Iroquois nation bound together by his prophetic teachings and guided by his hand was far from fulfillment. During his lifetime, Handsome Lake's spiritual claims were challenged by Iroquois religious traditionalists, by a few progressive secularists, and by a handful of Christian converts. His rivals sometimes claimed that they also had received revelations from the Great Spirit. Even Red Jacket at one point declared that he had learned in a dream that he, Red Jacket, was the Great Spirit's choice as leader of all the Iroquois and that terrible punishment would befall the people if they did not immediately acknowledge his elevation. Red Jacket never acquired stature as a visionary, but he remained an effective leader of those Senecas who doubted Handsome Lake's claim to speak for the Creator. There were other claimants to the prophetic mantle. Handsome Lake had few followers among the Tuscaroras, who adhered to the teachings of a female prophet whose name is lost to history. Many of the Oneidas were Christians, converted by the veteran missionary Samuel Kirkland. Others listened to the revelations of the Mohawk prophet, a traditionalist visionary who anticipated Handsome Lake in calling for a revival of the White Dog Ceremony. Elsewhere, traditionalists charged that Handsome Lake's innovations were offensive to the spirits and thereby endangered all Indians. Some continued to worry about Handsome Lake's meddling with the medicine societies, believing the societies "ministrations essential to protect against witches and the illnesses they inflicted."[73]

Although he never attained the political dominance he hoped for, Handsome Lake continued to win converts. He excelled as a religious teacher, traveling from village to village, excoriating sinners, condemning alcohol, promoting sobriety, and holding out the promise of a better life now and salvation in the world to come through the power of the Great Spirit. By 1806 the Oneidas were pondering stories about his revelations, particularly his warning that drunkards would be punished in hell and his exhortations calling for family harmony and racial peace. At first they seem to have misunderstood some of the prophet's teachings, believing that he had banned the White Dog Ceremony, instituted rituals of confession and absolution, and mandated observance of the Christian Sabbath. But visits from some of the prophet's converts removed most of those misconceptions. Although privately rather disdainful of Handsome Lake's pretensions, Kirkland avoided open criticism, as some members of his own congregation were attracted to his teachings. Handsome Lake achieved his greatest success among the Senecas and Onondagas, but he did not restrict his mission to the New York Iroquois. He traveled among the western Indians, visiting the Wyandots at Sandusky in 1806 and again in 1808, delivering his message of repentance and peace and speaking against the resumption of warfare with whites.[74]

As to the prophet's impact on the lives of his disciples, the Quaker Halliday Jackson in 1806 remarked, with some surprise, that "in the course of our travels among all the Indians on the Allegheny River, or either of the villages at Cararaugus we have not seen a Single individual the least intoxicated with Liquor." Other white observers testified that while alcoholism had not disappeared completely, its incidence had been greatly diminished since Handsome Lake began his ministry. Wallace captured the true significance of Handsome Lake's achievement when, after reviewing the available evidence, he contrasted the inner conflicts experienced by many Iroquois Christian converts with "the feeling of peace, confidence and strength that came to those who followed the *gaiwiio*."[75]

The rivalry between Handsome Lake's followers and the traditionalists continued for a number of years after the prophet's death. The opposition of clan mothers both delayed the acceptance of the Longhouse religion and forced modification of some of Handsome Lake's more radical teachings.[76] By the middle of the nineteenth century, however, traditional Iroquois living in New York and Canada (but not elsewhere) embraced the *gaiwiio*. That body of oral lore describes the life and teachings of Handsome Lake and memorializes his death, said to have been caused by the witchcraft of his enemies. As related by *gaiwiio* preachers, drawing upon variant oral traditions and supported by bands of wampum, the story of the life, visions, and passion of Handsome Lake provides the text recited at the great annual rituals of the Longhouse religion. Although Christianity has claimed many converts among the Iroquois and now commands the loyalty of a majority of those who claim to be believers, at least five thousand still follow Handsome Lake. Moreover, many Iroquoian members of Christian denominations also participate in the Longhouse ceremonies.

The current CD-ROM edition of the *Encyclopedia Britannica* classifies the religion of Handsome Lake as a Christian cult. [77] The influence of Christianity on Handsome Lake's thought and teaching is unmistakable, but so is the persistence of a system of values and beliefs that is not only not Christian or Euro-American but in many respects antithetical to both. Handsome Lake was indeed a moralist and a preacher whose code of personal conduct Christian missionaries found not only unexceptional but exemplary. But he was also a shaman, a healer, and a visionary possessed of a sense of personal spirit power that no Christian preacher could match or even comprehend. Most importantly, Handsome Lake's dream of a world redeemed by the power of the Great Spirit bore no real resemblance to that world of individualistic rural capitalism driven by the profit motive which Quakers and other whites envisioned as the Indian utopia. He remained to the end committed to Iroquois communalism, and soon after his death his teachings were invoked by nativists hostile to Quaker influence. The key issue was Quaker opposition to communal land ownership. Their advice that the Senecas divide their territory into individually owned plots alienated many of their earlier supporters. Often tactless in their criticisms of Seneca customs and culture, Quakers tried to teach the Senecas how to function in an economy grounded in individual ownership and private enterprise, thereby arousing deep suspicions about their motives and intentions. Some believed that the Quakers, who were in fact committed to the protection of reservations from speculators and land companies, intended to dispossess them.

A meeting of Senecas and other Iroquois at Tonawanda in the late summer of 1818 was marked by recollections of the visions of Handsome Lake as well as by strategy sessions on the organization of an inter-reservation resistance movement. In 1820, Cornplanter, who had been at odds with the Quakers since 1815, "experienced a series of visions that essentially recapitulated the teachings of Handsome Lake," particularly those rejecting both Christianity and capitalism. As nativist opposition mounted, the Society of Friends, deeply disappointed by the resistance of the "pagan party," abandoned their efforts to reshape Iroquois society.[78] The arrival of more aggressive missionaries representing various Protestant denominations deepened divisions on the Iroquois reservations. Cornplanter late in his life agitated against both Christianity and, it appears, some of the innovations of Handsome Lake as he labored to preserve the old creation stories the prophet had discarded.[79] Handsome Lake's disregard for some of those traditions notwithstanding, his main inspiration was certainly not Christian. Those who have seen Handsome Lake primarily as an advocate of acculturation misunderstand the nature of his mission, for it was the *gaiwiio* that provided the strongest ideological bulwark against those reformers, Quakers and others, who sought to "civilize" the Iroquois by persuading them to abandon their communal way of life. As his severest modern critic concedes, Handsome Lake "kept alive many truly authentic aspects of Houdensaunee culture that were threatened with extinction by a juggernaut of coerced assimilation." The

Longhouse religion he founded "had the dual effect of allowing the people at once to resist and to accommodate their invaders."[80] While some aspects of his teachings occasioned controversy and strife, the continued observance of the great religious festivals, the survival of clan organization, the communal ethic, and persistence of a distinctive Iroquoian sense of identity all reflect the influence of Handsome Lake.

6

The Kickapoo Prophet

Among the most stalwart of the tribes that had given support to the Shawnee prophet Tenskwatawa and his brother Tecumseh were the Kickapoos, a people closely related to the Shawnees. For most Kickapoos, the dream of a world restored to Indians through the power of the Great Spirit died with Tecumseh in 1813, but some came to follow a new prophet who also told them he had spoken with God. This prophet's message sometimes echoed the earlier revelations of Tenskwatawa, but more often it led his followers down a new and unfamiliar pathway. A glimpse of the Kickapoo prophet is found in the work of the painter George Catlin. On his way west to paint scenes of Indian life in 1831, Catlin visited a Kickapoo community on the Vermillion River in Illinois. The Kickapoos, as Catlin related, were "the remnant of a once numerous and warlike tribe" who now lived in poverty, their numbers reduced "by whisky and small-pox." The game they had once hunted had been "destroyed," and although the land they occupied was "one of the finest countries in the world," they now had little incentive "to build houses and cultivate their farms," for they knew that soon they would be dispossessed. There was no doubt that whites would force them "to sell out their country for a trifle, and move to the West."[1]

Catlin's assumption that the Kickapoos had little reason to hope they could stay in their homeland was well founded. In

1830 Congress had passed the Indian Removal Act, giving Pres. Andrew Jackson a mandate to negotiate treaties to relocate the remaining Indian nations on lands west of the Mississippi River. Jackson and his associates had no intention of abiding by the law's requirement that removal be voluntary. Through bribery, coercion, and intimidation, they were determined to remedy what the president in an unfinished private position paper had described as the "inconveniences" of having Indian tribes living within the states of the Union. [2] The future for the Kickapoos, as for other tribes slated for removal, looked fairly grim. Catlin was therefore surprised to discover that the members of the Kickapoo band he visited at Vermillion River, although impoverished, were not demoralized. They were sober, dignified, and surprisingly confident. The painter attributed their optimism to the influence of their "chief," a charismatic leader who regularly held "meetings in his tribe, on the sabbath, preaching to them and exhorting them to a belief in the Christian religion." "I went on the sabbath to hear this eloquent man preach, when he had his people assembled in the woods," Catlin related, "and although I could not understand his language, I was surprised, and pleased with the natural ease and emphasis, and gesticulation, which carried their own evidence of the eloquence of his sermon." Catlin painted the portrait of the chief, whose name he recorded as Kee-an-ne-kuk, and was struck that in posing, his subject appeared to be at prayer. In Catlin's portrait, the prophet, a dark-eyed visionary whose face conveys both gentleness and fervor, appears to be in a dream state as he gazes into space. [3]

The Teachings of the Kickapoo Prophet

Catlin was partly mistaken. Religion was, as he suspected, a source of hope and strength to the Vermillion River Kickapoos, but their leader was not a Christian. Kenekuk (as his name is now spelled) was the prophet of a new faith whose adherents among both the Kickapoos and the neighboring Potawatomis would prove to be tenacious in their resistance to the efforts of Christian missionaries. Catlin was not the last to mistake the nature of the prophet's message. Even those whites fluent in the Kickapoo dialect often misunderstood Kenekuk, assuming that he would prove an ally to those who labored to bring Indians to Christ. Their misconceptions were in part the product of perceptions of very real similarities between Christian, particularly Catholic, rites and the religious practices of the prophet's followers. But the prophet himself was directly responsible for the perpetuation of the notion that his spiritual teachings would serve as a force for cultural and spiritual assimilation, for in seeking to preserve the autonomy of his people, Kenekuk not infrequently sought to placate white authorities by telling them what they wanted to hear, at one point even allowing himself to be baptized by a Methodist missionary.[4] But, unlike some would-be Native American leaders who sought close association with government agents and Christian missionaries, Kenekuk cannot be dismissed as either a shallow manipulator or a self-serving opportunist. He was a man possessed of a rare genius for leadership, one of the few who was both a spiritual authority armed with charismatic power and a politician-diplomat of exceptional skill and shrewdness.

Kenekuk was born around 1790 in a village on the Wabash River. Kickapoo tradition, as related to anthropologist James Howard in 1960, tells us that he was a dissolute young man. After killing his uncle "in a drunken rage," Kenekuk was sent into exile and "went to live on the outskirts of the white frontier settlements, making a living doing odd jobs." He was hired by a "priest" who took the outcast into his home, employing him "as a helper around the house." After Kenekuk expressed curiosity about the contents of "some religious books in the priest's library," his employer agreed to give him religious instruction. Kenekuk was an apt pupil, so the priest suggested that "if he brought these good teachings back to his own people he would be forgiven by them for the murder of his uncle, as this would atone for his sin."[5] Around 1815, Kenekuk returned to the Kickapoos, preaching a gospel that stressed repentance for sins, moral reform to regenerate the Kickapoo community and secure individual salvation in the life to come, and peace with whites. Many of his fellow tribesmen, weary of war and disillusioned by the failure of the armed resistance preached by the Shawnee prophet and led by Tecumseh, "were ready to listen to the words of peace and coexistence that Kenekuk had brought with him." It was a message that white observers often misunderstood. As Kenekuk's biographer Joseph Herring tells us, their assumption that the Kickapoo prophet's teachings about peace and salvation were essentially Christian was mistaken. "It was Kenekuk's own interpretation of the Scriptures . . . that he preached to the Kickapoos and other Indians in the Indiana—Illinois region. In fact, his gospel departed significantly from conventional Christianity; it contained an implicit cultural nationalism that merged with, rather than superseded, traditional Indian beliefs."[6]

Christian missionaries to the Kickapoos, both Protestant and Catholic, at first did not understand Kenekuk's "cultural nationalism." Instead, they were struck by the strong resemblance between the religious practices of the devotees of Kenekuk's faith and Roman Catholicism, a resemblance that may have reflected the influence of Jesuit missionaries who had visited the Kickapoos when they resided in Wisconsin in the eighteenth century. It appears that in Kenekuk's teachings, "some Catholic rites" that had continued to be observed by the Kickapoos long after "they lost contact with the priests" were "reinforced and intensified." The Kickapoo prophet and his followers believed that Jesus, the Virgin Mary, and the saints were sacred beings. They also believed that in the afterlife they would be judged and admitted to heaven or condemned to hell or purgatory. They observed holy days. [7] In their worship they made use of chants and prayer sticks. As James Mooney noted, those prayer sticks contained characters "which bear some resemblance to the old black-letter type of a missal, while the peculiar arrangement [of the rows of characters] is strongly suggestive of the Catholic rosary with its fifteen 'mysteries' in three groups of five each." [8] Not surprisingly, a Jesuit priest who visited Kenekuk and his people in 1833 declared them "truly Catholic in desire." [9]

But there were significant differences. Reports of the religious services conducted by the Kickapoo prophet noted that the congregation gathered on Sundays and on certain holy days to listen to sermons, delivered by both the prophet and his assistants, and to sing hymns, but they employed no rite comparable to the Christian Eucharist. [10] While Jesus was revered in Kenekuk's teachings, the prophet did not regard Christ as his people's savior. A Methodist minister who spoke with Kenekuk in 1848 noted rather bitterly that the Kickapoo prophet had "persuaded scores of Indians to believe that white men killed Jesus Christ before he had made atonement for the Indians, and that he, Kenekuk, has been appointed by the Great Spirit to supply the deficiency." [11] Under the prophet's direction, his followers sought absolution from sin not through private confession, prayer, and reliance upon Christ's atonement but through a group ritual, held on Friday nights, wherein the wayward told the congregation about their misdeeds and submitted to public whippings. One observer, a white settler named Patrick Hopkins, witnessed a ceremony in which some fifty members of Kenekuk's congregation each received between fourteen and twenty-eight lashes on their bare skin, administered by a three-foot-long hickory rod, each stripe laid on with sufficient force to leave a mark. While the purpose of such flagellation was ostensibly to assure the forgiveness of sins and save the penitent from hellfire, Herring notes that whipping had another purpose: to ensure tribal solidarity. "Faced with the constant threat of expulsion from the Wabash area, Kenekuk and the other leaders employed the whippings to maintain unity and as an effective means of strengthening tribal unity." [12] Kenekuk's religious teachings and moral precepts had as their purpose not only salvation of the individual in the life to come but also preservation of tribal integrity in the face of the threat posed by whites in the here and now. Despite its resemblance to Christianity, the religion of Kenekuk was in its most fundamental aspects profoundly nativist. Englishman Charles Augustus Murray, to whose ear the singing or chanting of Kenekuk's congregation sounded "wild and peculiar," suspected that despite his understanding of the Christian gospel, the prophet retained "his Indian prejudices and superstitions." [13] When one discounts Murray's ethnocentrism and condescension, his remark is quite perceptive.

Closer scrutiny of the teachings and practices of Kenekuk and his followers reveals close affinities with the nativist gospels preached by Neolin and Tenskwatawa. Mooney, in his 1890 study of Native American prophetic movements, observed that Kenekuk's prayer stick "reminds us at once of the similar device of the Delaware prophet of 1764." [14] Kenekuk made use of a diagram of heaven and hell reminiscent of Neolin's "great book of writing." Like the Delaware prophet, he denounced shamanic practices. Claiming that the diagram had been given to him by the Great Spirit, Kenekuk outlined the Kickapoo journey through time, from past to present and into the future. A line running upward marked the progression to the point where the Great Spirit gave his first revelation to the prophet, a revelation that conveyed "blessings to the Indians" but also warned that they must destroy their medicine bags and follow a strict moral code that prohibited lying, quarreling, and homicide. The future lay beyond that point on the diagram. At the top of the chart was the place where Kenekuk was expected to meet again with the Great Spirit and receive a new revelation. But the pathway to that point of enlightenment and deliverance was not clear, for it was possible, the prophet warned, that the Kickapoos might disregard the commandments issued in the first revelation. In that case, they would need to "traverse a crooked path leading to a place of fire." Upon arriving at the edge of the inferno, they would encounter a "great preaching." If they listened carefully to the "commandments" they were given at that point, the Kickapoos would be empowered to pass through the fire, but if they remained recalcitrant, "then the Great Spirit would destroy everything and the world would be turned over." If they, and the world, survived the challenge of the place of fire, they would cross over water and enter a barren prairie, where "the sun will be hid from us by four black clouds." Soon thereafter, they would receive the final revelation from the Great Spirit. [15]

Kenekuk's prophecies and moral teachings had as their primary purpose the restoration and preservation of the integrity of the Kickapoo nation. While his gospel resembled Christianity in its promise of salvation of the righteous in the world to come and in its belief that the wicked would burn in hell, a close reading of the evidence available to us on the content of the Kickapoo prophet's preaching indicates that, like earlier revitalization leaders, Kenekuk offered a nativist answer to the question of why his people had suffered defeat and were afflicted by poverty and disease: Native Americans had offended the Great Spirit by embracing the vices of the white man. Like his predecessors, the Kickapoo prophet railed against alcohol and consigned to hellfire Indians "with bloated faces and swelled eyes occasioned by drunkenness." [16] Like other revitalization preachers, he warned that the Great Spirit could not tolerate witchcraft, deceit, and greed. The savior motif in Kenekuk's teachings was quite unlike the universal redeemer portrayed in the Christian gospel, for Kenekuk's deity was concerned with the worldly redemption of the Kickapoos. As Herring notes, Kenekuk taught that the Kickapoos "had wandered far from God's teachings. For this reason the Great Spirit had abandoned them." But, according to Kenekuk, "God felt lonely without and sorrowful without his beloved Kickapoos, and He now had returned to earth to redeem them." He had accordingly revealed himself through Kenekuk, the Indian Moses, and gave his chosen prophet his sacred black coat. "By wearing this black coat—God's holy garment—Kenekuk proved to all that he alone had been ordained to guide his people down the true path."[17]

In insisting on peaceful coexistence with whites, Kenekuk differed from some of the earlier prophets from whom he drew inspiration. He was eager to adopt Euro-American agricultural technology, believing that both resistance to white expansionism and rejection of white technology would be suicidal. His assessment was quite realistic. The Kickapoos by the early 1830s, according to Catlin, numbered no more than eight hundred.[18]

Even so, in the reports we have of Kenekuk's teachings there are hints that the Kickapoo prophet, like Neolin and Tenskwatawa before him, held out the hope of a supernatural restoration of many aspects of the world that had been lost. In explaining his map of the Kickapoos' journey to Superintendent of Indian Affairs George Clark at St. Louis in February 1827, Kenekuk related that the Great Spirit had assured him that once the Kickapoos had traveled through the places of fire and desolation, they would come to "a clear piece of land where you will all live happily." Moreover, in that place the people would see their "totems" again. Kenekuk used that revelation as the basis for appealing to Clark to delay once again enforcement of the Treaty of Edwardsville of 1819, which required that the Kickapoos relinquish their lands in Illinois "in exchange for a much smaller tract on the Osage river in Missouri and $3000 in goods."[19] Clark assumed, rather hopefully, that "the clear piece of land" Kenekuk spoke of might be the Osage tract, but there are hints in the prophet's speech of an apocalypse of the type prophesied many years before by Neolin. "My father, everything belongs to the Great Spirit. If he chooses to make the earth shake, or turn it over, all the skins, red and white, cannot stop it. . . . I trust to the Great Spirit."[20] The prophecy that foretold of the restoration of "totems" at the end of the journey outlined on the prophet's map certainly did not point to the eclipse of Kickapoo culture and the assimilation of white ways in a new homeland provided by whites. We do not really know just what message regarding their tribal future the Kickapoo prophet preached when whites were not present at his Sunday sermons. We do know that despite his conciliatory stance in dealing with white power, the prophet was at heart a nativist. It is not unreasonable to surmise that in his sermons he promised that adherence to the true path he revealed would empower the Kickapoos anew.

Fighting Removal

In his negotiations with various state and federal officials, Kenekuk used a variety of strategies to obstruct the implementation of the Jacksonian Indian removal program. In his meeting with Clark, he first issued a direct challenge: "My father, the Great Spirit has placed us all on this earth; he has given our nation a piece of land. Why do you want to take it away and give us so much trouble? We ought to live in peace and happiness among ourselves and with you." He promised that his people would be good neighbors, as the Great Spirit had revealed that they must "throw their tomahawks" into "the bad place," abandon vice and superstition, and live soberly and industriously. They would not make war in defense of their lands. "Some of the chiefs said the land belonged to us, the Kickapoo: but this is not what the Great Spirit told me—the lands belong to him. The Great Spirit told me that no people owned the land—that all was his, and not to forget to tell the white people that when we went into council." Kenekuk then told Clark that he could not agree to removal, because the Great Spirit had not told him to give up land. When he received such instructions from the true owner of the soil, he would comply. Meanwhile, he appealed to Clark to "take pity on us and let us remain where we are."[21]

The prophet had taken a similar tack with Indian agent Richard Graham at about the same time. Graham reported to Clark that Kenekuk had not rejected the idea of removal out of hand but rather had predicted "that God would talk to him again and he would let him know what he said." Meanwhile, Kenekuk promised to encourage other Kickapoos to agree to removal, even though he could not do so himself, not only because he had received no such instructions from the Great Spirit but because he needed to work on the moral reformation of his people. There were, Kenekuk told Graham, "many bad men yet among them." He assured the agent that "he would preach to his men and warn them from taking away or injuring the property of the white people, and if any white man struck him—to use his own expression—he would bow his head and not complain; he would stop any attempt to take revenge." The agent was deeply impressed by Kenekuk, a man of "wonderful influence" whose "eloquence, mildness and firmness of manner" convinced his people that he did indeed talk with God. [22]

Clark endeavored to persuade Kenekuk that his people would be far safer if they moved to the Osage lands, which were remote from white settlement. The prophet replied that "he feared to disobey the directions of the Great Spirit," who clearly did not want the Kickapoos to move at that time, and appealed for a year's delay. "If I do not act agreeably to His will, He will reduce us to nothing and finally destroy our nation." The superintendent was not persuaded by Kenekuk's argument that he needed more time to consult with the Great Spirit, writing that the prophet was "touched as usual by the colors of his fancy and mysteriously variegated by his divinity." But Kenekuk had implied that he needed time to prepare his people for a peaceful removal, and Clark, sympathetic to the Kickapoo leader's dilemma and also realizing that removal would be far easier to effect with Kenekuk's support than with his opposition, decided to agree to the requested postponement. Clark's decision was challenged by the Indian-baiting governor of Illinois, Ninian Edwards, who trafficked in contrived tales of Kickapoo outrages against whites and threatened to send in the state militia to deal with any act of savagery the Kickapoos might yet perpetrate. The Adams administration supported Clark. Secretary of War Peter B. Porter wrote to the Edwards to advise him on the wisdom of patience, assuring him that Kenekuk would arrange for the relocation of his band of Kickapoos to the Osage by May 1828.[23]

Kenekuk's promise to expedite removal a year hence had been hedged with references to the need to receive direction from the Great Spirit. In fact, as his biographer notes, "the Kickapoo prophet had no intention of ever taking his people west." Instead, he sought to persuade his white neighbors that the Kickapoos, now a sober, industrious, and peace-loving people, were no threat to anyone and should be allowed to remain on their lands on the Vermillion River. Kenekuk won numerous white allies to his cause, including Clark. Over the next few years the prophet continued to argue that the proper time for removal had not yet arrived, promising that he would facilitate the transfer of his people to the West when he received the proper guidance from the Great Spirit. The passage of Jackson's Indian Removal Act in 1830 intensified pressure on all of the Indian tribes remaining east of the Mississippi, but as Herring remarks, "despite the removal law, Kenekuk had successfully resisted every attempt to evict his people. Many times this master of delay had promised to leave, but he always found some last minute excuse for not complying with official orders to move. Because his followers were friendly and peaceful, moreover, the local settlers did not press the issue."[24]

Kenekuk, a master of diplomacy who knew how to tell whites what they wanted to hear, made every effort to assure his neighbors that the Kickapoos were no longer savages to be despised or feared. Preaching before a delegation of visitors from the town of Danville on July 17, 1831, he said that his followers had recently received directly from the Great Spirit "a knowledge of good and evil" not "by books" but through revelation of "His works." Thus, Kickapoos "do not shake their fists at you and abuse you, they do not quarrel with each other, they are not liars and tattlers," and they are no longer "fond of ridiculing old folks and children as they used to be." While they once strayed from the true way, "for a long time they have refrained from the bad practices of stealing and drunkenness." They believed, moreover, in universal brotherhood, knowing that the Great Spirit "loves His children, both red and white." [25] Kenekuk's white guests were profoundly impressed. Locally, among white settlers, Kenekuk was winning for his followers "a favorable reputation." [26]

But the goodwill of the whites who had settled near the Kickapoos on the Vermillion River was not sufficient. In 1832 an Illinois militia attack on a band of peaceful Sac and Fox Indians who had recrossed the Mississippi to visit their ancestral homeland ended in a rout of the militia and to renewed demands that all Indians be relocated in the West. In the so-called Black Hawk war that ensued, Kenekuk and his Kickapoos remained nonbelligerents, but Kenekuk had offered refuge to some of Black Hawk's people. Although both Winfield Scott, commander of the federal army that ultimately defeated Black Hawk, and Superintendent Clark, who was fully informed about Kenekuk's activities, both assured the people of Illinois that the prophet and his band of Kickapoos had kept their promise to remain at peace, state politicians and local newspaper publishers clamored for their expulsion. The *Vandalia Whig and Illinois Intelligencer* warned that bands of Kickapoos had been seen wandering the countryside. While they appeared to be friendly, "Indians never forget their cunning; our citizens should be cautious of trusting to their professions in whatever shape they come." [27] Illinois governor John Reynolds, angered by federal delays in securing total Indian removal, threatened to use the state militia to "exterminate all Indians who will not leave us alone." [28] Clark, assessing the political climate, advised Kenekuk that the time had come to "leave a country where you have long been looked upon with suspicion, and where you will shortly be treated as enemies." [29] With great reluctance, Kenekuk on October 24, 1832, signed the Treaty of Castor Hill, which, under the terms of the Indian Removal Act of 1830, committed the Kickapoos to leave Illinois. In the same treaty, a band of Kickapoos—sometimes referred to as the Prairie Kickapoos—who had earlier been resettled on the Osage lands in Missouri also agreed to resettlement in the West. [30]

As he had so many times in the past, Kenekuk pled for more time, saying that the Great Spirit had not yet blessed the removal enterprise. But his efforts were now unavailing, for Clark was bound by law to execute the terms of the Treaty of Castor Hill. In early 1833, Kenekuk's Kickapoos, joined by around a hundred Potawatomis who followed the prophet's new religion, crossed the Mississippi to resettle on lands in Kansas near Fort Leavenworth. The Kickapoo band from the Osage settled nearby, about a mile up the Missouri River. Relations between the two groups were far from cordial, as the Prairie Kickapoos, led by their chief, Kishko, rejected the teachings of the prophet and adhered to an older lifestyle that rejected agriculture and retained traditional, shamanistic religious practices that Kenekuk's revelations from the Great Spirit had condemned. Predictably, white visitors were partial to the prophet's band, generally praising the sobriety and industriousness of Kenekuk's followers while characterizing Kishko's people as a dirty, forlorn lot addicted to alcohol and gambling. Kishko was unhappy with the land he had been given in Kansas, as it had little game. Kenekuk's Kickapoos, by contrast, were reasonably satisfied, as the soil was rich and conducive to farming. When federal officials refused to give the Prairie Kickapoos new lands, Kishko and some of his compatriots defied orders to remain in Kansas and resettled in Texas and Mexico. [31]

Kishko's successor as leader of the Prairie Kickapoos was Pashishi, whom one missionary described as "a savage to the full extent of the term" who "paints his face black, with a little red around the eyes" and "glories in the fact that he has adopted no single article of the white man's dress." [32] It is no wonder that missionaries and government agents much preferred to deal with the black-coated and "civilized" Kickapoo prophet, particularly as Kenekuk was quite willing to assist in efforts to tame Pashishi's band, threatening at one point to use his shamanic powers to burn his rival to death if the latter did not do something to curb drunkenness among his followers. When Pashishi's people allegedly engaged in a drunken celebration of Colonel Dade's defeat at the hands of the Seminoles in 1836, Kenekuk joined with white officials in reprimanding Pashishi.[33] The Prairie Kickapoos, unable to live comfortably near Kenekuk's people, soon migrated, many to Kickapoo settlements in Mexico and Texas, some to a new village only some twenty miles distant. Although Capt. Matthew Duncan, an army officer who conducted a raid to seize Pashishi's whiskey store shortly after the so-called victory party, criticized the prophet as a "religious enthusiast" unduly intolerant of his pagan brethren, most whites regarded Kenekuk as a model Indian leader and his rival as an unregenerate savage.[34]

Kenekuk and Christian Missionaries

Without exception, those who had once been persuaded that Kenekuk would be a force for the conversion of the Kickapoos to the Christian faith concluded, sooner or later, that they had been victims of a deception. Kenekuk's relationship with both Protestant and Catholic missionaries revealed the same shrewd capacity to play on their hopes and prejudices that had characterized his earlier dealings with government officials and white settlers. In 1833 the Baptists, in response to a Kickapoo request for assistance in educating their children, sent Rev. Daniel French to Kansas. He found neither Kenekuk's congregation nor Pashishi's band interested in embracing Christian doctrine. Isaac McCoy, a prominent Baptist promoter of Indian missionary endeavors, was particularly angered by the stubbornness of Kenekuk's followers. While he had once believed that Kenekuk's teachings would provide a bridge from paganism to Christ, McCoy finally concluded that the Kickapoo prophet had led his people "from savage blindness into greater absurdity." The Baptists soon abandoned their Kickapoo mission.[35]

In the same year, a Jesuit priest, Fr. Benedict Roux, visited Kenekuk's people and reported that they were already on the road to the true faith. The Kickapoos who followed the prophet, Roux reported, "pray every day, morning, noon, and night and before meals; they sanctify Sunday as we do and spend it entirely in prayer. They do not swear nor wage war, nor lie, nor have more than one wife; they believe in Heaven, Purgatory and Hell, honor the Blessed Virgin and Saints." On a second visit, early in 1834, Kenekuk assured Father Roux that his people were eager to have the "blackrobes" tell them how to get to heaven. Roux took those words at face value, but as Kenekuk's biographer tells us, "the prophet had good reason for making a favorable impression on the priest. Kenekuk knew that the Indians' economic security would be enhanced if the federal government were to live up to its treaty commitment to provide money, farm tools, housing supplies and educational needs. Because the Kickapoos' repeated pleas for promised federal assistance had fallen on deaf ears, he decided to allow missionaries, who had greater influence over Washington bureaucrats, to proselytize among his people. Although he realized that the priests and ministers posed a threat to his authority, Kenekuk had enough confidence in his own religious powers to permit competition from outsiders."[36]

In 1835, inspired by Father Roux's report, Fr. Charles F. Van Quickenborne arrived in Kansas, determined to deliver the Kickapoos not only from their own errors but also from the Methodists, who had sent a missionary to Kenekuk's people the year before. Van Quickenborne's dealings with the prophet were rather bewildering, for Kenekuk vacillated between assertions that he himself possessed miraculous healing powers comparable to those of Jesus to a humble admission that he and his people needed religious instruction. But since both Kenekuk's band and his Prairie Kickapoo rivals expressed interest in receiving Catholic missionaries, Van Quickenborne sought and obtained federal assistance in the establishment of a mission and school in Kickapoo territory. The venture did not prosper. Although the missionary sent by the Society of Jesus, Fr. Christian Hoecken, learned the Kickapoo language quickly and was personally well liked, he found both Pashishi's people and Kenekuk's followers highly resistant to his efforts to bring them into the Catholic Church. Attempting to determine the reasons for the failure of the Kickapoo Jesuit mission, Fr. Pierre Jean De Smet, who visited the Kickapoos in 1838, blamed Kenekuk: "He calls himself the envoy of God, Christ under a new form, and invites all the nations of the earth to come and gather under his banner." De Smet, who believed that Kenekuk was "profoundly ignorant of Christian doctrines," was appalled that an unlettered "savage" had successfully sabotaged the work of showing "heathens" the true road to salvation. [37]

While Pashishi encouraged De Smet and others to believe that he and his band might one day embrace Catholicism, Kenekuk held out a comparable promise of conversion to the Methodists, who had established a mission and school in Kickapoo territory in 1834. The prophet invited Methodist missionary Jerome C. Berryman to preach at his Sunday meetings and then, along with some four hundred of his followers, accepted baptism into the Methodist Church. The missionary, believing that Kenekuk had been a Christian for a number of years, arranged for him to be licensed and salaried as a Methodist preacher. Soon the Methodist school Berryman founded was crowded with Kickapoo children. But the Methodists soon grew suspicious of Kenekuk's continuing control of his people. One Methodist visitor, after witnessing one of Kenekuk's flagellation rituals and talking with members of Kenekuk's congregation, concluded that "they seem to know little about Jesus Christ, and the way of salvation thru a Redeemer." Berryman himself was shocked to discover that Kenekuk "claimed to be the son of God come again in the flesh, and that the Father had sent him to the red people this time as he did to the white people before!" He was also deeply disturbed by the continuing belief in public whipping as the means of securing the forgiveness of sins and access to heaven. Kenekuk's followers did not understand the Christian doctrine of the Atonement, but believed that the blood drawn by Kenekuk's whippers was "expiatory in its effect; hence their willing submission to the lash." Kenekuk's apparent conversion to Methodism brought no real change in the religious practices of his people, who, after an initial period of apparent enthusiasm, withdrew most of their children from the Methodist school and avoided Methodist religious services. With some bitterness, Berryman now condemned Kenekuk as a shrewd, ambitious, and presumptuous fraud who played upon the "ignorance" and "superstition" of his flock. If men like Kenekuk were not held in check by some means, he believed, they would "in time barbarize the world."[38]

Berryman left the Kickapoo mission in 1841, and his successors were no more successful. They attributed the Kickapoos' refusal to embrace Methodism to the bad influence of the prophet, who, as Berryman's successor Nathaniel Talbot put it, "does all he can against the gospel." A visiting parson, William Patton, concurred, declaring that "Jesus Christ has no part in the religion of the prophet."[39] In 1848, Rev. Edmund Wright complained that the prophet had "persuaded scores of Indians to believe that the white man killed Jesus Christ before he had made an atonement for the Indians, and that he, Kenekuk, has been appointed to fill the deficiency." He found the prophet's pretensions deeply offensive.[40]

The Last Days of the Kickapoo Prophet
The missionaries were unable to shake the Kickapoos' faith in their prophet. A few years after Berryman's departure, the Methodists closed their mission. Kenekuk not only held onto his own followers, despite missionary opposition, but added several hundred Potawatomi converts, who were incorporated

into his community. Serving as both a religious leader and secular chief until his death from smallpox, during an epidemic in 1852, Kenekuk continued to preach sobriety, hard work, and peaceful coexistence with whites. Rejecting the traditional value system that defined male virtue in terms of prowess in warfare and success in the hunt, the prophet demanded that men labor in the fields. The Kickapoos would now live as farmers. Despite the failure of the federal government to provide support for their ventures in a timely way, Kickapoo farms in Kansas prospered. Kenekuk fended off a federal effort to eject his Potawatomi converts and finally won federal recognition for their adoption as Kickapoos.

The prophet's death stunned his followers. Many, however, believing that he would rise from the dead after three days, tried to rouse his corpse. As a result of that contact with the body of their deceased prophet, a number of them also contracted smallpox and died. [41] Although hard hit by disease and now surrounded by whites who poured into the territory in the 1850s, Kenekuk's community managed to salvage its identity, successfully resisting pressure to relocate in "Indian territory" (now Oklahoma) and gaining through negotiation a small permanent reservation in Kansas. That accomplishment, writes the prophet's biographer, "suggests that Kenekuk's religion was proof against all white men's schemes to assimilate or to dispossess the Vermillion people." [42] But both their numbers and their lands were radically diminished after Kenekuk's death.

The Kickapoo prophet defies easy classification. Viewed superficially, his teachings appear to owe more to Christian influence than to traditional Native American spirituality. The heavy emphasis on a judgmental supreme deity, the reverence for Jesus and Mary, the fear of hellfire, the rites of atonement through the shedding of blood, and an emphasis on a sober industriousness reminiscent of the Puritan work ethic all give evidence that Kenekuk was deeply affected by his exposure to Catholic and

Protestant doctrines. One is struck also by his apparent acceptance of much of the Euro-American condemnation of Indians
as lazy, dishonest, and violent and by his insistence that the
Kickapoos give up certain of their traditional behavior patterns.
But we must consider the context. Like other revitalization leaders
the world over, Kenekuk sought to identify and reform aspects
of the old culture that he held responsible for past catastrophes, but that does not mean he repudiated that culture. In
his claim of access to spirit power and in his assertions that he
could cure the sick and incinerate enemies through that power,
Kenekuk was operating as a shaman, not a priest. His teachings,
for all their obvious borrowings from Christianity, are basically
nativist in their thrust. While he called for peace with whites
and on occasion preached a gospel of universal brotherhood,
his was not a universal religion. The Great Spirit, in Kenekuk's
pronouncements as in the teachings of his prophetic forebears,
revealed the truth to Indians not in books but through an Indian
prophet. While he sometimes posed as a Christian for political
reasons, the syncretic religion Kenekuk founded essentially gave
divine sanction to efforts to preserve Indian identity. The Kickapoo
prophet was a spiritual heir of Neolin, Tenskwatawa, Handsome
Lake, and other prophets of the Great Spirit.

Conclusion

We began our story in a Delaware village on the Juniata River of Pennsylvania in 1744. In a confrontation of rival faiths, a medicine man whose name we do not know assured missionary David Brainerd that Indians had no reason to fear hellfire, as hell did not exist. One of the more striking of the prophetic innovations of the next century was the invention of an Indian hell where sinners who had offended the Creator would suffer horrendous torments after death. That innovation was a direct outgrowth of the prophets' belief in the Great Spirit's intimate involvement in the lives and destinies of his people. From Neolin through Kenekuk, the prophets of the Great Spirit promised the faithful not only a good life in the here and now, through regaining the favor of the maker of the universe, but also salvation from horrendous suffering in the life to come.

These were not familiar teachings. While their accounts of creation, of high gods, and of ever-present spirit beings varied greatly, all Native American peoples traditionally had portrayed the Creator (or creators) as remote, seldom if ever involved in daily life. Religious observances were driven by the need to avoid offending spirits and forces that could harm—and to enlist those who could benefit—both individuals and the community. While the Creator-God might well be the object of periodic (usually annual) rituals of thanksgiving and supplication, the notion of a Great Spirit watching over individuals, cataloging sins, and rendering final judgment after death was not part of Native American belief systems prior to European intrusions into the continent. Indian religious observances were about empowerment, not forgiveness. Preoccupation with individual sins against an omnipotent and omnipresent Creator and fear of hellfire were alien concepts. The Great Spirit spoken of by Native American revitalization prophets was an alien god stripped of his universalist pretensions and now enlisted in a nativist cause.

It would be easy to explain, and dismiss, the prophets' teachings about an omnipotent, omnipresent high god and about hell and a last judgment as examples of acculturation in the classic sense (as once described by anthropologists), that is, as the displacement of indigenous values and beliefs by the values and beliefs of the dominant colonizing power. But that explanation is too facile and too superficial. We are left with the following questions: Why were those ideas so attractive to the prophets and their followers? If it was simply a matter of embracing ideas from the "dominant culture" because that culture was perceived to be superior or more powerful, then why not simply convert to Christianity? Part of the answer can be found in the particular uses made of the concepts of sin, guilt, and punishment in the prophets' teachings. Their belief in divine judgment and punishment of sin in this world and the next offered a means of regaining power. Through acknowledgment of their faults, through repentance, and through fidelity to the new commandments of the Great Spirit, Indians could gain control of their lives and shape the future. They could not only enjoy the forgiveness of the Great Spirit and salvation in the world to come, but they could also regain his favor and enlist his power in their struggles with the white invader. Dreams of rebirth, of millennial expectation, permeated the thoughts of the prophets. Handsome Lake's declaration that "If all the world would repent, the earth would become as new again" blended a Christian emphasis on repentance with the belief in world renewal that underlay much of the ritual life of Native American peoples. [1] The prophets commonly held out the promise of a world renewed, a promise sometimes manifested in visions of the rolling up of the world, the disappearance of whites, and the return of game—and sometimes even the return of the ancestral dead. The dream of a world reborn through fidelity with prophetic revelations began in the forests of Pennsylvania and Ohio in the mid-eighteenth century but re-echoed throughout the continent. It would inspire the Ghost Dance and led to the tragedy at Wounded Knee on the high plains at the end of the next century.

The prophets did not agree on the place of whites in a renewed world. Handsome Lake preached racial tolerance, as did Wovoka, father of the Ghost Dance nearly a century later. Others who followed prophetic visions, including many of Wovoka's disciples on the high plains, held, with the Shawnee prophet Tenskwatawa, that whites were not the children of the Great Spirit. They would have nodded their heads in approval of a prophecy current among the Delaware in the late eighteenth century. As Moravian missionary John Heckewelder related it, the storytellers assured those who heeded their words that "when the whites shall have ceased killing the red men, and got all their land from them, the great tortoise which bears this island on his back, shall dive down into the deep and drown them all, as he once did before, a great many years ago, and that when he again rises, the Indians shall once more be put in possession of the whole country." [2] In its combination of a flood/world destruction myth, probably learned from missionaries, and the Earth Diver story common to many of the peoples of the eastern woodlands, that story illustrates the syncretic nature of much Indian prophecy. In its image of end times, of a termination of history and a rebirth of a world freed of the white man, it tells us much about the hope and desperation that inspired the prophets.

Although it was expressed in various and sometimes contradictory ways, overcoming the power of Euro-Americans was the central concern to all of the prophets. Through invoking the power of a Creator-God now concerned with the fate of his Indian children and willing, in recognition of their reformation, to endow them with power, the prophets hoped to make Indian survival possible in an increasingly forbidding world dominated by whites. They did not agree on the methods to be used to win the favor of the Great Spirit. For some, rejection of virtually all aspects of white culture, material as well as spiritual, was the essential first step. Those who, like Neolin and Tenskwatawa, lived in regions not yet completely occupied by whites made few compromises, rejecting everything from white clothing to white agricultural technology. Others, such as Handsome Lake and Kenekuk, had no illusions about the possibility of expelling whites and sought to fashion programs of accommodation and partial acculturation.

But while the Seneca prophet and the Red Sticks, to cite two extreme examples, would appear to have nothing in common, there is one theme that binds together the most diverse of the prophets. All recognized that if Native Americans were to survive spiritually and culturally as well as physically, they must find means to protect communal values from the corrosive and ultimately destructive effects of individualism and capitalism. From the late eighteenth century until the reforms of Commissioner of Indian Affairs John Collier in the mid-twentieth century, the consistent objective of white "friends of the Indians" and their Native American supporters was the elimination of communal land ownership and of the social values that mode of economic organization represented. This determination to teach Indians the value of property ownership and profit seeking was fundamental to the program of "civilization" that modern critics have described as "cultural genocide." When the earliest of the Delaware prophets warned that the Great Spirit was angry that his Indian children had become as greedy and selfish as the evil white men whose desecrating presence they tolerated on the lands made for the Creator's own children, they defined the central theme of Native American prophecy for many years to come. It is not surprising that Neolin, Tenskwatawa, and Handsome Lake, much as they differed on other matters, agreed that hell was the eternal abode of the greedy. Restoration of the world that had been lost, the prophets held, required that Native peoples embrace anew a mode of life radically incompatible with the plans of those who would transform Indians into capitalist farmers enamored of profit and individual gain.

Notes

Preface

1. No accurate count of the Native American population in 1492 or earlier or in the sixteenth, seventeenth, and eighteenth centuries is possible. Demographers differ widely in their estimates. For several very different assessments of the overall problem, see Dobyns, *Their Number Became Thinned*; Thornton, *American Indian Holocaust and Survival*; and Henige, *Numbers from Nowhere*. All authorities do agree that contact with Europeans from the early sixteenth century onward introduced epidemic diseases, which decimated Native American populations. It is not clear how extensive this process was prior to actual colonization. On the growth of the Euro-American population in the West see Frederick Jackson Turner, *The United States, 1830–1850*, 15.

2. A. F. C. Wallace, *Jefferson and the Indians*. The scholarly literature on this subject is rich and varied. Particularly useful, in addition to Wallace, are Pierce, *Savagism and Civilization*; Berkhofer, *The White Man's Indian*; and Sheehan, *Seeds of Extinction*.

Introduction

1. Kinietz and Voegelin, *Shawnese Traditions*, 56. C. C. Trowbridge, who would later serve as mayor of Detroit, assisted Cass in his ethnographic research. He kept notes on informants' responses to a series of standardized questions on Indian customs and beliefs. Those materials, including the interview with Tenskwatawa, were lost for many years but surfaced in 1939 in some family papers in the possession of Trowbridge's grandson, who made them available for publication by the Museum of Anthropology of the University of Michigan. Unfortunately, Trowbridge's notes of another interview with the Shawnee prophet, dealing with his life and with Tecumseh, have never been recovered. Trowbridge recalled that it was loaned to Thomas McKenney for use in the preparation of *The Indian Tribes of North America*, which McKenney published in collaboration with James Hall. On issues related these materials, see Schutz, "The

Study of Shawnee Myth," 28–32. It is not clear whether the idea that the world would end when the Shawnees returned from the West was original with Tenskwatawa. Jedidiah Morse reported that a similar claim was made by a Shawnee chief named Lewis Rogers. See Report to the Secretary of War, 236. But the particular emphasis on world destruction as the ultimate response to white expansionism was the prophet's.

2. Quoted in Mooney, The Ghost-Dance Religion, 696.

3. European observers in the sixteenth and seventeenth centuries had great difficulty comprehending Indian religious beliefs. They often misunderstood what they saw and what they were told. Their accounts contain both errors and inconsistencies. Some agreed with observers such as Columbus, Vespucci, and Verrazano, who reported that Native Americans had no religion. Others believed that they worshipped an evil spirit who resembled the Christian Devil. To cite a few representative examples, the sixteenth-century English travel accounts collected and published by Richard Hakluyt generally represented Indians as Satanists. In the next century, Capt. John Smith claimed, erroneously, that the Powhatans of Virginia sacrificed teenage boys to please their evil deity. Edward Winslow, writing from the Plymouth colony, was persuaded that the Algonquians had once worshipped God the Creator but now directed their prayers to the Devil. The idea that primitive peoples had once worshipped a single Creator-God but later degenerated into animism and polytheism was propounded by Andrew Lang in The Making of Religion (1895) and by Wilhelm Schmidt, S.J., in Der Ursprung der Gottesidee (1912) and numerous later works. It now has few if any scholarly adherents. The Jesuits of New France, often praised for their sagacious reports on Indian life and culture, were baffled by their religious practices. Some concluded that they served the Devil, others that they worshipped their dreams. The more knowledgeable understood that the Iroquois received messages from the spirits in those dreams and thus worshipped not the dreams themselves but the "will of God" that they revealed. The Jesuits were uncertain about the Indians' conception of a high god or creator. One report from Canada held that the Natives believed in two separate creators, the most recent of whom had restored the world after the deluge. It is clear that these accounts, the Jesuits' included, were all seriously flawed and provide only limited insights

into the real nature of traditional Native American spirituality. But it is significant that none of these early commentators described any deity even vaguely resembling the prophets' Great Spirit. For a summary of Hakluyt's reports see Cave, "Richard Hakluyt's Savages." An excellent overview of later English perceptions of Native American religious practices is found in Kupperman, *Indians and English*, 110–41. John Smith's early impressions are found in *A Map of Virginia* (1612) in Barbour, *Jamestown Voyages* 2:354, 364, 367, 372. For Edward Winslow see "Good Newes from New England" (1624) in Arber, *The Story of the Pilgrim Fathers*, 581–92. On the Jesuits of New France see Thwaites, *Jesuit Relations and Allied Documents*, 1:255–61, 288–89, 2:75, 3:75–77, 105–7, 6:157–227, 54:65–67, 55:61.

4. Underhill, *Red Man's Religion*, 3; Tedlock and Tedlock, *Teachings from the American Earth*, xvii–xviii.

5. Hultkrantz, *Religions of the American Indians*, 31. Paul Radin, "Monotheism among Native Americans," in Tedlock and Tedlock, *Teachings from the American Earth*, 119–47. See also Radin's *The Trickster*.

6. Cooper, "Northern Algonquian Supreme Being"; Hultkrantz, *Religions of the American Indians*, 15–27; Gill, *Native American Religions*, 15–38.

7. Hunter, "Delaware Nativist Revival," 47, 40.

8. Vibert, " 'The Natives Were Strong to Live,' " 204.

9. Wilson's *Magic and the Millennium* (1973) and Adas's *Prophets of Rebellion* remain the most valuable general surveys. An older study, Lanternari's *Religions of the Oppressed* (1963), although less sophisticated in analysis than Wilson's and sometimes inaccurate, is also useful. For an invaluable guide to the literature see Harold W. Turner's *Bibliography of New Religious Movements*, the second volume of which deals with North America. To place these movements in larger historical perspective see Cohn, *Chaos and the World to Come*.

10. A. F. C. Wallace, "Revitalization Movements." Wallace's essay has had enormous influence, but Wallace is not without critics. Dowd, in *A Spirited Resistance*, xix, argues that Wallace overlooked the interlinking of various eighteenth-century movements and the prophets' role in creating a pan-Indian consciousness.

11. Wilson, *Magic and the Millennium*, 1.

12. Translated in Znamenski, " 'White Faith' and 'White Czar,' " 6.

13. Weber, *Methodology of the Social Sciences*, 80.

14. Quoted in Martin, *Sacred Revolt*, x.

1. The Delaware Prophets

1. Bowden, *American Indians and Christian Missions*, 154; Sir William Johnson, "Review of the Trade and Affairs in the Northern District of America, September 22, 1767," in Alford and Carter, *Trade and Politics*, 52; Edwards, *David Brainerd*, 261–66; Pointer, " 'Poor Indians' and the 'Poor in Spirit,' " 414.

2. Edwards, *David Brainerd*, 229–30. The costume worn by the shaman probably represented the Masked Being, sometimes known as the Keeper or Master of Animals, a key figure in the Delaware pantheon.

3. Brainerd, *Life of John Brainerd*, 233–35; Dowd, *A Spirited Resistance*, 30.

4. [Benezet], *Some Observations*, 34; P. A. W. Wallace, *Conrad Weiser*, 88; Dowd, "Paths of Resistance," 286–90; White, *Middle Ground*, 281; Dowd, *A Spirited Resistance*, 29–32; Hunter, "Delaware Nativist Revival," 42.

5. Hays, "Diary and Journal of 1760," 76–77; Zeisberger, "Diaries," 24–25; Heckewelder, *History, Manners, and Customs*, 293–94; Dowd, *A Spirited Resistance*, 32–33; Hunter, "Delaware Nativist Revival," 42–43. The great buck in Wangomend's story may have been modeled after the Master of Animals.

6. M'Culloch, "Narrative," 1:273–74.

7. Champagne, *American Indian Societies*, 15–16; Newcomb, "Culture and Acculturation," 77. On the historical and cultural background, the following are of particular value: Kraft, *The Lenape*; Weslager, *The Delaware Indians*; Ives Goddard, "Delaware," in Trigger, *Handbook of North American Indians: Northeast*, 213–39. Lenape means the "people." Sometimes they are called the Leni Lenape. Lenni is often translated as "real" but more properly is a redundancy word adding emphasis, as in "we the people." Some eighteenth-century observers claimed that the Delawares had long been organized into three large tribal entities—the Unalachtegos (Turkey), a coastal nation; the Unamis (Turtle) in the adjacent interior; and the Munsis (Wolf) in the highlands—and a number of historians have followed their lead. However, as Grumet indicates, "the evidence suggests that those entities did not exist in the seventeenth century," but originated in exile communities in Pennsylvania and Ohio in the eighteenth century. Grumet, " 'We Are Not So Great Fools,' " 23. Fieldwork among the modern Delawares conducted by Jay Miller failed to confirm the existence of the Unalachtegos but did suggest

that a group once known as the Winetkoks merged with other refugee groups to form the historic Nanticokes. J. Miller, "The Unalachtigo?"

8. Champagne, American Indian Societies, 7.

9. Newcomb, "Culture and Acculturation," 85.

10. A. F. C. Wallace, "New Religions among the Delaware," 11. See also Champagne, American Indian Societies, 7, 17; Weslager, The Delaware Indians, 173–221; McConnell, A Country Between.

11. Jennings, The Ambiguous Iroquois Empire, 160–62, 204–5, 215, 245–49, 301–2; Jennings, Empire of Fortune, 29–30; Jennings, " 'Pennsylvania Indians' and the Iroquois," in Richter and Merrill, Beyond the Covenant Chain, 75–92; Fenton, The Great Law and the Longhouse, 398–516. See J. Miller, "The Delaware as Women," for a provocative discussion of the earlier history of Iroquois-Delaware relations. The relationship was not originally one of Delaware subjugation but rather one in which they played a ritual role as peacekeepers. The testimony of twentieth-century Delaware informants suggests that their acceptance of supernatural prohibitions against violence may have made them particularly vulnerable to aggressors. See J. Miller, "Kwulakan."

12. White, Middle Ground, 225; Aquila, The Iroquois Restoration, 196–97; Weslager, The Delaware Indian Westward Migration, 15; Jennings, Empire of Fortune, 266–67, 344–46; Fenton, The Great Law and the Longhouse, 414–15; A. F. C. Wallace, King of the Delawares, 56–115; Newcomb, "Culture and Acculturation," 87.

13. Bond, "The Captivity of Charles Stuart," 63.

14. For a superb modern history of the misnamed "French and Indian War" see Anderson, Crucible of War.

15. Johnson to Amherst, January 21, 1763, in M. W. Hamilton et al., Papers of Sir William Johnson, 10:621.

16. Champagne, American Indian Societies, 28. For a detailed study of Amherst's policies see Nester, "Haughty Conquerors."

17. Dowd, War under Heaven, 89, 94.

18. Dowd, War under Heaven, 94.

19. [Navarre], Journal of Pontiac's Conspiracy, 20–32.

20. Heckewelder, History, Manners, and Customs, 291–93.

21. M'Culloch, "Narrative," 1:273–76; Kenny, "Journal of James Kenny," 188; Neyon de Villiers to Jean-Jacques-Blaise D'Abbadie, December 1, 1763, in Alford and Carter, The Critical Period, 51–52. De Villiers

believed that the French were exempt from the Master of Life's condemnation.

22. Kraft, The Lenape, 162–66.
23. Dowd, A Spirited Resistance, 3.
24. Alexander, The Mythology of All Races, xxii.
25. Dankers and Sluyter, Journal, 150–51.
26. Harrington, Religion and Ceremonies of the Lenape, 23–25.
27. Kraft, The Lenape, 162–63.
28. Newcomb, "Culture and Acculturation," 59.
29. C. C. Trowbridge, "Account of Some of the Traditions, Manners, and Customs of the Lenee Lenaupaa or Delaware Indians," in Weslager, The Delaware Indians, 493.
30. Heckewelder, History, Manners and Customs, 212.
31. The most important of those public rituals was the Big House Ceremony. See J. Miller, "Old Religion among the Delaware"; J. Miller, "Structuralist Analysis." The most detailed account is Speck, A Study of the Delaware Indian Big House Ceremony, but Speck's work is somewhat flawed by his overreliance on an unreliable informant. See J. Miller, "Structuralist Analysis," 11. A valuable collection of documents and oral histories is found in Grumet, Voices from the Delaware Big House Ceremony. Other useful accounts of the Big House Ceremony may be found in Harrington, Religion and Ceremonies of the Lenape. Although some writers have maintained that this ceremony was the work of eighteenth- or early-nineteenth-century revitalization leaders, it probably originated much earlier through the consolidation of several ceremonies of considerable antiquity. Delaware folklore relating to the institution of this ceremony is varied, but it contains no hint that the prophets or their teachings played any role in its institution. See Bierhorst, Mythology of the Lenape, 39, 50–51, 66.
32. Harrington, Religion and Ceremonies of the Lenape, 18–19.
33. Lindstrom, Geographica Americae, 208.
34. Zeisberger, "History of the North American Indians," 127.
35. Lindstrom, Geographicae Americae, 208.
36. Gavalier, "The Empty Lot," 220.
37. Zeisberger, "History of the North American Indians," 53.
38. Lindstrom, Geographicae Americae, 207.
39. Zeisberger, "History of the North American Indians," 127.
40. Quotation from Tedlock and Tedlock, Teachings from the American

Earth, xviii. The literature on shamanism is extensive. Eliade's magisterial *Shamanism: Archaic Techniques of Ecstasy* (1964) provides an invaluable survey. See also Kehoe's critique of Eliade in *Shamanism and Religion*. For a comprehensive collection of recent articles on shamanism, consult Znamenski, *Shamanism*.

41. Grim, *The Shaman*, 13.

42. On Delaware Shamanism see Newcomb, "Culture and Acculturation," 69–70. Also of use are Brinton, *The Lenape and Their Legends*; Adams, *Ancient Religion of the Delaware*; and Harrington, *Religion and Ceremonies of the Lenape*. Contemporary reports of Delaware shamanic practices may be found in the writings of David Brainerd, John Heckewelder, David Zeisberger, Peter Lindstrom, and Daniel Denton cited earlier.

43. Weslager, *The Delaware Indians*, 68.

44. Kraft, *The Lenape*, 162–66.

45. Newcomb, "Culture and Acculturation," 60–61.

46. Cave, "Shawnee Prophet's Witch-Hunt," 447–51.

47. For evidence in support of the foregoing see Cave, "Indian Shamans and English Witches"; and Cave, "Shawnee Prophet's Witch-Hunt," 445–75. The *Jesuit Relations* and other French accounts describe a few instances in which Native shamans as well as French priests suspected of using supernatural power to spread disease were killed. But the only concrete instance I found of a witch hunt within a Native American village in the English colonies in the seventeenth century is a 1692 incident on Martha's Vineyard in which several Christian Indian converts threatened to lynch a traditionalist suspected of bewitching a sick man. This incident was probably the outgrowth of the influence of missionaries who insisted that all shamans were witches. See Cave, "Indian Shamans and English Witches," 253.

48. Kenny, "Journal," 34.

49. Zeisberger, *Diary*, 2:94; Zeisberger, "History of the North American Indians," 126.

50. John Brainerd to Ebenezer Pemberton, 1751, in Brainerd, *Life of John Brainerd*, 233–35; Dowd, *A Spirited Resistance*, 30.

51. Heckewelder, *History, Manners, and Customs*, 295; Cave, "Shawnee Prophet's Witch-Hunt," 451.

52. Edmunds, *Shawnee Prophet*, 42–66; Cave, "Shawnee Prophet's Witch-Hunt," 445–75.

53. Belief in the potential malevolence of shamans has persisted into

the twentieth century. One of Speck's Delaware informants declared that "some persons when endowed with shaman power, it is said, can use it against anyone when they are angry. And it is the cause of some persons' disability or the cause of persons going blind. And he may even kill with it." Speck, *Big House Ceremony*, 109. Rafert, *Miami Indians of Indiana*, 254, reports witchcraft accusations among the Miami Indians in Indiana in 1964. Fear of witchcraft is a deep-seated persuasion among Native peoples in the Southwest to this day. See Levy, Neutra, and Parker, *Hand Trembling, Frenzy Witchcraft, and Moth Madness.*

54. Loskiel quoted in Harrington, *Religion and Ceremonies of the Lenape*, 25. Loskiel's testimony was supported by both Brainerd and Zeisberger. A twentieth-century Delaware informant, Nora Thompson Dean, told anthropologist Herbert C. Kraft about Mahtantu, an evil spirit who spoiled the Creator's work by such malicious acts as adding thorns to berry bushes and creating stinging insects and poisonous reptiles. The antiquity of this belief is not clear, but it probably provided the basis for Neolin's reference to the "Evil One" cited above. But, as Kraft notes, while Mahtantu "introduced chaos and confusion" into the world, he "was not a devil in the Christian sense; the concept of the devil and hell did not exist among the Indians in prehistoric times, but were introduced by the Europeans." Kraft, *The Lenape*, 163. The evil spirit in Neolin's teachings was a Christian-style devil.

55. Edwards, *David Brainerd*, 329–30.

56. M'Culloch, "Narrative," 1:273–74.

57. Heckewelder, *History, Manners, and Customs*, 291–92.

58. M'Culloch, "Narrative," 1:273–74.

59. For a statement of this view see White, *Middle Ground*, 281.

60. M'Culloch, "Narrative," 1:273–76; Kenney, "Journal," 188. A teaching attributed to Neolin in one report from a Euro-American trader, unconfirmed—indeed, contradicted—in other sources, has erroneously been interpreted as an example of Christian influence. According to James Kenney, Neolin told his followers that they could not address the Creator directly but must pray instead to the "little god." Several scholars have identified the "little god" as Jesus Christ, but nothing in Kenny's report suggests that he Jesus was a messiah, savior, or human son of the Creator or that he underwent suffering to atone for human sins. If Kenny's report that

Neolin taught his people to pray to a "little God" is at all accurate, it is likely that we have here not a reference to Jesus but rather an allusion to the long-standing Delaware practice of appealing to a Creator—who, as we have noted was said to live in a twelfth heaven far above the earth and beyond reach of the human voice— by seeking the intercession of lesser spirits. This report may reflect either an early stage in the development of Neolin's thought or an inconsistency. In either case it probably offers us evidence of the persistence of traditionalist ideas about the Creator's relationship to the Lenapes. See Kenny, "Journal," 188.

61. White, *Middle Ground*, 283.
62. Kenny, "Journal," 188.
63. Dowd, *A Spirited Resistance*, 2.
64. Dowd argues that Neolin was not anti-French. See *War under Heaven*, 87–98. I believe that while Neolin may have been willing to collaborate with the French to win a war against the British, his overall message clearly called for the restoration of a world free of dependency on Europeans, a vision Pontiac shared.
65. White, *Middle Ground*, 269–314.
66. Steele, *Warpaths*, 246. Pontiac's role in the uprisings of 1763–64 has often been exaggerated; there was no "Conspiracy of Pontiac" but rather several regional anti-British uprisings.
67. Parmenter, "Pontiac's War," 631.
68. Croghan, "Journal, 1765," 7.
69. Dowd, *A Spirited Resistance*, 46; McConnell, *A Country Between*, 217; Parmenter, "Pontiac's War," 673; Beatty, *Journals*, 65–66.
70. E. P. Hamilton, *Adventure in the Wilderness*, 133.

2. The Shawnee Prophet

1. Zeisberger, "Diaries," 24, 188; Beatty, *Journals*, 23–35; Kenny, "Journal," 188; Dowd, *A Spirited Resistance*, 37–40.
2. Jones, *Journal of Two Visits*, 64.
3. J. M. Brown, *Captives of Abb's Valley*, 55–59.
4. O. Spencer, *Indian Captivity*, 95–96.
5. J. Spencer, "Shawnee Indians," 387.
6. The question of the location of Shawnee settlements is complex, often confusing, and quite controversial. For a succinct summary of possibilities see Clark, *The Shawnee*, 8–23. Mann, *Native Americans*,

119–27, offers an interesting analysis of evidence that suggests a southern origin for the Shawnees.

7. Charles Callender, "Shawnee," in Trigger, *Handbook of North American Indians: Northeast*, 622–47; Howard, *Shawnee*; Edmunds, *Shawnee Prophet*, 7–8; Sugden, *Blue Jacket*, 21–22. I follow Sugden's spelling of the divisional names.

8. Sugden, *Tecumseh*, 18.

9. Howard, *Shawnee*, 12–13.

10. Downes, *Council Fires*, 12.

11. Faragher, *Daniel Boone*, 83–97.

12. Sir William Johnson to the Earl of Dorchester, November 4, 1772, quoted in White, *Middle Ground*, 315.

13. Carter, *Correspondence of General Thomas Gage*, 1:152.

14. Quoted in White, *Middle Ground*, 317.

15. Gov. John Penn to Thomas Penn, September 12, 1766, quoted in Wainwright, *George Croghan*, 232.

16. Downes, *Council Fires*, 139.

17. Quoted in Sword, *Washington's Indian War*, 7.

18. Quotation from A. F. C. Wallace, *Death and Rebirth of the Seneca*, 125. On Lord Dunmore's War see Thwaites and Kellogg, *Documentary History of Dunmore's War*; Downes, *Council Fires*, 152–78; White, *Middle Ground*, 357–65.

19. Thwaites and Kellogg, *Documentary History of Dunmore's War*, 7–19.

20. A. F. C. Wallace, *Jefferson and the Indians*, 1.

21. Thwaites and Kellogg, *Documentary History of Dunmore's War*, 378.

22. White, *Middle Ground*, 350.

23. A. F. C. Wallace, *Jefferson and the Indians*, 7–8.

24. Drake, *Life of Tecumseh*, 35.

25. White, *Middle Ground*, 365.

26. Dowd, *A Spirited Resistance*, 76; Calloway, *American Revolution in Indian Country*, 167; Hurt, *The Ohio Frontier*, 68–69.

27. Calloway, *American Revolution in Indian Country*, 169.

28. Calloway, *American Revolution in Indian Country*, 171.

29. Boyd, *Papers of Thomas Jefferson*, 3:255, 276.

30. Quoted in Calloway, *American Revolution in Indian Country*, 174.

31. Calloway, *First Peoples*, 191–204; Dowd, *A Spirited Resistance*, 59–60.

32. Sugden, *Tecumseh*, 45.

33. Quoted in Sword, *President Washington's Indian War*, 6.

34. Sword, *Washington's Indian War*, 31–44; Calloway, *American Revolution in Indian Country*, 177.
35. Sword, *Washington's Indian War*, 41; Downes, *Council Fires*, 298.
36. Quoted in Sword, *Washington's Indian War*, 27.
37. Sword, *Washington's Indian War*, 73.
38. Sword, *Washington's Indian War*, 191.
39. *American State Papers*, 1:352.
40. Sword, *Washington's Indian War*, 79–191.
41. Quoted in Sugden, *Blue Jacket*, 107.
42. Quoted in Edmunds, *Shawnee Prophet*, 17.
43. Edmunds, *Shawnee Prophet*, 19.
44. Address of Arthur St. Clair to the Northwest Territorial Legislature, November 5, 1800, in W. H. Smith, *The St. Clair Papers*, 2:501–10.
45. "Message to the Legislature, August 17, 1807," in Esarey, *Messages and Letters*, 2:235–36.
46. Report of Rev. James B. Finlay, quoted in Schutz, "The Study of Shawnee Myth," 20.
47. The standard biography of Tenskwatawa is Edmunds, *Shawnee Prophet*. For an interesting suggestion concerning his relationship to later revitalization movements, see Thurman, "The Shawnee Prophet's Movement." The most detailed contemporary account of his teachings is found in a letter from Thomas Forsyth to Gen. William Clark, December 23, 1812, reprinted in Blair, *Tribes of the Upper Mississippi Valley*, 2:274–78. Also of value is a report from Shaker missionaries that is reprinted in MacLean, "Shaker Mission," and a sketch Forsyth dictated to Drake (Tecumseh Papers, microfilm, 9YY59, Draper Collection, State Historical Society of Wisconsin, Madison). The Shaker account dates from 1807 and is more sympathetic to the prophet than Forsyth's. In 1817 a Shaker spokesman informed Thomas Dean, a Quaker emissary seeking a land grant for the Brothertown Indians, that "Tecumseh and the Prophet had been much misrepresented, they and their people appeared to be a peaceable people, and that they were in his opinion Christian Indians opposed to war, and he thought it was an unguarded expression of General Harrison to one of the Potawatomis chiefs by the name of Winemack that caused the war. . . . [T]hey were well acquainted with the Prophet and believed him to be a peaceable and a good man." Dean, *Journal*, 308. The Shakers' perception of Tenskwatawa suggests that he possessed diplomatic

skills unrecognized by most writers, who contrast his presumed rude and violent temperament to his brother's more humane and moderate attitude.

48. This account is based on Tenskwatawa's 1824 description of hell. See Trowbridge, *Shawnese Traditions*, 41–42. For a similar but earlier and less-detailed version based on Tenskwatawa's conversations with the Shakers, see MacLean, "Shaker Mission."

49. Edmunds, *Shawnee Prophet*, 30–32.

50. Radin, *The Winnebago Tribe*, 70–72.

51. Thomas Forsyth to William Clark, December 23, 1812, in Blair, *Tribes of the Upper Mississippi Valley*, 2:274–78.

52. Shane interview, Tecumseh Papers, 12YY:12–13.

53. Trowbridge, *Shawnese Traditions*, 3; Edmunds, *Shawnee Prophet*, 36–37.

54. Wells to Harrison, August 2, 1807, in Esarey, *Messages and Papers*, 1:239.

55. Shane interview, Tecumseh Papers, 12YY:13.

56. Sugden, *Tecumseh*, 117.

57. Thomas Forsyth to William Clark, December 23, 1812, in Blair, *Tribes of the Upper Mississippi Valley*, 2:274–78.

58. Willig, "Prophetstown on the Wabash," 138–39. One white contemporary insisted that the prophet was dominated by his wife. See Law, *Colonial History of Vincennes*, 102.

59. Wells to Dearborn, April 23, 1808, in Carter and Bloom, *Territorial Papers*, 7:560.

60. Thomas Forsyth to William Clark, December 23, 1812, in Blair, *Tribes of the Upper Mississippi Valley*, 2:274–78.

61. Edmunds, *Shawnee Prophet*, 49; MacLean, "Shaker Mission," 224–25.

62. Tanner, *The Falcon*, 146.

63. Shane interview, Tecumseh Papers, 12:YY:4.

64. Indian agent Thomas Forsyth believed that the prophet had been influenced by Shaker missionaries who visited his village shortly before his first vision. See Forsyth's sketch of Tecumseh, Tecumseh Papers, 8YY54.

65. J. M. Ruddell to Lyman Draper, November 15, 1884, Tecumseh Papers, 8YY43.

66. Edmunds, *Shawnee Prophet*, 142.

67. Schutz, "The Study of Shawnee Myth," 108–9.

68. Schutz, "The Study of Shawnee Myth," 78–135.

69. Voegelin, "The Shawnee Female Deity," 3, 6, 8–9. It is not possible to say with certainty whether the Shawnee flood myth was indigenous or the result of Christian influences.

70. Voegelin, "The Shawnee Female Deity," 3–9.

71. Trowbridge, Shawnese Traditions, 2–32, 40–41.

72. Howard, Shawnee, 192.

73. Howard, Shawnee, 193.

74. Morse, Report to the Secretary of War, 236.

75. On Siberian shamanism see Eliade, Shamanism, 181–258.

76. Trowbridge, Shawnese Traditions, 36. Tenskwatawa was Trowbridge's informant.

77. Howard, Shawnee, 196.

78. Shane interview, Tecumseh Papers, YY12:9–10.

79. On Shawnee witchcraft see Howard, Shawnee, 145–47.

80. Willig, "Prophetstown on the Wabash," 132.

81. Voegelin, "The Shawnee Female Deity," 10, 18–19. It is not clear to what degree, if any, Tenskwatawa's exhortations against medicine bundles referred to tribal bundles believed to be gifts from the Creator. I am inclined to believe that since the overall tenor of his gospel was to stress obedience to moral precepts revealed by the Master of Life rather than reliance on access to supernatural power through such devices as sacred bundles, his failure to demand the destruction of all bundles was purely pragmatic. But one point is clear: reverence for the bundles proved far more durable than Tenskwatawa's movement.

82. Howard, Shawnee, 193–94; Voegelin and Voegelin, "Shawnee Name Groups," 630.

83. Trowbridge, Shawnese Traditions, 3–4.

84. Morris, Journal, 6.

85. Voegelin, "The Shawnee Female Deity."

86. Trowbridge, Shawnese Traditions, 43–46. Anthropologist Alanson Skinner, in fieldwork among the Menominis of Wisconsin in the early twentieth century, found that they also believed that witch bundles contained "portions of the body of the terrible Horned Hairy Snake." The origin of that belief is not clear. Skinner, Material Culture of the Menomini, 69. Another student of the Menominis reported that they were afraid of the witch bundles. It was believed that those who inherited witch bundles were obligated to kill two persons each

year through witchcraft in order to feed the bundle. Hilger, "Some Early Customs of the Menomini Indians," 56. Louise Spindler also reported that her Menomini informants "expressed great fear of the bags and desired to burn or destroy them." See Spindler, "Great Lakes: Menomini," 56. Did those ideas represent the persistence of aboriginal beliefs, or were they echoes of the anti-witchcraft teachings of revitalization prophets? While that question cannot be resolved, I am persuaded that fear of medicine bundles probably arose in response to the failures of shamans to cure diseases of European origin. The prophets—Neolin, Tenskwatawa, and others—interpreted that failure as evidence of witchcraft, believing that shamanic practices had in fact caused disease.

87. Heckewelder, *Narrative of the Missions*, 409–10.

88. Shane interview, Tecumseh Papers, 12YY:13.

89. For a thorough survey of the evidence relating to Delaware settlements in the White River region see Thurman, "The Delaware Indians," 125–35. For a more detailed account of the witchcraft controversies see Cave, "Shawnee Prophet's Witch-Hunt."

90. Gipson, *Moravian Mission*, 194–95, 346.

91. Gipson, *Moravian Mission*, 230–31.

92. Gipson, *Moravian Mission*, 333, 361–62, 402, 403, 407, 413–14, 620; Sugden, *Tecumseh*, 114; J. Miller, "The 1806 Purge."

93. J. Miller, "The 1806 Purge," 255. A comparative study of revitalization movements around the world discloses a ubiquitous belief that European colonizers used witchcraft against indigenous peoples. See Lanternari, *Religions of the Oppressed*.

94. Heckewelder, *Narrative of the Missions*, 416. Anthony Shane gave a different account of her execution, telling Drake that "They washed her for four days, calling on her each day to give up her charms and medicines, and just as she was dying, she explained that her grandchild had it, who was then hunting." Jay Miller comments on Shane's claim: "This was confusing until I discussed the text with Delaware elders, who thought that she was probably scrubbed with water mixed with wood ash or lye. Thus, she would have been both burned and washed at the same time. Since one of the major criticisms of her was that she kept a house like a white woman, a skill she learned from the Moravians, her fastidiousness was turned against her to make the punishment fit the crime." "The 1806 Purge," 256.

95. J. Miller, "The 1806 Purge," 255.

96. Gipson, Moravian Mission, 412–15; Shane interview, Tecumseh Papers, 12YY:14–15; Drake, Life of Tecumseh, 88. J. Miller, "The 1806 Purge," 254, conjectures that Coltos "was probably an outspoken critic of Beata, and as a Moravian, had probably been preaching conversion to her own relatives in opposition to the message of the apostate Beata."

97. Gipson, Moravian Mission, 413–16, 622.

98. Heckewelder, Narrative of the Missions, 411; Gipson, Moravian Mission, 190, 218, 358.

99. Gipson, Moravian Mission, 621.

100. Gipson, Moravian Mission, 407, 412–18, 420, 617–21.

101. Dunn, True Indian Stories, 67.

102. Shane interview, Tecumseh Papers, 12:YY-17–18; Drake, Life of Tecumseh, 89.

103. Gipson, Moravian Mission, 420–21.

104. Gipson, Moravian Mission, 624.

105. Thurman, "The Delaware Indians," 135–42. Thurman argues that the Big House Ceremony in particular was developed as an alternative to the new religion of the prophets. Delaware myths and legends, however, strongly suggest that the ceremony originated sometime before the mid-eighteenth century. See Bierhorst, Mythology of the Lenape, 39, 50–51, 66.

106. Deardorff, "The Religion of Handsome Lake," 101–2. See the analysis of the evidence on Delaware ritual practices in the White River region in Thurman, "The Delaware Indians," 135–42.

107. Edmunds, Shawnee Prophet, 48, interprets the response to Harrison as evidence that the Delaware villages of the White River region, although no longer engaged in witch-hunting, were still under the Shawnee prophet's influence. To the extent that they accepted his call for liberation from white influence, that is correct. But for the reasons given above, I believe that they repudiated the prophet's doctrine that the community must be purified through the killing of those whom he accused of witchcraft.

108. Sugden, Tecumseh, 125.

109. Badger, Memoir, 114, 145; Meek, "Tarhe—The Crane"; Edmunds, Shawnee Prophet, 46–47.

110. Sugden, Tecumseh, 209. For various other assessments of responsibility for the second Wyandot witch hunt, most blaming either

the prophet or Tecumseh, see Badger, Memoir, 125. Wyandots to William Hull, n.d., Lewis Cass Papers, William L. Clements Library, University of Michigan; Hull to John Johnson, September 27, 1810, in Thornbrough, Letter Book, 85; Heckewelder, History, Manners, and Customs, 297–98; Curry, "The Wyandot Chief"; Edmunds, Shawnee Prophet, 85, 97; Edmunds, Tecumseh, 127; Dowd, A Spirited Resistance, 137–38. On the Missouri witch hunt, Sugden relies on the account of Godfrey Lesieur that is found in the Tecumseh Papers, 8YY48. The absence of evidence that the prophet and Tecumseh were actively persecuting as late as 1810 supports Sugden's argument, as does the known affiliations of the victims of the second Wyandot and Missouri Shawnee witch killings.

111. Esarey, Messages and Letters, 1:182–84. A more comprehensive edition of Harrison's early papers is available on microfilm. See Douglas E. Clanin, ed., "The Papers of William Henry Harrison, 1800–1815" (microfilm, 10 reels, Indianapolis, 1999). For the reader's convenience I have cited the earlier letterpress edition where possible.

112. Shane interview, Tecumseh Papers, 12YY:20.

113. Esarey, Messages and Letters, 1:182–84.

114. Forsyth to Clark, December 25, 1812, in Blair, Tribes of the Upper Mississippi Valley, 2:278.

115. Tanner, The Falcon, 155–58, 178–79. While Tanner did not recognize the second visitor as a messenger from Tecumseh, one recent scholar states that "we have little doubt of it." Klinck, Tecumseh, 39–40.

116. Heckewelder, Narrative of the Missions, 416–17.

117. Shane interview, Tecumseh Papers, YY-12:1–40.

118. Edmunds, Tecumseh, 143–60. Bill Gilbert, in God Gave Us This Country, 223, argues that Tecumseh did nothing to discourage the witchcraft persecutions. Rev. Joseph Badger claimed that Tecumseh participated in the Wyandot witch hunt of 1810. See Memoirs, 125. But Edmunds in Tecumseh, 85, concludes that "Tecumseh opposed the killings. Although he believed that his brother had been chosen by the Master of Life, Tecumseh was repelled by the religious fanaticism apparent in many of the Prophet's followers. A practical man, the Shawnee war chief realized that the executions among the Delawares not only would alienate many of the Prophet's more moderate followers, but also would create alarm along the frontier

and cause problems with the Americans." Edmunds's assessment is consistent with the overall evidence regarding Tecumseh's temperament and behavior. Sugden, in his biography of Tecumseh, concurs.
119. Sugden, Tecumseh, 159.

3. Tenskwatawa, Tecumseh, and the Pan-Indian Movement

1. Shane interview, Tecumseh Papers, 12YY:19–20; Sugden, Tecumseh, 127–32.
2. MacLean, "Shaker Mission," 221; Andrews, "Shaker Mission," 113–20.
3. Sugden, Tecumseh, 130–31; Willig, "Prophetstown on the Wabash," 117.
4. Edmunds, Shawnee Prophet, 50; Esarey, Messages and Letters, 1:193–94.
5. Edmunds, The Potawatomis, 165.
6. Edmunds, Shawnee Prophet, 50.
7. "Talk Delivered at La Maioutinoy, entrance of Lake Michigan, by the Indian Chief Le Maigouis, or The Trout," National Archives, Record Group 107, M-222, roll 2, L-1807; Kendall, Travels, 287; William Wells to Henry Dearborn, April 2, 1808, in Carter and Bloom, Territorial Papers, 7:540; Dowd, A Spirited Resistance, 128–30, 144; Dowd, War under Heaven, 272–73; Edmunds, Shawnee Prophet, 51–52; Sugden, Tecumseh, 144–46; 157–61.
8. Edmunds, Shawnee Prophet, 54.
9. MacLean, "Shaker Mission," 215–29, quotes on 226, 228; Edmunds, Shawnee Prophet, 54–55.
10. Edmunds, Shawnee Prophet, 56–66; Sugden, Tecumseh, 159. Sugden notes that Blue Jacket, a highly acculturated Indian who owned a store, lived in a European-style house, drank heavily, and enjoyed the company of British and American military officials, was an unlikely convert to nativism. He attributes his support of the prophet to political ambition. Blue Jacket may have hoped to regain the power and prominence among the Shawnee that he lost after Fallen Timbers. Sugden, Tecumseh, 131–32.
11. William Wells to William Henry Harrison, August 20, 1807, in Esarey, Messages and Letters, 1:239–43. The British thought that the prophet might be a French agent, as he declined their offer to journey to Amherstburg in Upper Canada to confer on matters of mutual interest.

12. Sugden, *Tecumseh*, 148–50.

13. Shane interview, Tecumseh Papers, 12Y:44–67.

14. Harrison to Dearborn, September 5, 1807, in Esarey, *Messages and Letters*, 1:247–49.

15. Harrison to the Shawnees, in Esarey, *Messages and Letters*, 1:249–51.

16. Sugden, *Tecumseh*, 155.

17. Harrison to Secretary of War, July 10, 1811, in Esarey, *Messages and Letters*, 1:533.

18. Schoolcraft, *History of the Indian Tribes of the United States*, 35.

19. Shane interview, Tecumseh Papers, 12YY:28. Shane, who loathed the prophet, claimed he was a mercenary fraud who always collected money from the infirm before attempting a cure.

20. Wells to Henry Dearborn, April 20, 1808, in Carter and Bloom, *Territorial Papers*, 7:556; Wells to Dearborn, January 7 and April 2, 1808, quoted in Willig, "Prophetstown on the Wabash," 135.

21. Thomas Forsyth's Sketch of Tecumseh, Tecumseh Papers, 8YY54; R. David Edmunds, "Main Poc: Potawatomi Warrior," in Trafzer, *American Indian Prophets*, 22–23; Tanner, *The Falcon*, 122–23; Grim, *The Shaman*, 144–49; "Wabeno," in Hirschfelder and Molin, *Encyclopedia of Native American Religions*, 309.

22. Quoted in Sugden, *Tecumseh*, 5, 7.

23. The Prophet to Harrison, August 1807, June 29, 1808, August 1808, in Esarey, *Messages and Letters*, 1:251, 292, 299.

24. Bergh, *Writings of Thomas Jefferson*, 8:142–43; A. F. C. Wallace, *Jefferson and the Indians*, 311–12; Sugden, *Tecumseh*, 163.

25. John Sergeant to Rev. Dr. Marsh, March 25, 1808, in John Sergeant Letters, 1807–1624, Society for the Preservation of the Gospel, Phillips Library, Salem MA, MSS #48, box 4, folder 14, Missionary Papers. I am grateful to Rachel Wheeler for this citation.

26. Willig, "Prophetstown on the Wabash," 144.

27. Harrison to Dearborn, September 1, November 9, 1808, July 14, 1809, in Esarey, *Messages and Letters*, 1:302, 321–22, 355–56.

28. Harrison to Dearborn, May 18, 1808, in Esarey, *Messages and Letters*, 1:291; Sugden, *Tecumseh*, 168.

29. Wells to Harrison, April 8, 1809, and Harrison to Secretary of War, April 16, 1809, in Esarey, *Messages and Letters*, 1:337–38, 342; Edmunds, *Shawnee Prophet*, 76–77, 82; Willing, "Prophetstown on the Wabash," 141–42.

30. Willing, "Prophetstown on the Wabash," 146–47; Sugden, *Tecumseh*, 176–77.
31. Hull to Secretary of War, June 16, 1809, in Esarey, *Messages and Letters*, 1:348.
32. Harrison to Secretary of War, April 8, April 26, May 3, July 5, 1809, in Esarey, *Messages and Letters*, 1:340, 343, 345, 349.
33. For a typical example see Harrison to Eustis, May 15, 1810, in Esarey, *Messages and Letters*, 1:420–22.
34. Harrison to William Eustis, July 5, 1809, in Esarey, *Messages and Letters*, 1:349; Sugden, *Tecumseh*, 175–77.
35. Wells to Dearborn, April 22, 1808, in Carter and Bloom, *Territorial Papers*, 7:558–60.
36. Edmunds, *Shawnee Prophet*, 67–93, quote on 71.
37. Sugden, *Tecumseh*, 171–74.
38. Sugden, *Tecumseh*, 167–68.
39. "Journal of the Proceedings of a Treaty with the Indians at Fort Wayne and Vincennes," in Esarey, *Messages and Papers*, 1:362–83.
40. Jefferson, *Writings*, 1118.
41. Edmunds, *Shawnee Prophet*, 93.
42. Sugden, *Tecumseh*, 179–225.
43. Harrison to Secretary of War, August 22, 1810, in Esarey, *Messages and Papers*, 1:459–69.
44. Sugden, *Tecumseh*, 198–202.
45. Dawson, *Historical Narrative*, 158–59.
46. Harrison to Secretary of War, October 17, 1810, in Esarey, *Messages and Letters*, 1:480–81.
47. Annual Message, November 12, 1810, in Esarey, *Messages and Letters*, 1:487–89.
48. Esarey, *Messages and Letters*, 1:492–93.
49. Harrison to Secretary of War, December 24, 1810, in Esarey, *Messages and Letters*, 1:497.
50. Harrison to Secretary of War, August 28, 1810, in Esarey, *Messages and Letters*, 1:471.
51. Secretary of War to Harrison, July 15, 1809, in Esarey, *Messages and Letters*, 1:357.
52. See, e.g., William Patterson, a Delaware, to William Wells, April 5, 105, in Esarey, *Messages and Letters*, 1:121–23.
53. Annual Message, November 12, 1810, in Esarey, *Messages and Letters*, 1:491.

54. Sugden, *Tecumseh*, 266.

55. Harrison to Secretary of War, November 7, 1810, in Esarey, *Messages and Letters*, 1:483–84; Sugden, *Tecumseh*, 212–14.

56. Harrison to Secretary of War, October 10, 1810, in Esarey, *Messages and Letters* 1:480, 496; Sugden, *Tecumseh*, 211.

57. Sugden, *Tecumseh*, 223.

58. Harrison to Eustis, May 15, 1810, in Esarey, *Messages and Letters*, 1:420–22.

59. Keating, *Narrative*, 1:236. Keating's informant claimed that Tenskwatawa accompanied Tecumseh on his visit to the Sacs. Other sources indicate that the prophet did not leave Prophetstown but rather relied on emissaries to spread his message.

60. Black Hawk, *Life of Black Hawk*, 11.

61. Finley, *Life among the Indians*, 293.

62. Harrison to Secretary of War, June 19, 1811, in Esarey, *Messages and Letters*, 1:518.

63. Harrison to Secretary of War, July 10, 1811, in Esarey, *Messages and Letters*, 1:534.

64. Harrison to Secretary of War, June 19, 1811, in Esarey, *Messages and Letters*, 1:518.

65. Secretary of War to Harrison, July 20, 1811, in Esarey, *Messages and Letters*, 1:537.

66. Harrison to Secretary of War, August 6, 1811, in Esarey, *Messages and Letters*, 1:542–46.

67. Harrison to Secretary of War, August 7, 1811, in Esarey, *Messages and Letters*, 1:548.

68. "Message to the Legislature," August 17, 1807, in Esarey, *Messages and Letters*, 1:233–34.

69. "Message to the Legislature," November 3, 1806, in Esarey, *Messages and Letters*, 1:299–200.

70. Secretary of War to Harrison, July 20, 1811, in Esarey, *Messages and Letters*, 1:536–37.

71. Harrison to Secretary of War, August 13, 1811, in Esarey, *Messages and Letters*, 1:554.

72. Secretary of War to Harrison, August 22, 1811, in Clanin, "Harrison Papers," reel 4:735–36.

73. Secretary of War to Harrison, September 18, 1811, in Clanin, "Harrison Papers," reel 4:794–96.

74. Harrison to Secretary of War, April 23, June 6, June 19, 1811, in Esarey,

NOTES TO PAGES 116–120

Messages and Letters, 1:506–10, 512–19; Lalime to William Clark, May 26, 1811, and Harrison to Clark, June 19, 1811, in Esarey, *Messages and Letters*, 1:511, 519–21.

75. Edwards to Secretary of War, July 6, 1811, in Esarey, *Messages and Letters*, 1:530. William Clark at St. Louis concurred. See Clark to Secretary of War, July 3, 1811, in Esarey, *Messages and Letters*, 1:528–29.

76. John Johnson to editor of *Liberty Hall*, in Esarey, *Messages and Letters*, 1:559–60.

77. Harrison to Secretary of War, June 25, July 3, July 10, 1811, in Esarey, *Messages and Letters*, 1:524–28, 532–35.

78. Harrison to Secretary of War, October 28, 1811, in Esarey, *Messages and Letters*, 1:537.

79. Harrison to Secretary of War, June 25, 1811, in Esarey, *Messages and Letters*, 1:525.

80. Harrison to the Miami, Eel River, and Wea Tribes of Indians, September 11, 1811, in Esarey, *Messages and Letters*, 1:576–82.

81. Harrison to Secretary of War, August 7, August 13, September 3, September 17, September 25, October 18, October 29, November 2, 1811, in Esarey, *Messages and Letters*, 1:548–51, 554–55, 563–64, 557–75, 589–92, 599–603, 604–7; Edmunds, *Shawnee Prophet*, 99–104.

82. Harrison to Secretary of War, September 25, 1811, in Esarey, *Messages and Letters*, 1:589–92.

83. Harrison to Secretary of War, November 18, 1811, in Esarey, *Messages and Letters*, 1:618–30.

84. William Claus to Isaac Brock, June 16, 1812, in Esarey, *Messages and Letters*, 2:61–62. Claus was the deputy superintendent of Indian affairs in Upper Canada and had frequent contact with followers of the prophet.

85. Edmunds, *Shawnee Prophet*, 110–11. See also Drake, *Life of Tecumseh*, 152; Sugden, *Tecumseh*, 232; Gilbert, *God Gave Us This Country*, 270–71.

86. Most of the contemporary American sources cited in support of this reconstruction of events simply assume, without any particular evidence, that the prophet ordered the attack. The Shane interview (Tecumseh Papers, 12YY:27, 57), which is most often cited by those who do list sources, charges the prophet with responsibility for giving warriors false assurances of supernatural aid but does not

explain the exact circumstances precipitating the battle. Shane was not an eyewitness. The same statement applies to "Meeting of P. B. Whiteman and the Shawnees" (Tecumseh Papers, 5YY8). The Whiteman conference was conducted with members of Black Hoof's band, enemies of the prophet who assured Whiteman that they would kill him as soon as they had an opportunity. Another favored source must be used with even more caution. "Shabonee's Account of Tippecanoe," edited by Wesley Wicklar and published in the *Indiana Magazine of History* 21 (March 1921): 355–59, first appeared in 1864 in a book by Solon Robinson entitled *Me-Won-I-Toc*. Purportedly containing the reminiscences of an aging Potawatomi chief who fought for Tecumseh but later became pro-American (opposing Black Hawk), the account contains a number of obvious errors. Shabonee claimed to have been present at Tippecanoe, but his account of the battle for the most part reflects American propaganda and thus does nor ring true. He reports that British officers were in residence at Prophetstown and instigated the attack on Harrison, but all available evidence indicates that was not the case. He insists that Harrison harbored no aggressive designs against the prophet's community. And in a passage that must have delighted his white readers, the old chief purportedly declares that at the height of the battle "I could not lift my gun. The Great Spirit held it down. I knew then that the great white chief [Harrison] was not to be killed, and I knew that the red men were doomed." He is quoted as saying that Tippecanoe "was my last fight," when in fact the real Shabonee had fought with Tecumseh in Canada in 1812–13. His account of the prophet's role in Tippecanoe is contradictory, implying in some passages that Tenskwatawa orchestrated the attack, claiming in others that the British were in charge, and in another that the prophet lost control of the younger warriors. His claim that Tippecanoe ruined the prophet's reputation has been given a weight it does not deserve. The old chief may have been telling his white benefactors what they wanted to hear, or the account may be (at least in part) a forgery. I incline to the latter explanation. R. I. Snelling to Harrison, November 20, 1811, in Esarey, *Messages and Letters*, 1:643–46, often cited in accounts of the outbreak of the battle, contains a report from the Miami chief Little Eyes that implies but does not state explicitly that the prophet ordered the attack. Little Eyes, as we will note, related the anger of warriors who discovered that the prophet's war medicine was ineffective. A similar report is found in the journal of John Sergeant, based on a letter from Henry Aupaumut. A photocopy of the journal may be consulted at the Stockbridge Public Library, Stockbridge MA. I am grateful to Rachel Wheeler for bringing this source to my attention.

87. Elliott to Brock, January 12, 1812, in Esarey, *Messages and Letters*, 1:616–17.

88. "Speeches of the Indians at Massassinway," in Esarey, *Messages and Letters*, 2:51.

89. "Indian Speeches, 1816," Cass Papers.

90. Drake Memoranda, Tecumseh Papers, IYY:162.

91. Capt. R. I. Snelling to Harrison, November 18, 1811, in Esarey, *Messages and Letters*, 1:643–44.

92. Harrison to Secretary of War, April 15, 1812, in Esarey, *Messages and Letters*, 2:34–35.

93. Log of the Army to Tippecanoe, September 26 to November 18, in Esarey, *Messages and Letters*, 1:633–34; General Orders, December 20, 1811, in Esarey, *Messages and Letters*, 1:675–76; *Western Sun*, December 21, 1811, in Esarey, *Messages and Letters*, 1:676–77; Statement of William Brigham, in Adam Walker, *A Journal of Two Campaigns of the Fourth Regiment of U.S. Infantry in the Michigan and Indiana Territories*, in Esarey, *Messages and Letters*, 1:705; Edmunds, *Shawnee Prophet*, 114; Sugden, *Tecumseh*, 258, 236.

94. Statement of William Brigham, in Esarey, *Messages and Letters*, 1:705.

95. Harrison to Secretary of War, November 18, November 26, December 4, 1811, in Esarey, *Messages and Letters*, 1:629, 649–52, 656–58. See also Statement of William Brigham, in Esarey, *Messages and Letters*, 1:706–7.

96. Dowd, in "Thinking and Believing," 322–27, expresses some well-founded doubts about the claim that Tenskwatawa was discredited by Tippecanoe.

97. Harrison to Secretary of War, December 4, 1811, and Little Turtle to Harrison, January 25, 1812, in Esarey, *Messages and Letters*, 1:656, 2:18–19; Joseph Lalime to Benjamin Howard, February 4, 1812, and Ninian Edwards to Secretary of War, March 3, 1812, in Carter and Bloom, *Territorial Papers*, 14:536–37, 16:193–94; Sugden, *Tecumseh*, 258.

98. Acting Governor Attwater to Secretary of War, January 21, 1812, in Carter and Bloom, *Territorial Papers*, 10:376–77.

99. Harrison to Secretary of War, April 14, 1812, in Esarey, *Messages and Letters*, 2:32; *American State Papers*, 1:807.

100. William Claus to Isaac Brock, June 16, 1812, in Esarey, *Messages and Letters*, 2:61–62.

101. Drake, *Life of Tecumseh*, 157.

102. A man of mixed ancestry, half French and half Ottawa, Shane had lived among the Shawnees and was fluent in their language. From 1795 onward he made his living as an interpreter for the Americans and was closely associated with Indian agent William Wells at Fort Wayne. It must again be emphasized that those who use the account of Tecumseh's career that Shane and his wife dictated to Drake in 1822 would be well advised to consider Shane's prejudices and commitments. Despite his rather questionable claim that he understood Tecumseh, Shane was in fact an enemy. In 1813 he commanded a detachment of Shawnees that fought against Tecumseh at the Battle of the Thames. He was recommended to Drake by Richard Mentor Johnson, the man who purportedly killed Tecumseh. Tecumseh Papers, 12YY:46–47.

103. See, e.g., the account of Tecumseh's visit to the Sacs in Keating, *Narrative*, 1:236. Tecumseh's insistence on the destruction of medicine bags contributed to the failure of that visit, a failure that Black Hawk later lamented. See Black Hawk, *Life of Black Hawk*, 11. During his southern tour in 1811, many who heard Tecumseh believed that he was the prophet (see Choctaw notes, Tecumseh Papers, 4YY92). The efforts of white historians to represent Tecumseh as a pragmatic, secular war leader misrepresent the nature of his appeal. The deprecation of the prophet's religion was a major theme in nineteenth- and most twentieth-century Tecumseh literature. Writers who celebrated Tecumseh as a worthy (and dead) adversary were reluctant to admit that he believed in the prophet's message. In an entry that has influenced many later writers, Draper in his notes on Tecumseh summarized a story from the *Canadian Monthly* of December 1824 which asserted that Tecumseh "evinced little respect for the arts by which the Prophet has over-turned his unfortunate Tribe, and always spoke of him as 'his foolish brother.' " Overall, the *Monthly's* account of the movement is far from authoritative, containing many errors, including a claim that the Americans, not Indians, initiated

the fighting at Tippecanoe. On balance, there is little reason to believe that its unknown author was really privy to Tecumseh's personal remarks about the prophet. Stephen Ruddell told his son that "the Prophet exercised unbounded influence over him" and that "Tecumtha was the tool of the Prophet." Ruddell to Draper, November 15, 1884, Tecumseh Papers, 8YY:43.

104. It is not difficult to find indications that, after Tecumseh's death, whites who claimed to be knowledgeable spread the story that he and Tenskwatawa had been alienated by the events at Tippecanoe. Judge Law, for example, tells us that on returning from the South, Tecumseh "accused his brother of duplicity and cowardice, and it is said by those who knew him, never forgave him to the day of his death." *Colonial History of Vincennes*, 98. It is difficult to determine just who (other than the Shanes) the original sources of that information were. We do find in the account of Tippecanoe published in 1864 and attributed to the Potawatomi chief Shabonee the following statement: "He [Tecumseh] no longer declared that Elskatawwa was a Prophet and possessed of supernatural powers and knowledge. He called him by a most degrading epithet, that means far more than 'fool.' " Wicklar, "Shabonee's Account of Tippecanoe," 362. If that quotation was contemporary or even accurate, it would be highly significant, but we have already noted reasons for doubting the authenticity of this source. It must be borne in mind that both Stephen Ruddell, in his reminiscences to his family, and Tecumseh's contemporary friends (the British at Malden) believed that the prophet remained Tecumseh's close and trusted associate to the bitter end. If the disaffection was as great as the testimony of Shane and some others claimed some years after the fact, why was the prophet left in charge of the rebuilt Prophetstown during Tecumseh's absence in 1812? Why are there no references to his demotion in the contemporary sources?

105. Eliott to Brock, January 12, 1812, in Esarey, *Messages and Letters*, 1:616–17. While the Kickapoo account probably underestimates Indian casualties, authorities are agreed that Harrison's losses were higher. See Sugden, *Tecumseh*, 236. Sugden discounts the lower estimates and thinks that around 50 is a reasonable estimate of Indian deaths. Harrison lost 68 dead and 120 wounded. By whatever estimate we use, a large majority of the prophet's several hundred warriors left Tippecanoe unscathed.

106. Harrison to Secretary of War, December 11, 1811, in Esarey, *Messages and Letters*, 1:684–88.

107. Harrison to Secretary of War, January 29, 1812, in Esarey, *Messages and Letters*, 2:20–21.

108. Wells to Secretary of War, February 10, 1812, in Esarey, *Messages and Letters*, 2:21–22.

109. Snelling to Harrison, January 18, 1812, in Esarey, *Messages and Letters*, 2:15–17.

110. Harrison to Secretary of War, February 26, 1812, in Esarey, *Messages and Letters*, 2:27.

111. *New York Herald*, February 26, 1812.

112. Captain Starks to Col. D. Bissell, January 6, 1812, in Carter and Bloom, *Territorial Papers*, 14:506.

113. Governor Edwards to the Secretary of War, in Carter and Bloom, *Territorial Papers*, 16:193–94.

114. Forsyth to Governor Howard, June 9, 1812, in Carter and Bloom, *Territorial Papers*, 14:570–71.

115. Forsyth to Governor Edwards, July 13, 1812, in Carter and Bloom, *Territorial Papers*, 14:250.

116. Harrison to Secretary of War, December 4, 1811, and to Charles Scott, December 13, 1811, in Esarey, *Messages and Letters*, 1:658, 671.

117. Harrison to Charles Scott, December 13, 1811, and to Secretary of War, December 24, 1811, in Esarey, *Messages and Letters*, 1:666–72, 683–85.

118. For various public resolutions and testimonials celebrating Harrison's generalship, and a few statements critical of his conduct, see Esarey, *Messages and Letters*, 1:662–713. For a more extensive collection of documents bearing on this issue, consult reel 5 of Clanin, "Harrison Papers." For a good overview of the charges against Harrison, see Cleaves, *Old Tippecanoe*, 105–9.

119. Todd and Drake, *Sketches of the Civil and Military Services of William Henry Harrison*. For a typical example of the many other celebrations of Tippecanoe as one "of the brightest pages of Western History" and of Harrison as the savior of civilization in the wilderness, see Law, *Colonial History of Vincennes*, 97.

120. J. A. Green, *William Henry Harrison*, 133. Cleaves, *Old Tippecanoe*, 103–4, accepts at face value both Harrison's claims and the very questionable account of Shabonee. Webster, *Harrison's Administra-*

tion of Indiana Territory, 282, declares that Tippecanoe destroyed the prophet's influence.

121. Sugden, *Tecumseh*, 236. For a more detailed examination of this issue see Cave, "Shawnee Prophet, Tecumseh, and Tippecanoe."

122. Harrison to William Eustis, January 7, 1812, in Esarey, *Messages and Letters*, 2:4–5.

123. Secretary of War William Eustis to Harrison, January 12, 1812, in Esarey, *Messages and Letters*, 2:14.

124. Harrison to Secretary of War, February 19, 1812, in Esarey, *Messages and Letters*, 2:25; Stickney to Harrison, April 18, 1812, in Thornbrough, *Letter Book*, 105.

125. Harrison to Secretary of War, February 26, 1812, in Esarey, *Messages and Letters*, 2:26.

126. Wells to Secretary of War, March 1, 1812, in Esarey, *Messages and Letters*, 2:27.

127. Harrison to Secretary of War, March 4, 1812, in Clanin, "Harrison Papers," Reel 5:412–14.

128. Harrison to Secretary of War, April 14, 1812, in Esarey, *Messages and Letters*, 2:32–33.

129. Harrison to Secretary of War, April 15, 1812, in Esarey, *Messages and Letters*, 2:34–35.

130. Harrison to Secretary of War, April 22, 1812, in Esarey, *Messages and Letters*, 2:41.

131. Sugden, *Tecumseh*, 261.

132. Speeches of the Indians at the Massassinway, May 15, 1812, in Esarey, *Messages and Letters* 2:50–53; Harrison to Eustis, March 4, 1812, in Clanin, "Harrison Papers," reel 5:412–14.

133. Harrison to Secretary of War, June 3, 1812, in Esarey, *Messages and Letters*, 2:58–59.

134. Tecumseh to Elliott, June 8, 1812, in Esarey, *Messages and Letters*, 2:60–61.

135. A Declaration of Melessello a Sack Indian to John Johnson, July 3, 1812, in Carter and Bloom, *Territorial Papers*, 14:578–80; William Wells to Secretary of War, March 1, 1812, in Esarey, *Messages and Letters*, 2:27; Governor Edwards to Secretary of War, June 23, July 21, 1812, National Archives, M-271, frames 9415, 9431; Benjamin Stickney to William Henry Harrison, June 30, 1812, and to John Johnson, July 6, 1812, in Thornbrough, *Letter Book*, 149–52, 154–55.

136. "Narrative of the Expedition of Mr. Hunt," in Bradbury, *Travels in the Interior*, 227.

137. Sugden, *Tecumseh*, 271–74.

138. Rugley, "Savage and Statesman," 290.

139. Stickney to Governor Hull, June 20, 1812, in Thornbrough, *Letter Book*, 142–43.

140. John Johnson interview, Tecumseh Papers, 11YY9–11; Sugden, *Tecumseh*, 374.

141. Chambers to Proctor, August 12, 1811, in Esarey, *Messages and Letters*, 2:93.

142. Stickney to Secretary of War Eustis, July 19, 1812, in Thornbrough, *Letter Book*, 161–65.

143. Wells to Harrison, July 22, 1812, in Esarey, *Messages and Letters*, 2:77–78.

144. Stickney to the Secretary of War, July 19, 1812, and to Harrison, July 23, 1812, in Thornbrough, *Letter Book*, 161–65, 167–69.

145. Wells to Harrison, July 22, 1812, in Esarey, *Messages and Letters*, 2:76–78; Ninian Edwards to Secretary of War, in Carter and Bloom, *Territorial Papers* 16:244–47; Edmunds, *Shawnee Prophet*, 117–28.

146. Zachary Taylor to Harrison, September 10, 13, 1812, in Esarey, *Messages and Letters*, 2:124–28, 134.

147. Harrison to Shelby, September 18, 1812, and Harrison to Secretary of War, September 21, 24, 1812, in Esarey, *Messages and Letters*, 2:137–38, 143–47, 149–51.

148. Hopkins to Governor Shelby, November 27, 1812, in Esarey, *Messages and Letters*, 2:232.

149. Report of Auguste LaRoche and Lewis Chevalier, April 4, 1813, in Carter and Bloom, *Territorial Papers*, 14:554.

150. Harrison to the Secretary of War, February 13, 1813, in Esarey, *Messages and Letters*, 2:360.

151. Material in this paragraph and in the next two are based on Sugden, *Tecumseh's Last Stand*; Sugden, *Tecumseh*, 279–380; Edmunds, *Shawnee Prophet*, 127–64; and Sprague, "Death of Tecumseh."

152. Cass to the Secretary of War, April 24, 1816, in Carter and Bloom, *Territorial Papers*, 10:629.

153. "Journal of the Proceedings of the Commissioners Appointed to Treat with the Northwest Indians at Detroit, August 3–September 8, 1815," *American State Papers*, 2:17–25; Cass to the Secretary of

War, April 24, 1816, in Carter and Bloom, *Territorial Papers*, 10:630; Edmunds, *Shawnee Prophet*, 143–64.

154. Edmunds, *Shawnee Prophet*, 164–90.

155. Howard, *Shawnee*, 198; Radin, *The Winnebago Tribe*, 70–72.

4. The Red Sticks

1. "Sketch of Tecumseh, by Judge Jos[ephus] C. Guild," Tecumseh Papers, 8YY1.

2. The most detailed account of Tecumseh's travels through the South in 1811 is Halbert and Ball, *The Creek War*, 49–84. Halbert and Ball were fairly astute in their assessment of sources and rejected many of the more fanciful accounts. For an excellent modern assessment of the evidence see Sugden, "Early Pan-Indianism."

3. Halbert and Ball, *The Creek War*, 43–44; Sugden, *Tecumseh*, 243.

4. Quoted in Henri, *Southern Indians and Benjamin Hawkins*, 227.

5. Grant, *Letters of Benjamin Hawkins*, 1:184–85, 2:460, 594; Martin, *Sacred Revolt*, 121–23; Halbert and Ball, *The Creek War*, 75; Edmunds, *Tecumseh*, 220. On the controversy over the road, see Southerland and Brown, *The Federal Road through Georgia*.

6. Most draw upon the spurious "Tecumseh Speech" in Claiborne, *Mississippi as a Province*, 1:315–18. Sugden demonstrates that the speech is based on an account in the fanciful autobiography of a frontier settler named Samuel Dale. See Sugden, "Early Pan-Indianism," 288.

7. Remini, *Jackson and His Indian Wars*, 3; Owsley, *Struggle for the Gulf Borderlands*, 11–12, also accepts the report of Tecumseh's genocidal rant published by Claiborne. Halbert and Ball, cited earlier, effectively challenged the authenticity of that speech in 1895. See *The Creek War*, 69–70.

8. Hawkins to the Creek Chief, June 16, 1814, *American State Papers*, 1:845.

9. Hawkins to William Eustis, September 21, October 3, 1811, in Grant, *Letters of Benjamin Hawkins*, 2:591–92; Meigs to Eustis, December 4, 1811, National Archives, Record Group 107.

10. Pickett, *History of Alabama*, 2:243–44.

11. Henri, *Southern Indians and Benjamin Hawkins*, 11–12.

12. Stiggins, *Creek Indian History*, 85–86.

13. Halbert and Ball, *The Creek War*, 70–73; Edmunds, *Tecumseh*, 220.

14. Halbert asked the director of the Harvard College observatory to

assess the comet story. He reported that the comet had passed its peak by the time Tecumseh presumably flung his arm to heaven. Halbert and Ball, *The Creek War*, 122.

15. Deposition of Samuel Manac, A Warrior of the Creek Nation, August 9, 1813, in Halbert and Ball, *The Creek War*, 91.

16. Swanton, *Creek Religion and Medicine*, 487–88; Martin, *Sacred Revolt*, 22.

17. Martin, *Sacred Revolt*, 25.

18. Swanton, *Creek Religion and Medicine*, 478, 480.

19. Martin, *Sacred Revolt*, 26.

20. For a review of the evidence relating to Creek conceptions of the supreme being see Swanton, *Creek Religion and Medicine*, 480–89.

21. Adair, *Adair's History of the American Indians*, 37.

22. Swanton, *Creek Religion and Medicine*, 483, 485–86.

23. Bartram, *Travels and Other Writings*, 396; Bossu quoted in Martin, *Sacred Revolt*, 123.

24. Bartram, *Travels and Other Writings*, 390. For a detailed analysis of evidence relating to Creek shamanism see Swanton, *Creek Religion and Medicine*, 614–70. Like other Native American peoples, the Muskogees revered their shamans but also feared the abuse of shamanic power. Caleb Swan, an American army officer who visited them in 1791, related that Creek medicine men who cured their patients were amply rewarded "in skins and cattle," but "if after all the patient dies, the chance is two to one that the doctor is considered as a witch or sorcerer." Shamans deemed guilty of witchcraft, he reported, were "sometimes killed by the surviving relations." Caleb Swan, "Position and State of Manners and Arts in the Creek Nation, in 1791," in Schoolcraft, *Archives of Aboriginal Knowledge*, 5:271.

25. Swan, "Position and State of Manners and Arts," 266. See also Romans, *Concise Natural History*, 145–46.

26. Hudson, *The Southeastern Indians*, 226–29.

27. For a detailed description of Busk, see Swanton, *Creek Religion and Medicine*, 546–614.

28. Martin, *Sacred Revolt*, 34.

29. Stiggins, *Creek Indian History*, 63.

30. Swan, "Position and State of Manners and Arts," 268.

31. Martin, *Sacred Revolt*, 41.

32. Saunt, *A New Order of Things*, 14–15.

33. Crane, "The Origin of the Name of the Creek Indians," 339–42.

34. Wright, *Creeks and Seminoles*, 1–27, quote on 15. Swanton's *Early History of the Creek Indians and Their Neighbors* has been supplanted by several later studies, including Wright's, as it lacks interpretive insights, but it contains a wealth of factual information available nowhere else.

35. Braund, *Deerskins and Duffels*, 8.

36. Braund, *Deerskins and Duffels*, 4.

37. Adair, *Adair's History of the American Indians*, 285.

38. Saunt, *A New Order of Things*, 14–15.

39. Gallay, *The Indian Slave Trade*.

40. Braund, *Deerskins and Duffels*, 132.

41. Crane, *The Southern Frontier*, 260–63; Saunt, *A New Order of Things*, 26–27.

42. Braund, *Deerskins and Duffels*, 131.

43. Braund, *Deerskins and Duffels*, 118; Romans, *Concise Natural History*, 181.

44. On the economic and social transformations in Creek society, the recent monographs by Braund and Saunt are particularly valuable.

45. Quoted in Henri, *Southern Indians and Benjamin Hawkins*, 227–28.

46. Henri, *Southern Indians and Benjamin Hawkins*, 92–93.

47. Henri, *Southern Indians and Benjamin Hawkins*, 133.

48. Saunt, *A New Order of Things*, 272.

49. Grant, *Letters of Benjamin Hawkins*, 1:50, 241–42; Braund, *Deerskins and Duffels*, 72–75.

50. Braund, *Deerskins and Duffels*, 72.

51. Braund, *Deerskins and Duffels*, 178.

52. Grant, *Letters of Benjamin Hawkins*, 2:446, 476–77, 521, 524; Saunt, *A New Order of Things*, 314–15, 328–29.

53. *American State Papers*, 1:844–46.

54. Owsley, *Struggle for the Gulf Borderlands*, 14–15.

55. Quoted in Rogin, *Fathers and Children*, 24. See also *American State Papers*, 1:309; Halbert and Ball, *The Creek War*, 85–93.

56. Henri, *Southern Indians and Benjamin Hawkins*, 277–79.

57. Jackson to Creek Chiefs, September 4, 1815, in Moser et al., *Papers of Andrew Jackson*, 3:382.

58. This interpretation of the movement is developed most fully in Saunt, *A New Order of Things*, and Braund, *Deerskins and Duffels*. Braund notes that "the abandonment of traditional training in

native crafts and manufactures fractured the bind between generations of Creek men" (131) but concludes that class antagonisms
were more important as a source of the insurgency. See also Saunt,
" 'Domestick . . . Quiet being broke,' "; Waselkov and Wood, "The
Creek War of 1813–1814." Wright, *Creeks and Seminoles*, emphasizes
conflicts between Muskogean and non-Muskogean speakers. For an
interpretation that stresses intergenerational conflict see Hassig,
"Internal Conflict in the Creek War of 1813–1814."

59. McKenney and Hall, *Indian Tribes of North America*, 1:103; Halbert and
Ball, *The Creek War*, 68.

60. Cornells was a direct recipient of the prophets' wrath. Although they
were unable to carry out their threat to kill him, Red Stick raiding
parties burned his houses and killed his cattle in the early summer
of 1813. *American State Papers*, 1:845.

61. Hawkins to John Armstrong, July 20, 1813, in Grant, *Letters of
Benjamin Hawkins*, 2:647.

62. Dickens, "Archaeological Investigations at Horseshoe Bend National Park"; Fairbanks, "Excavations at Horseshoe Bend."

63. Quoted in Saunt, *A New Order of Things*, 259.

64. Saunt, *A New Order of Things*, 257.

65. Halbert and Ball, *The Creek War*, 251.

66. Manac Deposition, in Halbert and Hall, *The Creek War*, 92.

67. Stiggins, *Creek Indian History*, 91–93, 116–19, 121–22; Martin, *Sacred
Revolt*, 126–28, 134, 150, 160.

68. Stiggins, *Creek Indian History*, 134.

69. Grant, *Letters of Benjamin Hawkins*, 1:290.

70. Halbert and Ball, *The Creek War*, 93, 95–96.

71. Stiggins claims that the execution of Captain Isaacs was part of
a large-scale witch hunt. The prophets, he wrote, demanded the
execution of "those who were witches and who dealt with evil
spirits"; whenever a man was accused of sorcery, "he was seized
by a mob and tied to a tree with ropes, lighted wood was piled
around him, and set on fire." The Red Sticks' opponents, according
to Stiggins, were the objects of the witch hunts. "Many people who
were enlightened and disposed to peace were brought to this fiery
ordeal." Although this claim of extensive witch burnings cannot
be confirmed from other sources and probably reflects the writer's
bias, the evidence indicates that the prophets freely employed the

charge of witchcraft to justify their killing of political opponents during the Creek civil war. Stiggins, *Creek Indian History*, 88.

72. *American State Papers*, 1:846. Martin, in *Sacred Revolt*, 213–14, expresses doubts about the accuracy of Stiggins's account of Captain Isaacs. His status as a prophet cannot be confirmed from other sources.

73. Buchanan, *Jackson's Way*, 213. On resentment against acculturated women among the Creeks, see Saunt, " 'Domestick . . . Quiet being broke.' "

74. *American State Papers*, 1:849–50; Halbert and Ball, *The Creek War*, 94.

75. Saunt, *A New Order of Things*, 256.

76. *American State Papers*, 1:845–46.

77. On the early phases of the Creek War see Halbert and Ball, *The Creek War*, 105–265; Owsley, *Struggle for the Gulf Borderlands*, 6–60; Buchanan, *Jackson's Way*, 208–79; Heidler and Heidler, *Old Hickory's War*, 1–85.

78. Owsley, *Struggle for the Gulf Borderlands*, 17–29.

79. Stiggins, *Creek Indian History*, 98–103; Pickett, *History of Alabama*, 521–25; Halbert and Ball, *The Creek War*, 125–42.

80. Owsley, *Struggle for the Gulf Borderlands*, 32–33.

81. Halbert and Ball, *The Creek War*, 143–76; Owsley, "The Fort Mims Massacre"; Owsley, *Struggle for the Gulf Borderlands*, 32–36; Davis, " 'Remember Fort Mims.' "

82. Owsley, *Struggle for the Gulf Borderlands*, 36–39.

83. Kennedy to F. F. Claiborne, September 6, 1813, quoted in Owsley, *Struggle for the Gulf Borderlands*, 3.

84. Stiggins, *Creek Indian History*, 114–15.

85. Owsley, *Struggle for the Gulf Borderlands*, 48.

86. Owsley, *Struggle for the Gulf Borderlands*, 45–48.

87. Buchanan, *Jackson's Way*, 251–59.

88. The most thorough account of Jackson's early career is Remini, *Jackson and the Course of American Empire*.

89. Buchanan, *Jackson's Way*, 235–41, quotes on 237.

90. Wright, *Creeks and Seminoles*, 76.

91. Owsley, *Struggle for the Gulf Borderlands*, 64–69.

92. Quoted in Heidler and Heidler, *Old Hickory's War*, 19–20.

93. *American State Papers*, 1:845.

94. Stiggins, *Creek Indian History*, 136.

95. *American State Papers*, 1:85; Wright, *Creeks and Seminoles*, 177; Saunt,

A New Order of Things, 270; Heidler and Heidler, Old Hickory's War, 111–12, 145–46.

96. Wright, Creeks and Seminoles, 198–205.

97. Saunt, "Taking Account of Property"; Paredes, "Back from Disappearance."

98. Jackson to Henry Atkinson, May 15, 1819, in Moser et al., Papers of Andrew Jackson, 4:298.

99. Rogin, Fathers and Children, 72.

100. Jackson to James Monroe, November 20, 1814, in Moser et al., Papers of Andrew Jackson, 3:192.

101. Rogin, Fathers and Children, 157–59, 169–73. For correspondence between Jackson and various associates and officials that sheds light on this matter see Moser et al., Papers of Andrew Jackson, 3:72–75, 103–4, 109–11, 112–13, 377–78, 382–83, 385–86, 4:28–30, 32–33, 34–36, 36–38, 45–46, 50–51, 52–53, 63–64, 65–68, 69–70, 93–98, 280, 374, 378–79, 387–88. Jackson justified his disregard of the Treaty of Ghent by claiming that since his Indian land-cession treaty had been signed before the peace with England, the protective clause in the Ghent settlement did not apply. On this point, one historian notes: "This was, of course, a fraud since only the Indians in Jackson's army and one or two prisoners had signed the treaty [of Fort Jackson]." He adds that the administration had decided that, if the British pressed the matter by threatening the use of force to protect the Creeks, Jackson would be ordered to carry out the terms of the peace treaty and give the lands in question back to the Indians. The British made no such move. Frank L. Owsley, "Prophet of War: Josiah Francis and the Creek War," in Trafzer, American Indian Prophets, 47.

102. Heidler and Heidler, Old Hickory's War, 25.

103. Chief Tustunnugga to the Creek Council, September 18, 1815, Office of Indian Affairs, Record Group 75, Treaty File: Fort Jackson, microfilm, National Archives, Washington DC.

104. McLoughlin, Cherokees and Missionaries, 107; McLoughlin, Cherokee Ghost Dance, 111–52.

5. The Seneca Prophet

1. A. F. C. Wallace, Death and Rebirth of the Seneca, 184.

2. Graymont, The Iroquois in the American Revolution; A. F. C. Wallace, Death and Rebirth of the Seneca, 125–48.

3. Seaver, *Life of Mrs. Mary Jemison*, 58–59.
4. Stone, "Broadbent's Raid on the Seneca," 100.
5. Mann, *Iroquoian Women*, 45, 47.
6. Arthur C. Parker quoted in Mann, *Iroquoian Women*, 47.
7. There are no reliable figures on Iroquois casualties during the American Revolution. Rothenberg, "Friends Like These," 31–32, raises some serious questions about the claim, found in the writings of A. F. C. Wallace and elsewhere, that as many as half the Seneca people may have perished. Many found refuge with the British.
8. Swatzler, *A Friend among the Senecas*, 124–42; Manley, *The Treaty of Fort Stanwix*; Graymont, *The Iroquois in the American Revolution*, 272–73; Hauptman, *Conspiracy of Interests*.
9. Swatzler, *A Friend among the Senecas*, 144.
10. Fenton, *The Great Law and the Longhouse*, 104.
11. Swatzler, *A Friend among the Senecas*, 13–29.
12. A. F. C. Wallace, *Death and Rebirth of the Seneca*, 205.
13. Densmore, *Red Jacket*, 137–38.
14. Swatzler, *A Friend among the Senecas*, 104; Mann, *Iroquoian Women*, 168–70. Red Jacket's position was strongly supported by the clan mothers, whom he often served as speaker. See Rothenberg, " 'The Mothers of the Nation.' " Also of value is Rothenberg, "Friends Like These."
15. Deardorff, "The Cornplanter Grant in Warren County."
16. The Quaker missionary Halliday Jackson in 1799 noted that the Allegany Seneca hunters were still bringing in an abundance of venison. See A. F. C. Wallace, "Halliday Jackson's Journal," 134, 138, 141.
17. Swatzler, *A Friend among the Senecas*, 13. The Quakers did not make any direct effort to convert the Senecas, but they did encourage them to attend Quaker services.
18. Swatzler, *A Friend among the Senecas*, 42–46, 158–77.
19. Simmons quotations in Swatzler, *A Friend among the Senecas*, 52–53.
20. *Gaiwiio* ("good news") preachers recited events from the life of Handsome Lake and recounted his teachings at the great festivals of the Longhouse religion founded by the prophet. Edward Cornplanter's version, believed to be the most authoritative, had been passed down to him orally but was written down by him in the Seneca language in 1903. Arthur Parker published an English translation in 1913. The quotations and summary that follow are

taken from Parker, *Code of Handsome Lake*, 21–34. This text must, of course, be used with some caution, as some elements were added after the prophet's death. However, its account of Handsome Lake's visions is confirmed, for the most part, in contemporary reports from Quaker missionaries. See A. F. C. Wallace, "Halliday Jackson's Journal," 142, 332–33, 341–44; and Simmons, "Journal," June 15–October 7, 1799, 266–78. There are two earlier published versions of the *gaiwiio*. Jimmy Johnson's recitation at Tonawanda on October 2 and 3, 1845, was written down, at least in part, and translated into English. Arthur C. Parker published it in *The Life of General Ely S. Parker*, 251–61. A second version, said to come from Handsome Lake's grandson, was recorded and translated in 1848 by Ely Parker and published in Morgan, *League of the Iroquois*, 233–59. Although there are variations, these versions also confirm the essential accuracy of the more detailed Edward Cornplanter text.

21. Abortion was freely practiced among the Iroquois, and Handsome Lake's condemnation of the practice was controversial. Mann notes that the first written version of the *gaiwiio*, that of Jimmy Johnson (1845), soft-pedals and obscures Handsome Lake's teachings on the matter. She concludes that the opposition of the clan mothers was responsible, as they "were not willing to put up with such 'white talk' as a male ban on a female function." *Iroquoian Women*, 263.

22. Simmons, "Journal," June 15, 1799, 267.

23. A. F. C. Wallace, *Death and Rebirth of the Seneca*, 239.

24. Parker, *Code of Handsome Lake*, 62–80. A briefer account of this vision is found in Simmons, "Journal," August 7, 1799, 268–70. See also the summary in A. F. C. Wallace, *Death and Rebirth of the Seneca*, 242–48.

25. The identity of the chief has been a matter of some uncertainty. Edward Cornplanter believed he was Red Jacket, but Handsome Lake and Red Jacket had not quarreled at the time of this vision, so his inclusion among the damned is probably a later extrapolation. Deardorff believes Handsome Lake was referring to Farmer's Brother, who had recently been involved in a land deal that the prophet opposed. "The Religion of Handsome Lake," 150–51.

26. Throughout his prophetic career, Handsome Lake stressed the importance of the White Dog Ceremony. As described by Halliday Jackson, the dog, of pure white color, was always killed by strangulation so as not to shed blood or break bones. Its body was

decorated with red paint, white wampum, and ribbons of various colors. After being hung for a time from the statue of Tarachiwagon (son of sky woman and a creator), it was then either burned to ashes or, under exceptional circumstances, eaten. Jackson, *Sketches*, 25. Other descriptions of the ceremony varied only in some minor details. Lewis Henry Morgan, writing in 1851, refuted the notion that the dogs died to atone for the sins of the people (Halliday Jackson's interpretation). Instead, dogs, because of their fidelity, were considered excellent messengers to the Great Spirit, who was always pleased to receive them. *League of the Iroquois*, 216–17.

27. Simmons, "Journal," August 9, September 2 and 3, 1799, 271, 273–74; A. F. C. Wallace, *Death and Rebirth of the Seneca*, 247.

28. In the early nineteenth century the Quakers did not accept converts, so they made no effort to bring the Senecas into the Quaker fold. But they were less tolerant than many modern scholars realize. The missionaries hoped that the Senecas would abandon "Heathen ways" and adopt some form of Christianity. Halliday Jackson, after observing the Midwinter Ceremony at Cornplanter's village in 1799, wrote in his journal: "my heart was sorrowful because of the customs and traditions of the Heathen, for as I mused on these things I said in my head 'surely it availeth nothing your dancing and Musik and burnt offerings—your appointed Feasts and your sacrifices the Most high will not accept as an atonement for your sins." A. F. C. Wallace, "Halliday Jackson's Journal," 143.

29. Parker, *Code of Handsome Lake*, 40–48, 56; A. F. C. Wallace, *Death and Rebirth of the Seneca*, 97.

30. A. F. C. Wallace, *Death and Rebirth of the Seneca*, 250. See also Parker, *Code of Handsome Lake*, 42, 44, 47–50, 54–56, 58–59, 62.

31. One Seneca tradition holds that Handsome Lake's nephew Henry O'Bail told the prophet stories from the Christian Bible. One wonders if O'Bail may have been familiar with stories from Dante's *Divine Comedy* or from other nonbiblical portrayals of the sufferings of the damned.

32. Swatzler, *A Friend among the Senecas*, 203.

33. On witchcraft among the Iroquois, the following are particularly valuable: Shimony, *Conservatism among the Iroquois*, 262–68; Shimony, "Eastern Woodland: Iroquois of Six Nations," in Walker, *Witchcraft and Sorcery*, 141–65; A. F. C. Wallace, *Death and Rebirth of*

the Seneca, 254–62; Morgan, *League of the Iroquois*, 65–68; Swatzler, *A Friend among the Senecas*, 198–207.

34. *Jesuit Relations*, 33:217–19.

35. Swatzler, *A Friend among the Senecas*, 199. This view of witchcraft may reflect some white influences, for it is reminiscent of certain seventeenth-century European beliefs and of some later folklore.

36. Seaver, *Life of Mrs. Mary Jemison*, 184–85.

37. A. F. C. Wallace, "Halliday Jackson's Journal," 145–46; Swatzler, *A Friend among the Senecas*, 198.

38. Parker, *Code of Handsome Lake*, 49–50; A. F. C. Wallace, *Death and Rebirth of the Seneca*, 255.

39. Jackson, *Sketches*, 42; Swatzler, *A Friend among the Senecas*, 203–5; A. F. C. Wallace, *Death and Rebirth of the Seneca*, 259.

40. Jackson, *Sketches*, 24.

41. Iroquois creation stories, of which there are several versions, were translated into English by John Hewitt early in the twentieth century and are available in "Iroquoian Cosmology, Part 1," and "Iroquoian Cosmology, Part 2." The following brief summary is based on those texts. There are a number of summaries of the Iroquoian creation myths. One of the best is in Mann, *Iroquoian Women*, 32–35.

42. Some versions, however, say that Sky Woman, the grandmother, is the moon, placed in the sky by Sapling.

43. Swatzler, *A Friend among the Senecas*, 198.

44. Mann, *Iroquoian Women*, 89, 60.

45. Parker, *Code of Handsome Lake*, 39–40, 50; A. F. C. Wallace, *Death and Rebirth of the Seneca*, 252.

46. As noted earlier, in traditional Iroquois belief, if a witch were made to confess he or she would lose power. Parker relates a technique for fighting witchcraft that was still practiced in the early twentieth century. "To torture a witch, force a confession, and exact a promise of repentance, take a living bird, black in color, (a hen is now usually employed), and carry it into the woods at midnight. Here build a fire and then split open the bird's body, extract its beating heart, and hang it over a small fire to roast slowly. The witch will then exert every possible means to reach the spot and beg for the heart to be taken from the fire before it is consumed. At such a time, any promise may be extracted, for the witch is powerless. If the heart is consumed, the witch will die of a 'burnt heart.'" *Code of Handsome Lake*, 28n.

47. Parker, *Code of Handsome Lake*, 46–47; Jackson, *Civilization of the Indian Nations*, 49; A. F. C. Wallace, *Death and Rebirth of the Seneca*, 291–93; Swatzler, *A Friend among the Senecas*, 206–7. Barbara Mann argues that the stories about "death squads" were true. She dismisses the absence of mention of those incidents in the written record as reflective of a Quaker "conflict of *interest*" and concludes that later adherents to the Longhouse religion suppressed the facts about Handsome Lake's murderous activities in a bid to win support from clan mothers. *Iroquoian Women*, 321–24. I believe that whites hoping to dispossess the Iroquois as well as nativist opponents of the prophet's innovations would have had every reason to document the story of those atrocities had they occurred. The absence of references to multiple assassinations and witch killings in the contemporary records suggests that, with the exception of the two incidents that were recorded, they simply did not happen.

48. Jackson, *Civilization of the Indian Nations*, 43; A. F. C. Wallace, *Death and Rebirth of the Seneca*, 288. The idea that the Senecas could sell an agricultural surplus to whites was not realistic. The nearest market, Pittsburgh, was nearly two hundred miles away, so transport costs would eliminate any profit. Their most lucrative market proved to be for lumber, which could be floated downstream, although some funds still came from the sale of deer hides. Swatzler, *A Friend among the Senecas*, 242.

49. Parker, *Code of Handsome Lake*, 42.

50. Parker, *Code of Handsome Lake*, 38.

51. Jackson, *Civilization of the Indian Nations*, 50; Rothenberg, "Friends Like These," 142–216.

52. Deardorff, "The Religion of Handsome Lake," 94. See also Jensen, "Native American Women and Agriculture"; and J. K. Brown, "Economic Organization."

53. William Allinson quoted in Rothenberg, " 'The Mothers of the Nation,' " 77.

54. Swatzler, *A Friend among the Senecas*, 246; Rothenberg, "Friends Like These," 202–3, 215.

55. Quoted in A. F. C. Wallace, *Death and Rebirth of the Seneca*, 267–68.

56. A. F. C. Wallace, *Death and Rebirth of the Seneca*, 270–72; Jefferson to Handsome Lake, November 3, 1802, in Jefferson, *Writings*, 555–57.

57. A. F. C. Wallace, *Death and Rebirth of the Seneca*, 281; see also Parker, *Code of Handsome Lake*, 38.

58. Parker, Code of Handsome Lake, 38–39; 56. Despite the injunction that food should be free, the prophet declared that theft, even of food, was wrong. An offer to pay must be made. It would be best, he implied, if the food in question were then given free.

59. Tooker, "On the New Religion of Handsome Lake."

60. For a very perceptive account of Iroquois beliefs and practices in this area, see Mann, Iroquoian Women, 239–89.

61. Parker, Code of Handsome Lake, 31–35, 37. While Handsome Lake did not directly challenge the matrilineal clan structure, his teachings contributed to the loss of rights experienced by Iroquoian women in the nineteenth century. The constitution adopted by the Seneca nation in 1868 disenfranchised women and, by abolishing the clan basis of political life, eliminated the role of clan mothers in nominating and impeaching leaders. However, they did not lose their control of land, as the constitution required the consent of three-fourths of the clan mothers for land sales. Rothenberg, " 'Mothers of the Nation,' " 68.

62. Mann, Iroquoian Women, 22. For a thorough and perceptive analysis of misunderstandings about the status and role of Iroquois women, see also Foster, "Lost Women of the Matriarchy."

63. Mann, Iroquoian Women, 35–39. In some traditions, Adodaroh is the reincarnation of Flint and Deganawidah is the reincarnation of Sapling. Many accounts of the founding of the league omit or minimize the role played by the Jigonsaseh and the clan mothers. This, according to Mann, can be attributed in part to overreliance on traditions passed down by males and disregard of women's stories. But teachers of the Longhouse religion established by Handsome Lake are also responsible for loss of crucial parts of the tradition. Mann has relied on some women's stories recorded by Parker. For a comprehensive survey of all the material relating to the founding of the league, see Johansen and Mann, Encyclopedia of the Haudenosaunee, 265–85.

64. Some writers have claimed that the clan mothers had the sole power to appoint and remove chiefs, but that is incorrect. Their nominations required the assent of male leaders, as did their efforts to remove those who displeased them. When Iroquoian laws were codified in written form by several leaders in the late nineteenth century, there were some minor disagreements about the exact procedures to be used to appoint or remove a league chief, but all agreed that

clan mothers did not have absolute authority and could not act uni-
laterally. See Parker, *Constitution of the Five Nations*, 34–46; Fenton,
The Great Law and the Longhouse, 27–28, 212–14; Bilharz, "First among
Equals?" 102–7; Elizabeth Tooker, "Women in Iroquois Society," in
Foster, Campisi, and Mithun, *Extending the Rafters*, 109–23.

65. As Swatzler notes: "To be influential, and effective, a headman
    had to entertain freely and give gifts liberally. He depended on his
    lineage matrons to give feasts for the guests he entertained in large
    numbers. He therefore required his matron's unstinting support."
    A Friend among the Senecas, 215.

66. Mann, *Iroquoian Women*, 280.

67. Evidence of the extent of the problem of wife beating is not available,
    but it is telling that Simmons recorded two instances during his brief
    residence at Cornplanter's village. See Swatzler, *A Friend among the
    Senecas*, 207.

68. A. F. C. Wallace, *Death and Rebirth of the Seneca*, 285–87.

69. A. F. C. Wallace, *Death and Rebirth of the Seneca*, 287–89.

70. A. F. C. Wallace, *Death and Rebirth of the Seneca*, 285–96; Mann,
    Iroquoian Women, 317–19.

71. A. F. C. Wallace, *Death and Rebirth of the Seneca*, 292–94.

72. A. F. C. Wallace, *Death and Rebirth of the Seneca*, 294–96; Parker, *Code
    of Handsome Lake*, 43.

73. A. F. C. Wallace, *Death and Rebirth of the Seneca*, 308–9.

74. Deardorff, "The Religion of Handsome Lake," 102; A. F. C. Wallace,
    Death and Rebirth of the Seneca, 308.

75. Swatzler, *A Friend among the Senecas*, 158–77; A. F. C. Wallace, *Death
    and Rebirth of the Seneca*, 302.

76. Mann, *Iroquoian Women*, 324.

77. "Handsome Lake Cult," *Encyclopedia Britannica*, CD-ROM Edition,
    2003.

78. Swatzler, *A Friend among the Senecas*, 256; Rothenberg, "Friends Like
    These," 217–55.

79. Timothy Alden to Rev. Abiel Holmes, June 8, 1827, in Parker, *Notes
    on the Ancestry of Cornplanter*, 17–20.

80. Mann, *Iroquoian Women*, 315.

6. The Kickapoo Prophet

1. Catlin, *Letters and Notes*, 2:94.

2. Jackson, "Notes on Poinsett's Instructions," in Bassett, *Correspon-*

dence of Andrew Jackson, 4:59. On the various extralegal means employed by Jackson and his successor, Martin Van Buren, to force Indian removal, see Cave, "Abuse of Power."

3. Catlin, *Letters and Notes*, 2:94, 97–98.

4. Herring, *Kickapoo Prophet*, 100. This monograph remains the authoritative work on the subject.

5. Howard, "The Kenekuk Religion," 3–5. The identity of the "priest" is unknown. Herring, *Kickapoo Prophet*, 139, notes that circumstantial evidence suggests he may have been a Methodist minister.

6. Herring, *Kickapoo Prophet*, 27.

7. Herring, *Kickapoo Prophet*, 29.

8. Mooney, *The Ghost Dance Religion*, 699.

9. Garraghan, "Selected Letters from the Roux Correspondence," 92.

10. Dunbar and Allis, "Letters Concerning the Presbyterian Mission," 586.

11. Edmund Wright quoted in Herring, *Kickapoo Prophet*, 115.

12. Herring, *Kickapoo Prophet*, 31–32.

13. Murray, *Travels in North America*, 2:78–80.

14. Mooney, *The Ghost Dance Religion*, 693.

15. Mooney, *The Ghost Dance Religion*, 695.

16. Hubbard, "A Kickapoo Sermon," 473–76.

17. Herring, *Kickapoo Prophet*, 27.

18. Catlin, *Letters and Notes*, 2:97.

19. Mooney, *The Ghost Dance Religion*, 692.

20. Mooney, *The Ghost Dance Religion*, 696.

21. Mooney, *The Ghost Dance Religion*, 695–96.

22. Graham to Clark, February 22, 1827, quoted in Mooney, *The Ghost Dance Religion*, 694.

23. Mooney, *The Ghost Dance Religion*, 52–53.

24. Mooney, *The Ghost Dance Religion*, 64.

25. Hubbard, "A Kickapoo Sermon," 473–76.

26. Herring, *Kickapoo Prophet*, 66.

27. *Vandalia Whig and Illinois Intelligencer*, June 13, 1832, quoted in Herring, *Kickapoo Prophet*, 71.

28. Herring, *Kickapoo Prophet*, 69.

29. Clark to Kenekuk, August 31, 1832, quoted in Herring, *Kickapoo Prophet*, 72.

30. Herring, *Kickapoo Prophet*, 73.

31. Herring, *Kickapoo Prophet*, 77–90.

32. Quoted in Herring, *Kickapoo Prophet*, 84, 33.

33. Quoted in Herring, *Kickapoo Prophet*, 84.

34. Herring, *Kickapoo Prophet*, 81–86.

35. McCoy, *History of Baptist Indian Missions*, 456–57.

36. Herring, *Kickapoo Prophet*, 99.

37. Herring, *Kickapoo Prophet*, 98–102.

38. Berryman, "A Circuit-Rider's Frontier Experiences," 216–17.

39. Quoted in Herring, *Kickapoo Prophet*, 114.

40. Quoted in Herring, *Kickapoo Prophet*, 115.

41. Mooney, *The Ghost Dance Religion*, 700.

42. Herring, *Kickapoo Prophet*, 125–31.

Conclusion

1. Parker, *Code of Handsome Lake*, 43.

2. Heckewelder, *History, Manners, and Customs*, 345.

Bibliography

Primary Sources: Manuscripts
Lewis Cass Papers. William L. Clements Library, the University of Michigan.
"The Papers of William Henry Harrison, 1800–1815." Ed. Douglas E. Clanin. Microfilm, 10 reels. Indianapolis: Indiana State Historical Society, 1999.
Tecumseh Papers. In the Draper Collection. Microfilm. State Historical Society of Wisconsin, Madison.
United States: National Archives, Record Group 75: Bureau of Indian Affairs. From these materials, the following microfilm editions are available: M-271: Letters Received by the Secretary of War Relating to Indian Affairs; M-15: Letters Sent by the Secretary of War Relating to Indian Affairs.
United States: National Archives, Record Group 107. From this collection of materials relating to the War Department, the following microfilm editions are available: M-221: Letters Received by the Secretary of War, Registered Series; M-222: Letters Received by the Secretary of War, Unregistered Series.

Primary Source: Printed
Adair, John. *Adair's History of the American Indians.* Ed. Samuel Cole Williams. 1775. New York: Promontory Press, 1973.
Adams, John Quincy. *Memoirs of John Quincy Adams,Comprising Portions of His Diary from 1795 to 1848.* Ed. Charles Francis Adams. 12 vols. 1874. Freeport NY: Books for Libraries Press, 1969.
Alford, Clarence W., and Clarence E. Carter, eds. *The Critical Period, 1763–1765.* Springfield: Illinois State Historical Library, 1915.
———. *Trade and Politics, 1767–1769.* Springfield: Illinois State Historical Library, 1921.
American State Papers: Indian Affairs. 2 vols. Washington DC: Gales & Seton, 1832.
Arber, Edward, ed. *The Story of the Pilgrim Fathers.* 1895. New York: Kraus Reprints, 1969.

Badger, Joseph. *A Memoir of Rev. Joseph Badger.* Hudson OH: Sawyer, McGrath, 1851.

Barbour, Philip, ed. *The Jamestown Voyages under the First Charter.* 2 vols. London: Cambridge University Press, 1969.

Bartram, William. *Travels and Other Writings.* New York: Library of America, 1995.

Bassett, John Spencer, ed. *Correspondence of Andrew Jackson.* 7 vols. Washington DC: Carnegie Institution, 1926–35.

Beatty, Charles. *Journals of Charles Beatty, 1762–1769.* Ed. Guy Soulliard Klett. University Park: Pennsylvania State University Press, 1963.

[Benezet, Anthony]. *Some Observations on the Situation, Disposition, and Character of the Indian Nations of This Continent.* Philadelphia: Joseph Crukshank, 1784.

Bergh, Albert E., ed. *The Writings of Thomas Jefferson.* 20 vols. Washington DC: Thomas Jefferson Memorial Association, 1903–5.

Berryman, Jerome C. "A Circuit-Rider's Frontier Experiences." *Collections of the Kansas Historical Society* 16 (1923–25): 177–226.

Black Hawk. *Black Hawk: An Autobiography.* Ed. Donald Jackson. Champagne: University of Illinois Press, 1990.

———. *Life of Black Hawk.* 1834. New York: Dover, 1994.

Blair, Emma H., ed. *Tribes of the Upper Mississippi Valley and Regions of the Great Lakes.* 2 vols. Cleveland: Arthur H. Clark, 1912.

Bond, Beverley W., Jr., ed. "The Captivity of Charles Stuart." *Mississippi Valley Historical Review* 13 (1926): 58–81.

Boyd, Julian P., ed. *The Papers of Thomas Jefferson.* 30 vols. Princeton: Princeton University Press, 1950–.

Bradbury, John. *Travels in the Interior of America in the Years 1809, 1810 and 1811.* 1819. Lincoln: University of Nebraska Press, 1986.

Brown, James Moore. *The Captives of Abb's Valley.* 1853. New York: Garland, 1978.

Carter, Clarence E., ed. *Correspondence of General Thomas Gage with the Secretaries of State, 1763–75.* 2 vols. New Haven: Yale University Press, 1931.

Carter, Clarence E., and John Porter Bloom, eds. *Territorial Papers of the United States.* 27 vols. Washington DC: Government Printing Office, 1934–60.

Catlin, George. *Letters and Notes on the Manners, Customs and Conditions of North American Indians.* 2 vols. 1844. New York: Dover, 1973.

Croghan, George. "Journal, 1765." In *The New Regime, 1765–1767,* ed.

Clarence W. Alvord, 1–69. Springfield: Illinois State Historical Library, 1915.

Dankers, Jasper, and Peter Sluyter. *Journal of a Voyage to New York and a Tour of Several of the American Colonies in 1679–80.* New York: Long Island Historical Society, 1867.

Dean, John Camdee, ed. *The Journal of Thomas Dean: A Voyage to Indiana in 1817.* Indianapolis: Indiana State Historical Society, 1918.

Denton, Daniel. *A Brief Description of New York Formerly Called New Netherlands.* London: John Hancock and William Bradley, 1670.

Dunbar, John, and Samuel Allis. "Letters Concerning the Presbyterian Mission in the Pawnee Country, Near Bellevue, Neb., 1831–1849." *Collections of the Kansas State Historical Society* 14 (1918): 570–784.

Edwards, Jonathan. *The Life of David Brainerd.* Ed. Norman Petit. New Haven: Yale University Press, 1985.

Esarey, Logan, ed. *Messages and Letters of William Henry Harrison.* 2 vols. Indianapolis: Indiana State Historical Society, 1922.

Finley, James B. *Life among the Indians, or, Personal Reminiscences and Historical Incidents Illustrative of Indian Life and Character.* Cincinnati: Methodist Book Concern, 1859.

Garraghan, Gilbert J. "Selected Letters from the Roux Correspondence." *Catholic Historical Review* 4 (1918): 84–112.

Gipson, Lawrence Henry, ed. *The Moravian Mission on the White River: Diaries and Letters, May 5, 1779 to November 12, 1806.* Indianapolis: Indiana State Historical Society, 1938.

Grant, C. L. *Letters, Journals, and Writings of Benjamin Hawkins.* 2 vols. Savannah: Beehive Press, 1980.

Hamilton, Edward P., ed. *Adventure in the Wilderness: The American Journals of Louis Antoine de Bougainville, 1769–60.* Norman: University of Oklahoma Press, 1964.

Hamilton, Milton W., et al., eds. *The Papers of Sir William Johnson.* 13 vols. Albany: University of the State of New York, 1921–62.

Hays, John. "Diary and Journal of 1760." *Pennsylvania Archaeologist* 24 (1954): 63–84.

Heckewelder, John. *History, Manners, and Customs of the Indian Nations Who Once Occupied Pennsylvania and the Neighboring States.* 1818. Salem NH: Ayer, 1991.

———. *A Narrative of the Missions of the United Brethren among the Delaware and Mohegan Indians, from Its Commencement, in the Year 1704, to the Close of the Year 1808.* 1820. New York: Arno Press, 1971.

Hewitt, John. "Iroquoian Cosmology, Part 1." *Twenty First Annual Report of the Bureau of American Ethnology, 1899–1900,* 127–339. Washington DC: Government Printing Office, 1903.

———. "Iroquoian Cosmology, Part 2." *Forty-third Annual Report of the Bureau of American Ethnology, 1925–1926,* 453–819. Washington DC: Government Printing Office, 1928.

Hubbard, Gurdon S. "A Kickapoo Sermon." *Illinois Monthly Magazine,* October 1831, 473–76.

Jackson, Halliday. *Civilization of the Indian Nations.* Philadelphia: Marcus T. C. Gould, 1830.

———. *Sketches on the Manners, Customs, Religion, and Government of the Seneca Indians in 1800.* Philadelphia: Marcus T. C. Gould, 1830.

Jefferson, Thomas. *Writings of Thomas Jefferson.* Ed. Merrill D. Peterson. New York: Library of America, 1984.

Jones, David. *A Journal of Two Visits Made to Some Nations of Indians on the West Side of the River Ohio in the Years 1772 and 1773.* Burlington NJ: Isaac Collins, 1774.

Keating, William H. *Narrative of an Expedition to the Source of St. Peter's River.* 2 vols. London: C. B. Whitaker, 1825.

Kendall, Edward Augustus. *Travels through the Northern Part of the United States in the Years 1807 and 1808.* New York: I. Riley, 1809.

Kenny, James. "Journal of James Kenny, 1761–1763." Ed. John Jordan. *Pennsylvania Magazine of History and Biography* 31 (1913): 152–201.

Kinietz, Vernon, and Erminie Voegelin. *Shawnese Traditions: C. C. Trowbridge's Account.* Ann Arbor: University of Michigan Press, 1939.

Klinck, Carl F., ed. *Tecumseh: Fact and Fiction in Early Records,* Englewood Cliffs NJ: Prentice Hall, 1961.

Law, John. *The Colonial History of Vincennes under the French, British, and American Governments.* Vincennes: Harvey, Mason, 1858.

Lindstrom, Peter. *Geographica Americae with an Account of the Delaware Indians.* Trans. Amadeus Johnson. 1656. Philadelphia: Swedish Colonial Society, 1925.

Loskiel, George Henry. *History of the Mission of the United Brethren among the Indians of North America.* London: Brethren's Society for the Furtherance of the Gospel, 1794.

MacLean, J. P. "Shaker Mission to the Shawnee Indians." *Ohio Archaeological and Historical Society Publications* 11 (1903): 216–29.

McCoy, Isaac. *History of the Baptist Indian Missions.* New York: H. S. Rayor, 1840.

M'Culloch, John. "A Narrative of the Captivity of John M'Culloch, Esq." In *Archibald Loudon, A Selection of Some of the Most Interesting Narratives of Outrages Committed by the Indians in Their Wars with the White People*, 1:268–303. Carlisle PA: A. Loudon, 1808.

Morris, Thomas. *The Journal of Captain Thomas Morris from Miscellanies in Prose and Verse*. Ann Arbor: University Microfilms, 1966.

Morse, Jedidiah. *A Report to the Secretary of War of the United States on Indian Affairs*. 1822. New York: A. M. Kelley, 1970.

Moser, Harold D., et al., eds. *The Papers of Andrew Jackson*. 15 vols. Knoxville: University of Tennessee Press, 1980–.

Murray, Charles Augustus. *Travels in North America during the Years 1834, 1835, and 1836*. 2 vols. London: Richard Bentley, 1839.

[Navarre, Robert]. *Journal of Pontiac's Conspiracy*. Trans. R. Clyde Ford. Detroit: Speaker-Hines, 1912.

Parker, Arthur C. *The Code of Handsome Lake: The Seneca Prophet*. In *Parker on the Iroquois*, ed. William N. Fenton. Syracuse: Syracuse University Press, 1958.

Pilkington, Walter. *The Journal of Samuel Kirkland*. Clinton NY: Hamilton College, 1980.

Romans, Bernard. *A Concise Natural History of East and West Florida*. Ed. Kathyrn E. Holland Braund. 1775. Tuscaloosa: University of Alabama Press, 1999.

Schoolcraft, Henry R. *Archives of Aboriginal Knowledge Containing All the Original Papers Laid before Congress Respecting the History, Antiquities, Language, Ethnology, Pictography, Rites, Superstitions, and Mythology of the Indian Tribes of the United States*. 6 vols. Philadelphia: Lippincott, 1868.

Seaver, James E. *A Narrative of the Life of Mrs. Mary Jemison*. 1823. Syracuse: Syracuse University Press, 1990.

Simmons, Henry. "Journal." In John Swatzler, *A Friend among the Seneca: The Quaker Mission to Cornplanter's People*, 257–78. Mechanicsburg PA: Stackpole, 2000.

Smith, William Henry, ed. *The St. Clair Papers*. 2 vols. 1882. Freeport NY: Books for Libraries Press, 1970.

Snyderman, George S. "Halliday Jackson's Journal of a Visit Paid to the Indians of New York." *Proceedings of the American Philosophical Society* 101 (1957): 565–88.

Spencer, Oliver. *Indian Captivity: A True Narrative of the Capture of Rev. O. M.*

Spencer by the Indians in the Neighborhood of Cincinnati. New York: B. Waugh & C. T. Mason, 1835.

Stiggins, George. Creek Indian History: A Historical Narrative of the Genealogy, Traditions, and Downfall of the Ispocaga or Creek Indian Tribe of Indians. Ed. Virginia Pounds Brown. Birmingham: Birmingham Public Library Press, 1989.

Tanner, John. The Falcon: A Narrative of the Captivity and Adventures of John Tanner. 1830. New York: Penguin Books, 1994.

Thornbrough, Gail, ed. Letter Book of the Indian Agency at Fort Wayne 1809–1815. Indianapolis: Indiana State Historical Society, 1961.

Thwaites, Reuben Gold. The Jesuit Relations and Allied Documents. 73 vols. Cleveland: Burrows, Brown Bros., 1896–1901.

Thwaites, Reuben Gold, and Louise P. Kellogg, eds. Documentary History of Dunmore's War. Madison: Wisconsin Historical Society, 1908.

Wallace, Anthony F. C., ed. "Halliday Jackson's Journal to the Seneca Indians, 1798–1800." Pennsylvania History 19 (1952): 117–47, 325–49.

Wallace, Paul A. W., ed. Thirty Thousand Miles with John Heckewelder. Philadelphia: University of Pennsylvania Press, 1958.

Wicklar, Wesley, ed. "Shabonee's Account of Tippecanoe." Indiana Magazine of History 21 (March 1921): 355–59.

Zeisberger, David. "David Zeisberger's History of the North American Indians." Ed. Archer Butler Hulbert and William Nathaniel Schwarze. Ohio Archaeological and Historical Quarterly 19 (1910): 1–189.

———. "The Diaries of David Zeisberger Relating to the First Mission in the Ohio Basin." Ed. Archer Butler Hurlbut and William Nathaniel Schwarze. Ohio Archaeological and Historical Quarterly 21 (1921): 8–115.

———. Diary of David Zeisberger: A Moravian Missionary among the Indians of Ohio. Ed. Eugene Bliss. 2 vols. Cincinnati: M. Clarke, 1885.

Secondary Sources

Adams, Richard C. The Ancient Religion of the Delaware Indians and Observations and Reflections. Washington DC: Law, 1904.

Adas, Michael. Prophets of Rebellion: Millenarian Protest Movements against the European Colonial Order. Cambridge: Cambridge University Press, 1979.

Alexander, Hartley B. The Mythology of All Races: North America. Boston: Marshall Jones, 1916.

Anderson, Fred. *Crucible of War: The Seven Years' War and the Fate of Empire in British North America*. New York: Knopf, 2000.

Andrews, Edward Demming. "The Shaker Mission of the Shawnee Indians." *Winterthur Portfolio* 7 (1972): 113–28.

Aquila, Richard. *The Iroquois Restoration: Iroquois Diplomacy on the Colonial Frontier, 1701–1754*. 1984. Lincoln: University of Nebraska Press, 1997.

Axtell, James. *Beyond 1492: Encounters in North America*. New York: Oxford University Press, 1992.

———. *The European and the Indian: Essays in the Ethnohistory of Colonial North America*. New York: Oxford University Press, 1981.

———. *The Invasion Within: The Contest of Cultures in Colonial North America*. New York: Oxford University Press, 1985.

———. *Natives and Newcomers: The Cultural Origins of North America*. New York: Oxford University Press, 2009.

Barber, Bernard. "Acculturation and Messianic Movements." *American Sociological Review* 6 (1941): 663–69.

Barton, Lois. *A Quaker Promise Kept: Philadelphia Friends Work with Allegany Senecas, 1795–1960*. Eugene OR: Spencer Butte Press, c. 1990.

Beauchamp, William M. "The New Religion of the Iroquois." *Journal of American Folklore* 9 (1896): 269–77.

Benn, Carl. *The Iroquois in the War of 1812*. Toronto: Toronto University Press, 1998.

Berkhofer, Robert F., Jr. "Faith and Factionalism among the Seneca: Theory and Enthnohistory." *Ethnohistory* 12 (1965): 99–112.

———. *Salvation and the Savage: An Analysis of Protestant Missions and American Indian Response, 1787–1862*. Lexington: University of Kentucky Press, 1965.

———. *The White Man's Indian: Images of the American Indian from Columbus to the Present*. New York: Knopf, 1978.

Bierhorst, John. *Mythology of the Lenape: Guide and Texts*. Tucson: University of Arizona Press, 1995.

Bilharz, Joy. "First among Equals? The Changing Status of Seneca Women." In *Women and Power in Native North America*, ed. Laura F. Klein and Killian A. Ackerman, 102–12. Norman: University of Oklahoma Press, 1995.

Blau, Harold. "The Iroquois White Dog Sacrifice: Its Evolution and Symbolism." *Ethnohistory* 11 (1964): 97–119.

Bonvillain, Nancy. "Gender Relations in Native North America." *American Indian Culture and Research Journal* 13 (1989): 1–28.

Bowden, Henry Warner. *American Indians and Christian Missions: Studies in Cultural Conflict.* Chicago: University of Chicago Press, 1981.

Brainerd, Thomas. *The Life of John Brainerd: Brother of David Brainerd, and His Successor as Missionary to the Indians of New Jersey.* Philadelphia: Presbyterian Publication Committee, 1865.

Braund, Kathyrn E. Holland. *Deerskins and Duffels: Creek Indian Trade with Anglo-America, 1685–1815.* Lincoln: University of Nebraska Press, 1993.

Brinton, Daniel G. *The Lenape and Their Legends.* Philadelphia: D. G. Brinton, 1885.

———. *The Myths of the New World: A Treatise on the Symbolism and Mythology of the Red Man in America.* 1868. Baltimore: Clearfield, 1982.

Brown, Judith K. "Economic Organization and the Position of Women among the Iroquois." *Ethnohistory* 17 (1970): 151–67.

Buchanan, John. *Jackson's Way: Andrew Jackson and the People of the Western Waters.* New York: Wiley, 2001.

Burridge, Kenelon O. L. *New Heaven, New Earth: A Study of Millenarian Activities.* Blackwell: Oxford, 1969.

Calloway, Colin G. *The American Revolution in Indian Country: Crisis and Diversity in Native American Communities.* Cambridge: Cambridge University Press, 1995.

———. *First Peoples: A Documentary Survey of American Indian History.* Boston: Bedford/St. Martin's, 1999.

Campisi, Jack, and William A. Starna. "On the Road to Canadaigua: The Treaty of 1794." *American Indian Quarterly* 19 (1995): 467–90.

Cave, Alfred A. "Abuse of Power: Andrew Jackson and the Indian Removal Act of 1830." *Historian* 65 (winter 2003): 1130–53.

———. "The Delaware Prophet Neolin: A Reappraisal." *Ethnohistory* 46 (1999): 265–90.

———. "The Failure of the Shawnee Prophet's Witch-Hunt." *Ethnohistory* 42 (1995): 445–75.

———. *The French and Indian War.* Westport CT: Greenwood Press, 2004.

———. "Indian Shamans and English Witches in Seventeenth Century New England." *Essex Institute Historical Collections* 128 (October 1992): 239–54.

———. "Richard Hakluyt's Savages: The Influence of Sixteenth Cen-

tury Travel Narratives on English Indian Policy in North America."
International Social Science Review 60 (winter 1985): 3–24.

————. "The Shawnee Prophet, Tecumseh, and Tippecanoe: A Case
Study of Historical Myth-Making." *Journal of the Early Republic* 22
(2002): 637–74.

Chafe, Wallace L. "Linguistic Evidence for the Relative Age of Iroquois
Religious Practices." *Southwestern Journal of Anthropology* 20 (1964):
278–85.

Champagne, Duane. *American Indian Societies: Strategies and Conditions of
Political and Cultural Survival.* Cambridge MA: Cultural Survival, 1989.

Chazanof, William. *Joseph Ellicot and the Holland Land Company: The Opening
of Western New York.* Syracuse: Syracuse University Press, 1970.

Churchill, Ward. *A Little Matter on Genocide: Holocaust and Denial in the
Americas 1492 to the Present.* San Francisco: City Lights Books, 1997.

Claiborne, J. F. H. *Mississippi as a Province, Territory, and State.* 2 vols.
Jackson MS: Power & Barksdale, 1880.

Clark, Jerry E. *The Shawnee.* Lexington: University of Kentucky Press, 1993.

Cleaves, Freeman. *Old Tippecanoe: William Henry Harrison.* New York:
Scribner, 1939.

Cohn, Norman. *Chaos and the World to Come.* New Haven: Yale University
Press, 1993.

Coker, William S., and Thomas D. Watson. *Indian Traders of the Southeastern Borderlands: Panton, Leslie and Company and John Forbes and Company, 1783–1847.* Gainesville: University Presses of Florida, 1986.

Cooper, J. M. "The Northern Algonquian Supreme Being." *Primitive Man*
6 (1933): 41–111.

Cotterill, R. S. *The Southern Indians: The Story of the Civilized Tribes before
Removal.* Norman: University of Oklahoma Press, 1954.

Crane, Verner W. "The Origin of the Name of the Creek Indians."
Mississippi Valley Historical Review 5 (1918): 539–24.

————. *The Southern Frontier, 1670–1782.* Ann Arbor: University of Michigan Press, 1956.

Curry, William L. "The Wyandot Chief, Leatherlips." *Ohio Archaeological
and Historical Publications* 12 (January 1903): 30–36.

Custer, Milo. "Kannekuk or Keeanakuk: The Kickapoo Prophet." *Illinois
State Historical Society Journal* 2 (1918): 48–56.

Davis, Karl. " 'Remember Fort Mims': Reinterpreting the Origin of the
Creek War." *Journal of the Early Republic* 22 (2002): 611–36.

Dawson, Moses. *Historical Narrative of the Civil and Military Services of Major General William Henry Harrison.* Cincinnati: M. Dawson, 1824.

Deardorff, Merle H. "The Cornplanter Grant in Warren County." *Western Pennsylvania Historical Magazine* 24 (1941): 1–21.

———. "The Religion of Handsome Lake: Its Origins and Development." In *Symposium on Local Diversity in Iroquois Culture,* ed. William N. Fenton, 77–107. Bureau of American Ethnology Bulletin no. 149. Washington DC: Smithsonian Institution, 1951.

Densmore, Christopher. *Red Jacket: Iroquois Diplomat and Orator.* Syracuse: Syracuse University Press, 1999.

Dickens, Ray S. "Archaeological Observations at Horseshoe Bend National Park, Alabama." *Alabama Archaeological Society Special Publications* 3 (1979).

Doster, James F. *The Creek Indians and Their Florida Lands, 1740–1823.* 2 vols. New York: Garland, 1974.

Dowd, Gregory Evans. "Paths of Resistance: American Indian Religions and the Quest for Unity, 1745–1815." Ph.D. diss., Princeton University, 1986.

———. *A Spirited Resistance: The North American Indian and the Struggle for Unity. 1745–1815.* Baltimore: Johns Hopkins University Press, 1992.

———. "Thinking and Believing: Nativism and Unity in the Ages of Pontiac and Tecumseh." *American Indian Quarterly* 16 (1992): 309–35.

———. *War under Heaven: Pontiac, the Indian Nations, and the British Empire.* Baltimore: Johns Hopkins University Press, 2002.

Downes, Randolph. *Council Fires on the Upper Ohio: A Narrative of Indian Affairs in the Upper Ohio Valley until 1795.* Pittsburgh: University of Pittsburgh Press, 1940.

Dobyns, Henry F. *Their Number Became Thinned: Native American Population Dynamics in Eastern North America.* Knoxville: University of Kentucky Press, 1983.

Drake, Benjamin. *Life of Tecumseh.* 1841. New York: Arno Press, 1969.

Drinnan, Richard. *Facing West: Metaphysics of Indian Hating and Empire Building.* Minneapolis: University of Minnesota Press, 1980.

Dunn, Jacob Pratt. *True Indian Stories, with a Glossary of Indiana Indian Names.* Indianapolis: Sentinel, 1909.

Edmunds, A. David. *The Potawatomis: Keepers of the Fire.* Norman: University of Oklahoma Press, 1978.

———. "The Prairies Potawatomi Removal of 1833." *Indiana Magazine of History* 68 (1973): 240–53.

———. *The Shawnee Prophet.* Lincoln: University of Nebraska Press, 1983.

———. *Tecumseh and the Quest for Indian Leadership.* Boston: Little, Brown, 1984.

Ehle, John. *Trail of Tears: The Rise and Fall of the Cherokee Nation.* New York: Anchor Books, 1988.

Eliade, Mircea. *Shamanism: Archaic Techniques of Ecstasy.* Trans. William R. Trask. Princeton: Princeton University Press, 1964.

Fairbanks, Charles. "Excavations at Horseshoe Bend, Alabama." *Florida Anthropologist* 15 (1962): 41–56.

Faragher, John Mack. *Daniel Boone: The Life and Legend of an American Pioneer.* New York: Henry Holt, 1992.

Fenton, William N. *The False Faces of the Iroquois.* Norman: University of Oklahoma Press, 1987.

———. *The Great Law and the Longhouse: A History of the Iroquois Confederacy.* Norman: University of Oklahoma Press, 1998.

———. "Iroquois Studies at Mid-Century." *Proceedings of the American Philosophical Society* 95 (1951): 296–310.

Foreman, Grant. *Indian Removal.* Norman: University of Oklahoma Press, 1932.

Foster, Martha Harroun. "Lost Women of the Matriarchy: Iroquois Women in the Historical Literature." *American Indian Culture and Research Journal* 19 (1995): 121–40.

Foster, Michael K., Jack Campisi, and Marianne Mithun, eds. *Extending the Rafters: Interdisciplinary Approaches to Iroquoian Studies.* Albany: State University of New York Press, 1984.

Gallay, Alan. *The Indian Slave Trade: The Rise of the Indian Empire in the American South, 1670–1717.* New Haven: Yale University Press, 2002.

Garraghan, Gilbert J. "The Kickapoo Mission." *St. Louis Catholic Historical Review* 4 (1918): 84–100.

Gavalier, Christopher P. "The Empty Lot: Spiritual Contact in Lenape and Moravian Religious Beliefs." *American Indian Quarterly* 18 (1994): 215–28.

Gibson, Arrell M. *The Kickapoo: Lords of the Middle Border.* Norman: University of Oklahoma Press, 1963.

Gilbert, Bill. *God Gave Us This Country: Tekamthi and the First American Civil War.* New York: Doubleday, 1989.

Gill, Sam D. *Native American Religions: An Introduction*. Belmont CA: Wadsworth, 1982.

Goebel, Dorothy B. *William Henry Harrison: A Political Biography*. Indianapolis: Historical Bureau of the Indiana Library, 1926.

Graymont, Barbara. *The Iroquois in the American Revolution*. Syracuse: Syracuse University Press, 1972.

Green, James A. *William Henry Harrison: His Life and Times*. Richmond: Garrett and Massie, 1941.

Green, Michael. *The Politics of Indian Removal: Creek Government and Society in Crisis*. Lincoln: University of Nebraska Press, 1984.

Griffith, Benjamin W. *McIntosh and Weatherford: Creek Indian Leaders*. Tuscaloosa: University of Alabama Press, 1988.

Grim, John A. *The Shaman: Patterns of Religious Healing among the Ojibway Indians*. Norman: University of Oklahoma Press, 1983.

Grumet, Robert Steven. " 'We Are Not So Great Fools': Changes in Upper Delawarean Socio-Political Life 1630–1758." Ph.D. diss., Rutgers, 1978.

―――, ed. *Voices from the Delaware Big House Ceremony*. Norman: University of Oklahoma Press, 2001.

Halbert, H. S., and Ball, T. H. *The Creek War of 1813 and 1814*. 1895. Tuscaloosa: University of Alabama Press, 1995.

Harrington, Mark R. *Religion and Ceremonies of the Lenape*. New York: Museum of the American Indian, Heye Foundation, 1921.

Hassig, Ross. "Internal Conflict in the Creek War of 1813–1814." *Ethnohistory* 21 (1974): 251–71.

Hauptman, Lawrence. *Conspiracy of Interests: Iroquois Dispossession and the Rise of New York*. Syracuse: Syracuse University Press, 1999.

Heidler, David S., and Jeanne T. Heidler. *Old Hickory's War: Andrew Jackson and the Quest for Empire*. Mechanicsburg PA: Stackpole, 1996.

Henige, David. *Numbers from Nowhere: The American Indian Contact Population Debate*. Norman: University of Oklahoma Press, 1998.

Henri, Florette. *The Southern Indians and Benjamin Hawkins, 1796–1816*. Norman: University of Oklahoma Press, 1986.

Herring, Joseph R. "Cultural and Economic Resilience among the Kickapoo Indians of the Southeast." *Great Plains Quarterly* 6 (1986): 263–75.

―――. *Kenekuk, the Kickapoo Prophet*. Lawrence: University of Kansas Press, 1988.

————. "Kenekuk, the Kickapoo Prophet: Acculturation without Assimilation." *American Indian Quarterly* 9 (1985): 295–307.

————. "The Vermillion Kickapoo of Illinois: The Prophet Kenekuk's Peaceful Resistance to Indian Removal, 1819–1833." In *Selected Papers in Illinois History, 1983*, 28–38. Springfield: Illinois State Historical Society, 1985.

Hertzberg, Hazel. *The Great Tree of Peace: The Culture of the Iroquois.* New York: Macmillan, 1978.

Hilger, Sister M. Inez. "Some Early Customs of the Menomini Indians." *Journal de la Societe de Amercanistes* 44 (1960): 45–68.

Hinderacker, Eric. *Elusive Empires: Constructing Colonialism in the Ohio Valley, 1673–1800.* Cambridge: Cambridge University Press, 1997.

Hirschfelder, Arlene, and Paulette Molin. *The Encyclopedia of Native American Religions.* New York: Facts on File, 1992.

Howard, James H. "The Kenekuk Religion: An Early Nineteenth Century Revitalization Movement 140 Years Later." *Museum News: South Dakota Museum* 26 (1965): 1–49.

————. *Shawnee! The Ceremonialism of a Native American Tribe and Its Cultural Background.* Athens: Ohio University Press, 1981.

Hudson, Charles. *The Southeastern Indians.* Knoxville: University of Tennessee Press, 1976.

Hunter, Charles. "The Delaware Nativist Revival of the Mid-Eighteenth Century." *Ethnohistory* 18 (1971): 31–49.

Hurt, R. Douglas. *The Ohio Frontier: Crucible of the Old Northwest, 1720–1830.* Bloomington: Indiana University Press, 1996.

Hultkrantz, Ake. *The Native Religions of North America.* San Francisco: Harper, San Francisco, 1987.

————. "The Problem of Christian Influence on Northern Algonkian Eschatology." In *Belief and Worship in Native North America,* ed. Christopher Vecsey, 187–211. Syracuse: Syracuse University Press, 1981.

————. *The Religions of the American Indians.* Trans. Monica Setterwall. Berkeley: University of California Press, 1980.

Jacobs, Wilbur R. *Dispossessing the American Indians: Indians and Whites on the Colonial Frontier.* New York: Scribner, 1972.

Jennings, Francis. *The Ambiguous Iroquois Empire: The Covenant Chain Confederation of Indian Tribes with English Colonies from Its Beginnings to the Lancaster Treaty of 1744.* New York: Norton, 1984.

———. *Empire of Fortune: Crowns, Colonies, and Tribes in the Seven Years War in America*. New York: Norton, 1988.

———. *The Invasion of America: Indians, Colonialism, and the Cant of Conquest*. Chapel Hill: University of North Carolina Press, 1975.

Jensen, Joan. "Native American Women and Agriculture: A Seneca Case Study." In *Unequal Sisters: A Multicultural Reader in U.S. Women's History*, ed. Ellen Carol Dubois and Vicki L. Ruiz, 51–65. New York: Routledge, 1990.

Johansen, Bruce, and Barbara Mann, eds. *Encyclopedia of the Haudenosaunee*. Westport CT: Greenwood Press, 2000.

Kehoe, Alice. *The Ghost Dance: Ethnohistory and Revitalization*. New York: Holt, Rinehart and Winston, 1989.

———. *Shamanism and Religion: An Anthropological Exploration in Critical Thinking*. Prospect Heights IL: Waveland Press, 2000.

Kelsay, Isabel Thornton. *Joseph Brant, 1747–1807: Man of Two Worlds*. Syracuse: Syracuse University Press, 1984.

Kraft, Herbert C. *The Lenape: Archaeology, History and Ethnography*. Newark: New Jersey Historical Society, 1986.

Krech, Shepard, III. *The Ecological Indian: Myth and History*. New York: Norton, 1999.

Krusele, R. "The Origin of the Mask Concept in the Eastern Woodlands of North America." *Man in the Northeast* (1986): 1–47.

Kupperman, Karen Ordhal. *Indians and English: Facing Off in Early America*. Ithaca: Cornell University Press, 2000.

Lanternari, Vittorio. *Religions of the Oppressed: A Study of Modern Messianic Cults*. New York: Knopf, 1963.

Levy, Jerrod E., Raymond Neutra, and Dennis Parker. *Hand Trembling, Frenzy Witchcraft, and Moth Madness: A Study of Navaho Seizure Disorders*. Tucson: University of Arizona Press, 1987.

Linton, Ralph. "Nativistic Movements." *American Anthropology* 45 (1943): 230–40.

Lutz, J. J. "The Methodist Missions among the Indian tribes of Kansas." *Transactions of the Kansas State Historical Society* 9 (1905–6): 160–235.

Mancall, Peter C. *Deadly Medicine: Indians and Alcohol in Early America*. Ithaca: Cornell University Press, 1995.

Manley, Henry S. *The Treaty of Fort Stanwix, 1784*. Rome NY: Sentinel, 1932.

Mann, Barbara. *Iroquoian Women: The Gantowisas*. New York: Peter Lang, 2000.

———. "The Lynx in Time: Haudenosaunee Women's Traditions and History." *American Indian Quarterly* 21 (1997): 423–49.

———. *Native Americans, Archaeologists, and the Mounds.* New York: Peter Lang, 2003.

Mann, Barbara, and Jerry L. Fields. "A Sign in the Sky: Dating the League of the Iroquois." *American Indian Cultural and Research Journal* 21 (1997): 105–63.

Martin, Joel. *Sacred Revolt: The Muskogees' Struggle for a New World.* Boston: Beacon Press, 1991.

McConnell, Michael N. *A Country Between: The Upper Ohio Valley and Its Peoples, 1724–1774.* Lincoln: University of Nebraska Press, 1992.

McKenney, Thomas, and James Hall. *The Indian Tribes of North America with Biographical Sketches and Anecdotes of the Principal Chiefs.* 3 vols. Philadelphia: D. Rice & A. A. Hart, 1859.

McLoughlin, William G. *Cherokee Ghost Dance: Essays on the Southeastern Indians, 1789–1861.* Macon GA: Mercer University Press, 1984.

———. *Cherokee Renascence in the New Republic.* Princeton: Princeton University Press, 1986.

———. *Cherokees and Missionaries, 1789–1839.* New Haven: Yale University Press, 1984.

Meek, Basil. "Tarhe—The Crane." *Ohio Archaeological and Historical Society Publications* 20 (January 1911): 64–72.

Merrill, James H. *Into the American Woods: Negotiators on the Pennsylvania Frontier.* New York: Norton, 1999.

Miller, Christopher. *Prophetic Worlds: Indians and Whites on the Columbia Plateau.* New Brunswick NJ: Rutgers University Press, 1985.

Miller, Jay. "The Delaware as Women: A Symbolic Solution." *American Ethnologist* 1 (1974): 507–14.

———. "The 1806 Purge among the Indiana Delaware: Sorcery, Gender, Boundaries, and Legitimacy." *Ethnohistory* 41 (spring 1994): 255–66.

———. "High Minded High Gods." *Anthropos* 75 (1980): 916–19.

———. "Kwulukan: The Delaware Side of Their Movement West." *Pennsylvania Archaeologist* 45 (1975): 45–46.

———. "Old Religion among the Delaware: The Gamwing (Big House Rite)." *Ethnohistory* 44 (1997): 113–34.

———. "A Structuralist Analysis of the Delaware Big House Rite." *University of Oklahoma Papers in Anthropology* 12 (1980): 107–33.

———. "The Unalachtigo?" *Pennsylvania Archaeologist* 44 (1974): 7–8.

Mooney, James. *The Ghost Dance Religion and Wounded Knee*. 1896. New York: Dover, 1973.

Morgan, Lewis Henry. *The League of the Iroquois*. 1851. New York: Citadel Press, 1962.

Nester, William R. *"Haughty Conquerors": Amherst and the Great Indian Uprising of 1763*. Westport CT: Greenwood Press, 2000.

Newcomb, William W., Jr. "The Culture and Acculturation of the Delaware Indians." *Anthropological Papers, Museum of Anthropology, University of Michigan*, no. 10. Ann Arbor: University of Michigan Press, 1956.

Owsley, Frank Lawrence, Jr. "The Fort Mims Massacre." *Alabama Review* 24 (July 1971): 194–204.

———. *The Struggle for the Gulf Borderlands: The Creek War and the Battles of New Orleans, 1812–1815*. 1981. Tuscaloosa: University of Alabama Press, 2000.

Paredes, Anthony. "Back from Disappearance: The Alabama Indian Community." In *Southeastern Indians since the Removal Era*, ed. Walter L. Williams, 123–41. Athens: University of Georgia Press, 1979.

Parker, Arthur C. *The Constitution of the Five Nations, or, The Iroquois Book of the Great Law*. Albany: University of the State of New York, 1916.

———. *The Life of General Ely S. Parker: The Last Grand Sachem of the Iroquois and General Grant's Military Secretary*. Buffalo NY: Buffalo Historical Society, 1919.

———. *Notes on the Ancestry of Cornplanter*. 1927. New York: Kraus Reprints, 1970.

Parmenter, Jon William. "Pontiac's War: Forging New Links in the Anglo-Iroquois Covenant Chain." *Ethnohistory* 44 (1997): 617–54.

Pierce, Roy Harvey. *Savagism and Civilization: A Study of the Indian and the American Mind*. Rev. ed. Berkeley: University of California Press, 1988.

Pickett, Albert J. *History of Alabama and Incidentally of Georgia and Mississippi from the Earliest Period*. 1851. Birmingham: Birmingham Book and Magazine Co., 1962.

Pointer, Richard W. " 'Poor Indians' and the 'Poor in Spirit': The Indian Impact on David Brainerd." *New England Quarterly* 67 (1994): 403–26.

Radin, Paul. *The Trickster: A Study in American Indian Mythology*. 1956. New York: Schocken, 1972.

———. *The Winnebago Tribe: Bureau of American Ethnology 37th Annual Report*. Washington DC: Smithsonian Institution, 1923.

Rafert, Stuart. *The Miami Indians of Indiana: A Persistent People, 1654–1994.* Indianapolis: Indiana Historical Society, 1996.

Remini, Robert. *Andrew Jackson and His Indian Wars.* New York: Viking, 2001.

———. *Andrew Jackson and the Course of American Empire, 1767–1821.* New York: Harper and Row, 1997.

Ricciardelli, Alex F. "The Adoption of White Agriculture by the Oneida Indians." *Ethnohistory* 10 (1963): 309–28.

Richter, Daniel K. *Facing East from Indian Country: A Native History of Early America.* Cambridge: Harvard University Press, 2001.

———. *The Ordeal of the Longhouse: The People of the Iroquois League in the Era of European Colonization.* Chapel Hill: University of North Carolina Press, 1992.

———. "War and Culture: The Iroquois Experience." *William and Mary Quarterly* 40 (1983): 528–59.

Richter, Daniel K., and James H. Merrill, eds. *Beyond the Covenant Chain: The Iroquois and their Neighbors in Indian North America.* Syracuse: Syracuse University Press, 1987.

Rogin, Michael Paul. *Fathers and Children: Andrew Jackson and the Subjugation of the American Indians.* New York: Vintage Books, 1975.

Rothenberg, Diane. "Erosion of Power: An Economic Basis for the Selective Conservatism of Seneca Women in the Nineteenth Century." *Western Canadian Journal of Anthropology* 6 (1978): 106–22.

———. "Friends Like These: An Ethnographic Analysis of the Interaction between Allegheny Senecas and Quakers. 1798–1823." Ph.D. diss., City University of New York, 1976.

———. " 'The Mothers of the Nation': Seneca Resistance to Quaker Intervention." In *Women and Colonization: Anthropological Perspectives,* ed. Mona Etienne and Eleanor Leacock, 62–83. New York: Praeger, 1980.

Rugley, Terry. "Savage and Statesman: Changing Historical Interpretations of Tecumseh." *Indiana Magazine of History* 85 (1989): 289–311.

Satz, Ronald. *American Indian Policy in the Jacksonian Era.* Lincoln: University of Nebraska Press, 1973.

Saunt, Claudio. " 'Domestick . . . Quiet being broke': Gender Conflict among the Creek Indians in the Eighteenth Century." In *Contact Points: American Frontiers from the Mohawk Valley to the Mississippi, 1750–1830,* ed. Andrew R. L. Cayton and Frederika Teute, 151–71. Chapel Hill, 1998.

————. *A New Order of Things: Property, Power, and the Transformation of the Creek Indians, 1733–1816.* Cambridge: Cambridge University Press, 1999.

————. "Taking Account of Property: Stratification among the Creek Indians in the Early Nineteenth Century." *William and Mary Quarterly* 3rd ser., 57 (October 2000): 733–60.

Schmidt, Wilhelm. *High Gods in North America.* Oxford: Oxford University Press, 1933.

Schoolcraft, Henry Rowe. *History of the Indian Tribes of the United States: Their Present Condition and Prospects and a Sketch of Their Ancient Status.* Philadelphia: Lippincott, 1857.

Schultz, George A. *An Indian Canaan: Isaac McCoy and the Vision of an Indian State.* Norman: University of North Carolina Press, 1972.

————. "Kenekuk, the Kickapoo Prophet." *Kansas History* 3 (1980): 38–46.

Schutz, Noel. "The Study of Shawnee Myth in an Ethnographic and Ethnohistorical Perspective." Ph.D. diss., Indiana University, 1975.

Sheehan, Bernard. *Seeds of Extinction: Jeffersonian Philanthropy and the American Indian.* Chapel Hill: University of North Carolina Press, 1973.

Shimony, Annie Marie. *Conservatism among the Iroquois at the Six Nation Reserve.* 1961. Syracuse: Syracuse University Press, 1994.

Skinner, Alanson. *Material Culture of the Menomini.* Heye Foundation Indian Notes and Monographs 4. New York: Heye Foundation, 1921.

Smith, De Cost. "Witchcraft and Demonism of the Modern Iroquois." *Journal of American Folklore* 2 (1889): 184–93.

Sosin, Jack. *Whitehall and the Wilderness: The Middle West in British Colonial Policy, 1760–1775.* Lincoln: University of Nebraska Press, 1961.

Southerland, Henry DeLeon, Jr., and Jerry E. Brown. *The Federal Road through Georgia, the Creek Nation, and Alabama, 1803–1836.* Tuscaloosa: University of Alabama Press, 1989.

Speck, Frank C. *Midwinter Rites of the Cayuga Long House.* Philadelphia: University of Pennsylvania Press, 1945.

————. *A Study of the Delaware Indian Big House Ceremony.* Harrisburg: Pennsylvania Historical Commission, 1931.

Spencer, Jacob. "The Shawnee Indians: Their Customs, Traditions, and Folklore." *Transactions of the Kansas Historical Society* 10 (1908): 382–402.

Spindler, Louise. "Great Lakes: Menomini." In *Witchcraft and Sorcery of the*

Native American Peoples, ed. Duward E. Walker Jr., 39–74. Moscow: University of Idaho Press, 1989.

Sprague, Stuart S. "The Death of Tecumseh and the Rise of Rumpsey Dumpsey." *Filson Club Historical Quarterly* 59 (1985): 455–61.

Steele, Ian. *Warpaths: Invasion of North America*. New York: Oxford University Press, 1994.

Stone, Rufus B. "Broadbent's Raid on the Seneca." *Western Pennsylvania Historical Magazine* 7 (1924): 88–101.

Sugden, John. *Blue Jacket: Warrior of the Shawnees*. Lincoln: University of Nebraska Press, 2000.

——. "Early Pan-Indianism: Tecumseh's Tour of the Indian Country, 1811–1812." *American Indian Quarterly* 10 (fall 1986): 273–304.

——. *Tecumseh: A Life*. New York: Henry Holt, 1998.

——. *Tecumseh's Last Stand*. Norman: University of Oklahoma Press, 1985.

Swanton, John R. *Creek Religion and Medicine*. 1928. Lincoln: University of Nebraska Press, 2000.

——. *Early History of the Creek Indians and Their Neighbors*. 1922. Gainesville: University Presses of Florida, 1998.

——. *Myths and Tales of the Southeastern Indians*. 1929. Norman: University of Oklahoma Press, 1995.

Swatzler, John. *A Friend among the Senecas: The Quaker Mission to Cornplanter's People*. Mechanicsburg PA: Stackpole, 2000.

Sword, Wiley. *President Washington's Indian War: The Struggle for the Old Northwest, 1790–1795*. Norman: University of Oklahoma Press, 1985.

Tanner, Helen Hornbeck. "Coocooche: Mohawk Medicine Woman." *American Indian Culture and Research Journal* 3 (1979): 23–42.

——, ed. *Atlas of Great Lakes Indian History*. Norman: University of Oklahoma Press, 1987.

Tedlock, Dennis, and Barbara Tedlock, eds. *Teachings from the American Earth: Indian Religion and Philosophy*. New York: Liveright, 1992.

Thornton, Russell. *American Indian Holocaust and Survival: A Population History since 1492*. Norman: University of Oklahoma Press, 1987.

Thrupp, Sylvia L. *Millenial Dreams in Action: Studies in Revolutionary Religious Movements*. New York: Stocken Books, 1970.

Thurman, Melburn D. "The Delaware Indians: A Study in Ethnohistory." Ph.D. diss., University of California, Santa Barbara, 1973.

——. "The Shawnee Prophet's Movement and the Origins of the Prophet Dance." *Current Anthropology* 25 (1984): 530–31.

Todd, Charles S., and Benjamin Drake. *Sketches of the Civil and Military Services of William Henry Harrison*. Cincinnati: U. P. James, 1840.

Tooker, Elizabeth. *The Iroquois Ceremonial of Midwinter*. Syracuse: Syracuse University Press, 1970.

―――. "The Iroquois White Dog Sacrifice in the Latter Part of the Eighteenth Century." *Ethnohistory* 12 (1965): 129–40.

―――. "On the Development of the Handsome Lake Religion." *Proceedings of the American Philosophical Society* 133 (1989): 35–50.

―――. "On the New Religion of Handsome Lake." *Anthropological Quarterly* 41 (1968): 187–200.

―――, ed. *Native American Spirituality of the Eastern Woodlands: Sacred Myths, Dreams, Visions, Speeches, Healing Formulas, Rituals, and Ceremonials*. New York: Paulist Press, 1979.

Trafzer, Clifford E., ed. *American Indian Prophets: Religious Leaders and Revitalization Movements*. Newcastle CA: Sierra Oaks, 1986.

Trigger, Bruce, ed. *Handbook of North American Indians*. Vol. 15, Northeast. Washington DC: Smithsonian Institution, 1978.

Trowbridge, C. C. *Shawnese Traditions*. Ed. Vernon Kienitz and E. W. Voegelin. Occasional Contributions from the Museum of Anthropology, University of Michigan, no. 9. Ann Arbor: University of Michigan Press, 1939.

Turner, Frederick Jackson. *The United States, 1830–1850*. 1935. New York: Norton, 1965.

Turner, Harold W. *Bibliography of New Religious Movements in Primal Societies*. 6 vols. Boston: C. K. Hall, 1978.

Underhill, Ruth. *Red Man's Religion: Beliefs and Practices of the Indians North of Mexico*. Chicago: University of Chicago Press, 1965.

Vaughan, Alden T. *Roots of American Racism: Essays on the Colonial Experience*. New York: Oxford University Press, 1995.

Vecsey, Christopher. "The Story and Structure of the Iroquois Confederacy." *Journal of the American Academy of Religion* 54 (1986): 79–106.

―――, ed. *Belief and Worship in Native North America*. Syracuse: Syracuse University Press, 1981.

―――, ed. *Religion in Native North America*. Moscow: University of Idaho Press, 1990.

Vibert, Elizabeth. " 'The Natives Were Strong to Live': Reinterpreting Nineteenth-Century Prophetic Movements in the Columbia Plateau." *Ethnohistory* 42 (1995): 198–229.

Viola, Herman J. *Thomas McKinney: Architect of America's Early Indian Policy, 1816–1830.* Chicago: Swallow Press, 1974.

Voeglin, C. F. "The Shawnee Female Deity." *Yale University Publications in Anthropology* 10 (1936): 3–21.

Voeglin, C. F., and E. W. Voegelin. "Shawnee Name Groups." *American Anthropologist* 37 (1935): 617–35.

Wainwright, Nicholas B. *George Croghan, Wilderness Diplomat.* Chapel Hill: University of North Carolina Press, 1959.

Walker, Duward E., Jr., ed. *Witchcraft and Sorcery of the Native American Peoples.* Moscow: University of Idaho Press, 1989.

Wallace, Anthony F. C. *The Death and Rebirth of the Seneca.* New York: Knopf, 1970.

———. "Dreams and Wishes of the Soul: A Type of Psychoanalytic Theory among Seventeenth Century Iroquois." *American Anthropologist* 60 (1958): 234–48.

———. *Jefferson and the Indians: The Tragic Fate of the First Americans.* Cambridge: Belknap Press of Harvard University Press, 1999.

———. *King of the Delawares: Teedyuscung, 1700–1763.* 1949. Freeport NY: Books for Libraries Press, 1970.

———. *The Long, Bitter Trail: Andrew Jackson and the Indians.* New York: Hill and Wang, 1993.

———. "New Religions among the Delaware." *Southwestern Journal of Anthropology* 12 (1958): 1–21.

———. *Prelude to Disaster: The Course of Indian-White Relations Which Led to the Black Hawk War of 1832.* Springfield: Illinois State Historical Library, 1970.

———. "Revitalization Movements." *American Anthropologist* 58 (1956): 264–81.

Wallace, Paul A. W. *Conrad Weiser, 1696–1760: Friend of the Colonist and the Mohawk.* New York: Russell & Russell, 1945.

Waselkov, Gregory A., and Brian M. Wood. "The Creek War of 1813–1814: Effects on Creek Society and Settlement Patterns." *Journal of Alabama Archaeology* 32 (1986): 1–24.

Weber, Max. *The Methodology of the Social Sciences.* Trans. E. A. Shills and H. A. Finch. Glencoe IL: The Free Press, 1949.

Webster, Homer J. *William Henry Harrison's Administration of Indiana Territory.* Indianapolis: Sentinel, 1907.

Weslager, C. A. *The Delaware Indians: A History.* New Brunswick NJ: Rutgers University Press, 1989.

————. The Delaware Indian Westward Migration: With the Text of Two Manuscripts, 1821–22, Responding to General Lewis Cass's Inquiries about Lenape Language and Culture. Wallingford PA: Middle Atlantic Press, 1978.

White, Richard. The Middle Ground: Indians, Empires, and Republics in the Great Lakes Region, 1650–1815. Cambridge: Cambridge University Press, 1991.

Wilkinson, Norman B. "Robert Morris and the Treaty of Big Tree." Mississippi Valley Historical Review 40 (1953): 257–78.

Willig, Timothy D. "Prophetstown on the Wabash: The Native Spiritual Defense of the Old Northwest." Michigan Historical Review 23 (1997): 115–58.

Wilson, Bryan R. Magic and the Millennium: A Sociological Study of Religious Movements of Protest among Tribal and Third World Peoples. New York: Harper and Row, 1973.

Wright, J. Leitch, Jr. Creeks and Seminoles. Lincoln: University of Nebraska Press, 1986.

————. The Only Land They Knew: The Tragic Story of the American Indians in the Old South. New York: Free Press, 1981.

Young, Mary. "Indian Removal and Land Allotment: The Civilized Tribes and Jacksonian Justice." American Historical Review 64 (1958): 31–45.

Znamenski, Andrei. " 'White Faith and White Czar': Ethnicity, Misrepresentation, and Native Religious Revival in Altai, 1905." Unpublished paper.

————, ed. Shamanism: Critical Concepts in Sociology. 3 vols. London: Routledge Curzon, 2004.

Index